THE Image of Man

Studies in the History of Sexuality
Guido Ruggiero, *General Editor*

IMMODEST ACTS
The Life of a Lesbian Nun in Renaissance Italy
Judith Brown

THE EVOLUTION OF WOMEN'S ASYLUMS SINCE 1500
From Refuges for Ex-Prostitutes to Shelters for Battered Women
Sherrill Cohen

AUTHORITY AND SEXUALITY IN EARLY MODERN BURGUNDY (1500–1730)
James R. Farr

SEXUALITY IN THE CONFESSIONAL
A Sacrament Profaned
Stephen Haliczer

COMMON WOMEN
Prostitution and Sexuality in Medieval England
Ruth Mazo Karras

HOMOSEXUALITY IN MODERN FRANCE
edited by Jeffrey Merrick and Bryant T. Ragan, Jr.

THE IMAGE OF MAN
The Creation of Modern Masculinity
George L. Mosse

MASCULINITY AND MALE CODES OF HONOR IN MODERN FRANCE
Robert A. Nye

FORBIDDEN FRIENDSHIPS
Homosexuality and Male Culture in Renaissance Florence
Michael Rocke

THE BOUNDARIES OF EROS
Sex Crime and Sexuality in Renaissance Venice
Guido Ruggiero

THE MYSTERIOUS DEATH OF MARY ROGERS
Sex and Culture in Nineteenth-Century New York
Amy Gilman Srebnick

Further volumes are in preparation

THE Image of Man

The Creation of Modern Masculinity

GEORGE L. MOSSE

Oxford University Press
New York Oxford

Oxford University Press

Oxford New York
Athens Auckland Bangkok Bogota Bombay Buenos Aires
Calcutta Cape Town Dar es Salaam Delhi Florence Hong Kong
Istanbul Karachi Kuala Lampur Madras Madrid Melbourne
Mexico City Nairobi Paris Singapore Taipei Tokyo Toronto Warsaw

and associated companies in

Berlin Ibadan

First published in 1996 by Oxford University Press, Inc.
198 Madison Avenue, New York, New York 10016

First issued as an Oxford University Press paperback, 1998

Library of Congress Cataloging-in-Publication Data

Mosse, George L. (George Lachmann), 1918–
The image of man : the creation of modern masculinity / George L. Mosse.
p. cm. — (Studies in the history of sexuality)
Includes index.
ISBN 0-19-510101-4
ISBN 0-19-512660-2 (pbk.)
1. Masculinity (Psychology) 2. Stereotype (Psychology) 3. Men—Psychology. 4. Men—Sexual behavior. I. Title. II. Series.
HQ1090.M67 1996
155.3'32—dc20 95-16987

Printing (last digit): 1 3 5 7 9 8 6 4 2

Printed in the United States of America on acid-free paper

ACKNOWLEDGMENTS

This book focuses on the history of the masculine stereotype and its political consequences; it addresses a normative and widespread manly ideal. I have incurred many debts of gratitude in this quest. The British Library, the Wiener Library, London, The Hebrew National and University Library, and the libraries of the University of Wisconsin have become a home away from home over the years. At the same time, the Staatsbibliothek, Berlin-West, the Cambridge University Library, and the Olin Library at Cornell University were generous with their help. Howard Fertig used his unparalleled skills to make me refine and clarify my thoughts and style. Paul Breines and Anson Rabinbach read and greatly improved the text. To Dawn Barclift I owe thanks for her indefatigable research that enriched much of the book. I am grateful for the support of Sander Gilman, who shared his vast knowledge of stereotypes. Lois Corcoran, with the greatest patience, typed and retyped the manuscript and then helped read the proof. I owe a very special debt to John Tortorice for the environment he created, his support and help, which made the writing of this book so much more rewarding.

Parts of Chapter 5 were included in "Masculinity and the Decadence," in *Sexual Knowledge, Sexual Science*, ed. Roy Porter and Mikulas Teich (Cambridge: Cambridge University Press, 1994), while passages from Chapter 6 appear in "Manliness and War," in *Violence and Human Survival*, ed. Charles Strozier and Michael Flynn (Lanham, Md.: Bowman and Littlefield, 1996).

CONTENTS

THE Image of Man

1

INTRODUCTION: THE MASCULINE STEREOTYPE

Distinct images of masculinity—the way men assert what they believe to be their manhood—have been all pervasive in Western culture. The ideal of masculinity was invoked on all sides as a symbol of personal and national regeneration, but also as basic to the self-definition of modern society. Manliness was supposed to safeguard the existing order against the perils of modernity, but it was also regarded as an indispensable attribute of those who wanted change. Indeed, the exhortation "to be a man" became commonplace, whether during the nineteenth century or the first half of the twentieth. The word *man* as constantly used in this book denotes gender and never refers to people in general.

What, then, was the meaning of a concept which has been so ubiquitous that historians have usually taken it for granted? The concept of modern masculinity stood for a definite view of human nature and human actions that could serve a variety of causes and that left hardly one modern ideology untouched. Nevertheless, as a theory of human nature, it was concrete and definite enough, constituting a coherent system that can easily be examined. This the more so, as during its relatively short life—from the second half of the eighteenth century onwards—the manly ideal changed very little, projecting much the same so-called manly virtues, such as will power, honor, and courage. These and other so-called attributes of manliness that fill this book remain near the center of our language to this very day. There have been no dramatic transformations, even if towards the end of the twentieth century the pace of change has accelerated.

Though I myself have dealt with the concept of masculinity in various contexts, nationalism among them, it constituted merely a subtext; the focus was upon a different framework, such as right-wing movements or the reshaping of the memory of the world wars. But the manly ideal deserves to hold the center of the stage as well, for it not only played a determining role in fashioning ideas of nationhood, respectability, and war, but it was present and influenced almost every aspect of modern history. And though modern masculinity must be analyzed as a historical phenomenon in its own right, it was nevertheless closely tied to the fears and hopes of modern society. Examining the manly ideal means dealing not only with nationalism or fascism, usually regarded as "masculine," but also with socialism, communism and, above all, the ideals and functioning of normative society.

Modern masculinity helped to determine, and was in turn influenced, by what were considered normative patterns of morality and behavior, that is to say, typical and acceptable ways of behaving and acting within the social setting of the past centuries. Though, as we shall see presently, the middle classes were instrumental in the formation of that society, its standards spread to both the aristocracy and working class as well. Indeed, the manly ideal was so well established from the start of the nineteenth century onwards, that every western European movement had to face it and accept it, emphasizing at times one or another of its attributes or even trying a change in direction, until it faced its stiffest challenge as we end this book.

This book is concerned with the evolution of a stereotype that became normative, and not with the multitude of personal definitions of manhood or even with an ideal such as that of the "sensitive man" which informed the romantic movement[1] at the same time that the building blocks of the dominant modern masculine stereotype were put into place. There are many ways in which the history of modern masculinity can be explored and focused: it is possible, for example, to concentrate upon several of its attributes, such as will power or self-restraint ("real men do not cry"), and yet, in order to get closer to the way in which manhood was actually perceived at the time we must see it as a totality.

Masculinity was regarded as of one piece from its very beginning: body and soul, outward appearance and inward virtue were supposed to form one harmonious whole, a perfect construct where every part was in its place. Modern masculinity was a stereotype, presenting a standardized mental picture, "the unchanging representation of another," as *Webster's Dictionary* defines stereotypes. Such a picture must be coherent in order to be effective, and, in turn, the internalized visual image, the mental picture, relies upon the perception of outward appearance in order to judge a person's worth. Stereotypes objectify human nature, making it easy to understand at a glance and to pass judgment.

Stereotypes came into their own with the modern age as part of a general quest for symbols in order to make the abstract concrete within the bewildering changes of modernity. Modern stereotypes did not exist in earlier ages, even if appearances mattered and men were supposed to walk and stand in a proper manner. The concept of male honor had been important for a long time, and its transition to modernity will occupy us later. It is impossible to point to a precise moment when the ideal of modern masculinity was born and became part of modern history, other than it happened sometime between the second half of the eighteenth century and the beginning of the nineteenth. The building blocks of modern masculinity existed, but they were systematized, formed into a stereotype, only at the start of the modern age. Now the importance of the actual structure of the human body became equal to—if not greater than—the importance of its adornments. The stereotype of masculinity was conceived as a totality based upon the nature of man's body.

At a time when political imagery like the national flag or the Jacobin's *cocarde* became potent symbols, the human body itself took on symbolic meaning. With the second half of the eighteenth century, western Europe was entering an ever more visually oriented age, exemplified not only by national symbols but also by the effect of sciences such as physiognomy and anthropology, with their classification of men according to standards of classical beauty. The masculine stereotype became integral to an ever more visually centered age and its quest for symbols when, as the French Revolution proclaimed, "new symbols" could make new men.[2] As the human body took on symbolic form, its construction and its beauty became of increasing importance. Modern masculinity was to define itself through an ideal of manly beauty that symbolized virtue. That is why we shall deal so extensively with both the ideal male body and its attributes.

In our time stereotypes have become the equivalent of a negative judgment; it is those marginalized by society who are said to be stereotyped. So-called stereotypes of Jews or blacks are common currency and provide justification for discrimination. Negative stereotypes did play an important role in the construction of modern masculinity, as we shall see; however, we are focusing upon what was regarded as a positive stereotype. Ideals can take on human shapes most easily through the objectification of beauty. The stereotype of true manliness was so powerful precisely because unlike abstract ideas or ideals it could be seen, touched, or even talked to, a living reminder of human beauty, of the proper morals, and of a longed-for utopia. This book, then, focuses upon a specific stereotype, not a negative stereotype but a stereotype that was regarded as positive, as a motor that drove the nation and society at large.

Stereotyping meant that men and women were homogenized, considered not as individuals but as types. The fact that stereotyping depended upon unchanging mental images meant that there was no room for individual variations. Moreover, the new sciences of the eighteenth and nineteenth centuries in their passion for classification sought to analyze men in groups rather than as individuals. Stereotyping meant giving to each man all the attributes of the group to which he was said to belong. All men were supposed to conform to an ideal masculinity.

The masculine stereotype was strengthened, however, by the existence of a negative stereotype of men who not only failed to measure up to the ideal but who in body and soul were its foil, projecting the exact opposite of true masculinity. Groups marginalized by society, such as Jews or blacks, fulfilled this role, and indeed racism was based upon stereotypes and stereotyping. Those who were said not to fit into settled and respectable society were transformed into countertypes to the ideals that society cherished and that manliness represented so well. They were supplied with all the features that in an unambiguous manner told everyone who had eyes to see of the evil they portended. Their misshapen bodies were in themselves a sign of their degeneration. At the beginning of the nineteenth century in a book about the character and destiny of manhood, Friedrich Ehrenberg, a leading German Protestant clergyman, asserted that the ideal of the true man must be kept clearly in view, without the least hesitation, opposed as it was to immoral, weak and servile men.[3]

The public nature of a stereotype needs emphasis. It made the invisible both visible and public, and it was in this manner that stereotypes gained their social and political importance. At the end of the nineteenth century an English phrenological magazine expressed this visibility in a striking manner when it wrote that "man may be considered in the light of a placard, hung up on the wall to be read," and went on to state that "our virtues, vices, excellences, culture or barbarism, can be seen by those who have eyes sufficiently educated to read and understand their external manifestations."[4]

To educate such eyes was, during the second half of the eighteenth century, the work of scientists and theologians, among others, who discussed how one could read faces at a glance or draw conclusions from the structure of the human body. Artists played their part as well or, rather, a new artistic sensibility that became crucial in defining the beauty of manliness. Social and political movements also educated the eye, for they had to make themselves widely understood through visual images in an age in which, as the French Revolution had taught, the support of the masses counted. Nationalism, a movement which began and evolved parallel to modern masculinity, will play an important role as such an educator, for it adopted the masculine stereotype as one means of its self-representation. However, in the last resort, as we shall see throughout this book, it was modern society itself that diffused the ideal of masculinity. Middle-class society helped to create and supported the masculine stereotype that differed from the aristocratic ideal of masculinity as it yielded to bourgeois sensibilities.

The masculine stereotype was not bound to any one of the powerful political ideologies of the previous century. It supported not only conservative movements, as is often maintained, but the workers' movement as well; even Bolshevik man was said to be "as firm as an oak."[5] Modern masculinity from the very first was co-opted by the new nationalist movements of the nineteenth century and yet it could also exist against a background of the cosmopolitan Enlightenment. Thus Friedrich Ehrenberg wrote that the image of true masculinity must be easy to read because it sets the goal for man's education. Living a virtuous life and maintaining self-control at all times were part of true manliness, but a strong sense of liberty, a commitment to freedom, was for him an equally important ingredient.[6] Indeed, typically enough, at this stage in the history of modern nationalism, fatherland and humanity were often paired in the Enlightenment manner; the love of one did not exclude love for the other. Here the male stereotype, in what Ehrenberg calls its beauty of form and power of will,[7] was not an enemy of liberty but its friend. True manhood had become the goal of what the Germans called *Bildung*, that is, the self-cultivation of the individual. But although in its origin this was supposed to be an open-ended process, now it was given a definite goal.

The manly ideal in this particular context demonstrates the limited extent to which it could coexist with the autonomy of the individual. Johann Gottfried von Herder had written in the 1770s that through self-cultivation every man must grow like a plant toward the unfolding of his personality until he becomes a harmonious, autonomous individual, exemplifying both the continuing quest for knowledge and the moral imperative.[8] But this growth was cut short if the manly stereotype provided the paradigm, the goal for man's education. Though the masculine stereotype could exist regardless of political and ideological background, as a stereotype it necessarily restricted individual freedom, because, as we mentioned before, stereotypes were classified not individually but in groups; manliness and what it stood for hardly varied, always reflecting society's traditional values. Thus when society showed a greater tolerance for the so-called abnormal or attempted to legitimize the unconventional—as in the twentieth century—manliness pulled in the reins. At that point, just as it had helped cut short the open-ended process of *Bildung* earlier, it became a conservative force reflecting and upholding the traditional standards of a society that threatened to depart from the very norms that had sustained it for such a long time.

The male stereotype remained intact in spite of the structural changes that modern society experienced; it was apparently not dependent upon a specific economic, social and political constellation. However, masculinity was in fact dependent upon a certain moral imperative, upon certain normative standards of appearance, behavior, and comportment. And when the traditional value system of the middle class was endangered, the ideal of masculinity was threatened as well.

Here the position of manliness was not unlike that of femininity; masculine and feminine figures, for example, became public symbols at the same time representing the nation. Women as national symbols, however, did not embody generally valid norms such as the virtues that masculinity projected but, instead, the motherly qualities of the nation, and pointed to its traditions and history. Such feminine images usually wore ancient dress, looking backward, like Germania, Brittania, or even Marianne, who after the revolution was for the most part matronly in appearance. They were not usually dependent upon changes in the nation itself, monarchical or republican, and represented through their constant visual presence the ancient values that the nation was supposed to hold dear. Thus even if Marianne was rejected for a short time because of her association with revolution, she was soon back in favor.[9] To be sure, woman as a public symbol also exemplified normative social values through her sedate appearance and passive posture. In countless illustrations, like those which, for example, accompanied Goethe's phenomenally successful *Die Leiden des jungen Werthers* (The Sorrows of the Young Werther, 1774), she was surrounded by trees and flowers (testifying to her natural innocence), as well as by sweet little children (Figure 1.1). Women as public symbols did not reflect the needs and hopes of society directly, but the male body, as we shall see, was thought to symbolize society's need for order and progress, as well as middle-class virtues such as self-control and moderation. Woman as a public symbol was a reminder of the past, of innocence and chastity; manliness could also recall such virtues, but much more besides.

This comparison reenforces the crucial role played by modern masculinity in upholding the clear division between men and women, so basic to modern society over the past centuries. At the beginning of the nineteenth century women lost whatever small gains they had made during the eighteenth century Enlightenment and were confined to a sphere clearly distinct from that assigned to men: their task was governing the household and educating the children; unlike the female national symbols, women as individuals had no place in public life. This division of labor did not mean that women were necessarily inferior to men, but that they had different functions: men and women were thought to complement each other.

This difference was all-important in the construction of modern masculinity, which, as we mentioned, defined itself against a countertype but also in connection with the differences between the sexes. For example, the word *effeminate* came into general usage during the eighteenth century indicating an unmanly softness and delicacy. Gender division and its meaning for the strengthening and support of the ideal male type remained in place, though challenged by the women's rights movements from the end of the nineteenth century onward. These movements were followed by the emergence of the so-called new woman, largely after the First World War: self-employed, wearing mannish clothes, hair bobbed, puffing a cigarette (Figure 1.2). During the Ger-

1.1 This representation of Werther's Charlotte with her children by Bartolozzi (1792) contains other symbols of femininity as well: Eros blowing a trumpet, the church, and verdant Nature. (*Werther Illustrationen*, Stadtmuseum Ratingen. Ed. Ursula Mildner-Flesch and Heinz Kruger, Ratingen, 1982. By permission.)

man Weimar Republic the lifestyles of the sexes among the intelligentsia and some of the middle classes seemed to be converging.[10] But the alarm that the so-called new women caused among men was largely premature. Stefan Zweig, the popular German novelist, for example, saw a sea change in morality taking place after the First World War as the relationship between the sexes seemed to become liberated from false morality and false shame, but this did not touch the womanliness

1.2 *Sylvia von Harden*, a Journalist, by Otto Dix (1926). (Musée National d'Art Moderne, Centre National d'Art et de Culture Georges Pompidou. By permission.)

of women, whose chief asset, he believed, was their beauty and their figure, whose contours were happily transparent in modern dress.[11]

Although, as Ute Frevert has shown for Germany, most middle-class women were religious and conservative,[12] this did not diminish the threat men perceived in the relaxation of the barriers between the sexes. Nevertheless, women had a status different from the counter-types, those who symbolized the very opposite of normative masculinity and who were said to lack all qualities either men or women as members of established society were thought to possess. Women who left their prescribed roles, however, joined the countertypes as the enemies against whom manliness sharpened its image. We return to a point made earlier in this introduction and extend it: just as modern masculinity reflected the ideals and hopes of society, so its enemies were the enemies of society. Here manliness fulfilled its task of strengthening normative society against those who supposedly wanted to destroy its fabric, and who through their looks and comportment made clear their evil intentions.

The durability of the late eighteenth century masculine ideal in modern times has determined the structure of this book. The first chapters establish the manly ideal, the standards to which it was held and how these were to be reached. Once the foundations of modern manliness have been laid, the most important aspects of its history are explored: events or movements that have extended its dimensions, attempted to change its direction or to heighten features latent in the stereotype. Movements such as the decadence at the turn of the century, the First World War, and the new political movements in its aftermath are some of the events that left their mark on the normative definition of masculinity. Here the normative and not the exceptional definitions of manliness concern us. We are often so fascinated by the exceptional, the especially interesting or challenging, that we forget that it is the normative—that which is considered normal—which motivates most people and determines their perceptions of society and their place within it.

The countertype to the manly ideal also receives special attention. We have already mentioned that masculinity reaffirmed and strengthened its image in confrontation with its enemies, who represented all that the manly man was not, figures constructed largely in direct opposition to the masculine stereotype. The history of racism and anti-Semitism has, up to now, all but ignored the important part modern manliness played in the patterns of prejudice, that the standards by which such outsiders were judged were for the most part measured against the bodily structure and spirit of the masculine ideal. Any Jewish or black male or any male thought to be of inferior race can, through his own experience, substantiate this fact. How many of such outsiders have attempted to become insiders through reconstructing their bodies and adjusting their comportment according to the male aesthetic ideal? Bodybuilding, nose straightening, and hair straightening are only some of the devices that have been used to accomplish this end.

These countertypes were the traditional "outsiders" such as Jews or gypsies (there were, after all, very few blacks in Europe) and also those who had repudiated or did not fit in with social norms, such as vagrants, the insane or habitual criminals and, last but not least, "unmanly" men and "unwomanly" women. Towards the end of the nineteenth century, lesbians and homosexual men became more visible, and a few even began to flaunt their differences from the accepted norm. All "outsiders," as we shall see, were stereotyped in much the same manner as they faced the manly ideal. Because this ideal was set, its countertype had no room for maneuver; it could not change either its looks or character. We will meet the "outsiders" often, trying to become "real men" but eventually founding their own liberation movements partly to escape and mock all that the male stereotype symbolized. There was a very significant dialectic involved here whose implications are of importance to this study. Modern masculinity needed the countertype, and those stigmatized as countertypes either attempted to imitate the ideal type or defined themselves in opposition to the dominant stereotype. Either way, escape was difficult.

The passive image of woman in society and politics in general tended to remain constant until well after the First World War, in spite of the various movements for women's rights that agitated for an end to women's exclusion from public life. The male stereotype, as has been mentioned, was unchanging as well, for neither stereotypes nor symbols are easily altered. Yet it seems that the male stereotype was more consistent over time than that of women. Even when there was talk about a "new man," as we shall see, he was often merely the old man writ large, but the "new woman" represented a substantive change. Men's imagination toyed with the stereotypes of women such as the *femme fatale* or the Amazon (woman as a national symbol was, of course sacred), yet women had no real chance to manipulate the public representation of men. Still, by and large, the substance of the ideal of femininity remained intact, even among those who wanted women to take a meaningful part in public life.

Some men themselves attempted to put forward alternative views of masculinity that did not correspond to the normative stereotype. Here it was principally the socialist intellectuals who constructed what they called a "new man" who would continue the tradition of the Enlightenment, which the normative stereotype in its nationalism and latent aggressiveness seemed to have rejected. Men such as Max Adler, at the beginning of this century, returned to the ideas of the Enlightenment put forward nearly a hundred years earlier. These socialists were on the whole concerned not with bodily images, but with a humanistic spirit which the new man must possess. Yet this effort to change the normative male stereotype failed, even among the rank and file of the socialists. The stereotype that is our principal concern fulfilled too many social needs and had become too deeply rooted; it dominates the discussion of masculinity throughout this book.

Stereotypes, however, can be eroded at the same speed with which society itself produces or seems to tolerate a loosening of those manners and morals, the virtues that up to that point had been considered vital for its cohesion. Nationalism can decline sharply as well, and with it the symbolic value of manliness within that framework. We shall try to determine at the conclusion of this book if such erosion of traditional stereotypes, of hitherto congenial symbols, took place in western Europe after the Second World War or if modern masculinity still constitutes an ideal to be aimed at. Does true manliness remain the potent political and social force that had made it so important during the nineteenth century and throughout most of the twentieth?

If our discussion of manliness focuses upon its stereotype and its impact upon public life, it is contained by the geographical boundaries we have set for ourselves. Germany is at the center here, but examples mostly from England, France, and Italy have also been used to give a wider dimension to our analysis. However, it is difficult to write about France after the Revolution in this context because comparatively little research exists that deals with the general stereotype of masculinity in that country. We have confined ourselves to that part of the continent that, broadly speaking, followed Western traditions, and that here includes Germany and Austria as parts of western Europe. The United States makes a dramatic entrance in the last chapter of this book through the vast influence it exercised upon European culture after the Second World War. Through such a focus, we can look at the construction of modern masculinity in some depth and at the same time present a paradigm for analyzing modern masculinity in other parts of Europe or even the United States.

Though nothing specific is said in this book about masculinity and empire, empires, such as the British Empire, were exceedingly masculine affairs. R. S. S. Baden-Powell, the founder of the Boy Scouts, wrote that Africans were as dull as oxen, inert men. They may be our brothers, he went on, but they certainly are not men.[13] Rudyard Kipling, to take another famous example, in his writings about pioneers of empire, was apt to combine good looks with masculine virtues.[14] But, above all, as Martin Green has rightly told us, in Kipling's works men were conduits of power: it is inflicted upon them by their superiors and they inflict it upon others.[15] Still, even the British Empire did not allow such power full play; it had to be coupled with self-control and the restraint of reckless impulses.[16] Such self-restraint was a key attribute of the masculine stereotype, as we shall see; a true man must know how to master his passions. The British Empire, in places such as the Indian subcontinent, became an arena in which to test and reinforce the Victorian character.[17] Here any discussion of modern masculinity in western Europe itself applies with some national modifications to the rulers of empire as well. The use of power, inherent in modern masculinity, was always restrained by other manly virtues.

Masculinity cannot be reduced to the sole exercise of raw power in the empire, society or family, or nation; it was never so one-dimensional. Instead, modern masculinity contained a whole series of attributes that reflected both social realities and the hope for the future. Middle class sensibilities, as we shall see, demanded a "quiet strength" that did not conflict with virtues such as fair play, harmony, and order, which an undue display of power must not disrupt. Moreover, when in the next chapter we discuss male honor and the duel, the warrior image will be shown as giving way to some efforts at reconciliation.

The stereotype of those who ruled empires certainly corresponds to that of modern masculinity in general, even if the reality may have been closer to the bored, exhausted, and indifferent French colonial officers described so well by Louis Ferdinand Céline in *Journey to the End of the Night* (1936). But we are concerned with an ideal type of masculinity that was to inform the normative concept of manliness. No matter how much the male stereotype varied in detail, wherever masculinity in modern times became a major political and social force, it served as a symbol for the ideals and hopes of society. Change has come only recently at a point when important segments of society themselves seems to have embarked upon a new course whose limits cannot as yet be predicted.

2

SETTING THE STANDARD

I

The construction of modern masculinity was closely linked to the new bourgeois society that was in the making at the end of the eighteenth century. It was then that a stereotype of manliness emerged that we recognize even today. Yet, the contribution that past ideas of manhood made to the modern stereotype cannot be neglected. If the idea of manhood changed direction in the late eighteenth century, from what did it change?

The break with older, aristocratic ideas of manhood was not abrupt. Medieval ideals such as chivalry and institutions such as the duel lasted well into modern times. The earlier ideals of manhood, confined to the aristocracy, were, to a large extent, based upon a warrior caste; however, the refinement and ritual of court society had tempered such an image of masculinity long before the end of the eighteenth century. Nevertheless, medieval tournaments were more like war games than the rituals of chivalry, which, in any case, were associated with knighthood in its decline—when strong rulers had placed limits upon violence.[1] Duels—the combat between two men in front of witnesses—had become ritualized ever since the sixteenth century.[2] Calling for a judgment from God was embedded in a ritual of confrontation that stripped away uncontrolled violence and cruder symbols of domination (as when the victor put his foot on the chest of the vanquished).

The duel was fought for the sake of male honor, and the concept of honor was to last, associated with courage or the sangfroid needed to defend it. Aristocratic honor was linked to the power of blood, it was attached to noble lineage and descent. The denial of respect due one's rank was one of the most frequent causes for dueling. Honor, in accordance with the tradition of chivalry, was attached to the individual himself, to his reputation, standing, and dignity. But the concept of honor also entailed an ideal of manliness—to be called a coward was the worst insult. Edmund Burke was not the only writer who equated chivalry and manliness, meaning heroism and generosity of feeling.[3] Courage and daring were some of the virtues that a man must possess; he was also supposed to be compassionate, loyal, and ennobled by the pure love of a woman. This ideal of chivalry was produced by feudal society in its decline, when the aristocracy clung to a code of honor as a symbol of its autonomy. As military officers, courtiers, and civil servants, the aristocracy now cultivated a code of honor linked on the one hand to the performance of duties and, on the other, to trying to preserve self-respect and sense of caste.[4]

The so-called manly qualities of aristocratic honor were to last, as was the ideal of chivalry, not just as a much-used metaphor but as a means of tempering the harshness of masculinity. Anatole France wrote in 1886, at a time when the duel had undergone an astonishing revival in France, that the sword was "the first tool of civilization, the only means man has found to reconcile his brutal instincts and his ideal of justice."[5] Here was a code of behavior that could be transmitted into a time when proper comportment such as that of the English gentleman had become an important component of masculinity. The Romantic revival of the early nineteenth century strengthened the concept of chivalry, as for example, in Sir Walter Scott's novels, and the French Revolution caused Edmund Burke to write in revulsion against the Jacobins that manners, including chivalric behavior, were more important than laws.[6] And indeed many of the qualities a perfect knight was supposed to possess, as summed up in Alan Chartiers's fifteenth-century ballad *Les Breviaires des Nobles* (The Catechism of Nobles), such as loyalty, righteousness, prowess, sobriety, and perseverance, were singularly adaptable and would fit the definition of modern masculinity.[7] And yet, this aristocratic ideal lacked the firm contours and moral imperatives essential to modern masculinity. Chivalry, in any case, was an ideal to be aimed at and not one that was well kept in a more violent age.

The adjustment of such aristocratic ideas to middle-class sensibilities, at least from the eighteenth century onward, was an important step in the construction of modern masculinity. If the characteristics of courage, sangfroid, and even compassion remained as ideals, they were now changed, stripped of much of their remaining violence, and imbedded in moral imperatives. The idealized platonic love of a noble lady that was supposed to spiritualize knighthood was now made commonplace through the monopoly exercised by the institution of marriage. Still more important, physical appearance would now assume an importance it did not have earlier; not only comportment but looks mattered. Such an aesthetic of masculinity was crucial to the formation of a stereotype that, as we saw in the last chapter, must be based upon visually-oriented perceptions. And this stereotype will determine to a large degree attitudes toward modern masculinity. A consistent and all-embracing male stereotype had not yet emerged before the end of the eighteenth century, one that took in the whole personality and set a definite standard for masculine looks, appearance, and behavior.

Nevertheless, aristocratic ideas of manliness made their contribution, even if they were changed in the process. The duel strengthened the feeling of autonomy, of personality, but also that of class and caste; as such it became in the nineteenth century part of the life of officers and students, politicians and businessmen, as well as Jews, who used it to disprove their unmanly, cowardly stereotype.[8] Theodor Herzl in Vienna, for example, dreamt of dueling and defeating Austrian anti-Semites. The "code of honor" in central Europe was a means for officers as well as students in elite university fraternities, which set great stock in the fighting of duels, to maintain their status. Now, in a nonaristocratic society, it mattered with whom one could fight a duel, for the choice was no longer confined to one hereditary caste and therefore social distinctions became a test for combat. To be worthy of dueling meant being given the same social status as the adversary. The bourgeoisie in German-speaking countries adopted the male code of honor as a status symbol and as a set of standards they could set for themselves.[9] Jews in central Europe, but not in France, were gradually excluded; indeed, here was a ready way to draw the line between those who were acceptable to society and those whom society attempted to marginalize or to exclude from power.

While in central Europe manly honor based upon aristocratic models was cultivated, above all, in the officer corps and by students, the officer corps was more than just a military institution; students in Germany became officers in the reserves, which gave them social status for the rest of their lives, a status that was confirmed by the marks of the duel, which scarred their faces for all to see. Elite student fraternities made dueling compulsory—it became almost a sport—partly because under the spell of aristocratic custom members sought to increase their status, partly because it cemented their camaraderie and, not least, because it made them into an elite in comparison to their fellow students. Moreover, in student duels the casualty figures were low.[10] Yet students and officers were not alone in fighting duels; Karl Marx, for example, challenged an opponent to such a fight. For all that, it has been estimated that only 5 percent of German society was considered honorable enough to give satisfaction.[11] In contrast to Germany, in France everyone could duel, and the duel was less a sign of caste than an instrument of civic manhood; the art of fencing produced the "virile hearts and vigorous bodies"[12] needed in a nation that in 1871 had been defeated and humiliated by Prussia.

But despite their survival, these aristocratic contributions to a construction of the manly ideal were changed from their earlier forms. To be sure, the duel as a defense of manly honor remained ritualized: there was the insult to manly honor, the challenge, the formal appointment of seconds, the witnesses, the order of combat, and, now, the choice of weapons between the sword and the pistol. All this was regulated much as it had been since the Baroque, but the analogy to war had some credence only in Germany. The duel still used sometimes deadly force to settle quarrels, but taking into account middle-class sensibilities, it usually dressed up this force in moral considerations of justice and virtue.[13] Basing honor on the power of blood or noble descent was irrelevant in the modern age; instead, as Robert Nye has written, bourgeois critics of the feudal order hoped to replace honor with virtue.[14] Yet in reality the duel continued to be used as a defense of honor even if so-called manly qualities and the defense of virtue were substituted for the trappings of aristocracy.

Still, the goal of the duel in fin-de-siècle Germany, unlike France, was to kill the opponent, for pistols, not sabers, were usually used.[15] Self-control, steadfastness, and the disregard of danger were emphasized; there was no defense against the bullet, while duelers could defend themselves with the sword. German duels were deeply serious affairs; French duels had an extremely low fatality rate.[16] The military cast of German duels was absent in France. German fraternity students, however, did use swords in fencing, which had become a sport that mimicked duels. The wounds inflicted must not elicit a single cry (shades of Laocoön).[17] But even so, masculine bravery and courage included other virtues as well: uprightness, honesty, and lack of passion. Moreover, myriad restrictions inhibited challenges and their acceptance;[18] the duel itself was ritualized in an almost bureaucratic fashion.

The German duel assimilated modern masculinity in its fashion. The new social reality was present, not in the brutality but in the normative aspects of masculinity and in the emphasis on justice—going to great lengths to give each combatant an equal chance.[19] The introduction of a new social reality into an aristocratic custom was clearest in France. The goal of the duel was no longer to kill the enemy but to display rather than demonstrate manly virtues. But here an even deeper change in direction took place than an increased emphasis upon justice and equality. It was best voiced toward the end of the nineteenth century—a time when many duels were fought: "If a man defends his honor for the sole purpose of appearing honorable, the honor code ceases to fulfill its original function and becomes a travesty."[20] The function that the honor code was now supposed to fulfill, even if it failed to do so in practice, at least in Germany, was best summed up by a French work on duels published in 1900 that repeats many of the themes we have addressed already: the duel makes man strong and independent, it takes up the cause of justice the minute the law abandons it, and penalizes scorn and insult that the laws are unable to punish.[21] In this way the sensibilities of the law-abiding citizen were eased. But the duel also served to contain quarrels lest they get out of hand. Men who cross swords were said to form a kind of "free masonry" of mutual regard. Thus the duel was embedded in ideals of justice and manly virtue and also exemplified principles of good order, so important to bourgeois society.

Male honor had to be informed by a moral purpose, and here justice, equality, and good order were signs of a more fundamental change in line with the passing from an aristocratic to a middle-class society. Male honor defined as courage, sangfroid, and pride in one's status was no longer enough. Dueling and fencing—a necessary skill for fighting duels—were now regarded as a school for character.[22] Just so, a general uneasiness that had not existed before informed some of those who resorted to duels, even in Germany. For example, the cuckolded husband in Theodor Fontane's novel *Effi Briest* (1895), who has just killed his wife's seducer in a duel, has bouts of conscience in spite of the fact that he repeats to himself constantly that "everything had happened as it was bound to happen."[23] Moreover, duels were now fought in private, where before they had largely been public events.[24] Even despite the maintenance of traditional ritual, to which we have already referred, the duel had made concessions to bourgeois sensibilities. Nothing sums up this change better, even beyond the bad conscience of Effie Briest's officer husband, than the fact that duels now had to end with a handshake between the duelers. And though some duels still ended in death, for the most part they had become character-building exercises or tests of manliness rather than an often fatal judgment by God.

While parliaments at the end of the nineteenth century debated the abolition of duels, rulers encouraged "courts of honor" that might adjudicate disputes without resorting to force. Nevertheless, dueling lasted until well after the First World War. The duel as a proof of manly qualities and as a badge of belonging to the established order is documented in Germany as late as 1926 by the last remaining Jewish member of an elite student fraternity. He accepted the challenge to fight a duel even though its cause had been settled in a court of honor, in order to defend the social position of all German Jews.[25] Through such an assertion of manly honor a discriminated minority hoped to become part of the respectable bourgeoisie. This was by then a minority opinion, but it demonstrates the persistence of what had once been an aristocratic ideal. In the end, however, not even adjustment to moral sensibilities could save the duel from collapsing under the onslaught of those who condemned as barbaric this manner of settling disputes or of rulers who did not want to lose some of their best officers.

The importance of the duel has only recently been rediscovered by historians. During the past century, those who wanted to outlaw duels included an ever-greater number, perhaps the majority, of the European middle classes and intellectuals. But for our purposes the actual controversies that the duel inspired are not important. Instead, the duel is significant as an aristocratic concept of male honor making its own contribution to the construction of a modern masculinity that was now tied to significant moral and physical principles. The manly qualities of courage, sangfroid, pride, and a sense of justice remained intact. The concept of chivalry, also coming from the past, became generalized, as we have mentioned; it meant a certain attitude and behavior linked, for example, in England, where it was strong, to compassion, straightforwardness, and patriotism. There dueling had ended in the early nineteenth century, and the so-called chivalric ideals were absorbed into middle-class manners and morals as part of what was regarded as respectable behavior.

Chivalry and manly honor, in the modern age, meant not only moral but also general physical toughness. Physical skill and dexterity had always been prized as necessary to defend one's honor, but now the new society in the making looked at the entire male body as an example of virility, strength, and courage expressed through the proper posture and appearance. We hear much about knightly conduct in earlier times but rarely about physical appearance and never—except perhaps for the darkest of villains—of how the human body itself set a standard for judging conduct. To be sure, looks had always counted; thus in the medieval and early modern period dress had been a sign of rank and status often fixed by royal ordinance. Comportment had been important as well, a certain manly bearing and courtesy. But what had been present earlier in a fragmented manner was now systematized, formed into a totality in which not merely dress and bearing but the male body itself became the focus of attention, judged, as we shall see, according to a set standard of beauty. A stereotype was fashioned that would determine the perceptions of manhood in the modern age, when earlier times knew no such method of classification.

The construction of a masculine stereotype occupies us throughout this book as the key to modern perceptions of manhood. Such stereotyping symbolized the physical and moral values of a new age, but it also presupposed an emphasis upon visual perceptions that had not existed before in this manner. It was not enough to rejoice in a beautiful landscape or a beautiful painting; public life itself had to become suffused with symbols and symbolic meaning related to beauty as well as to power or history. The nation and society represented themselves and competed for the people's attention through the use of easily understood and transparent symbols. Indeed, the masculine ideal itself in its strength and beauty became a symbol of society and nation. Secular symbols took on a new importance as an increasing number of people were drawn into public life and as the new concept of "the people" was concretized in the upheavals of the French Revolution and through the newly awakened national consciousness. These symbols were used in profusion during the French Revolution, but the nation started to represent itself through secular symbols as well. It is striking to what extent, during and after the age of the French Revolution, we confront descriptions of manly beauty as symbolic of both moral and physical worth. At the same time, in the French Revolution and the Napoleonic Wars, men seemed to become more self-conscious about their manhood; we find masculinity emphasized even where it should have been obvious, as for example in the repeated exclamation during the German wars of liberation that "we return from a bloody battle fought among men."[26] That the divide between the sexes became wider as well—each confined to its own sphere of influence and the foil of the other—added to the imperative of constructing an ideal male stereotype.

The joining of the outward to the inward projected a stereotype that took in the whole personality, and through the shape of body and face made it easy to "read" the supposed worth of an individual. But such a stereotype could make sense only if there was a standard of beauty to which it was held. Otherwise no judgment of the whole personality was possible based upon looks and comportment. This concept of beauty, in turn, had to rest upon a generally received consensus of what was deemed beautiful in the male figure. Such a consensus came about at the end of the eighteenth century and, as exemplified through the ideal of masculinity, was to last into our own time.

II

The linking of body and spirit was basic to the ideal of beauty and to the stereotype it projected. During medieval and early modern times most men believed that a living soul inhabited an inert body. The eighteenth-century Enlightenment's ideal of nature was instrumental in the joining of body and soul. This is not the place for a detailed analysis of the Enlightenment, but suffice it to say that the belief in unity—in the interrelationship of men, women, and nature—was decisive here. The exploration of nature, central to Enlightenment thought, meant learning to read nature's innermost purpose through outward appearances, decoding that which could be seen, touched, measured, and dissected. Many examples of this new attitude specifically toward man and nature come to mind as building blocks for a modern stereotype. Matter alone, Pierre Bayle tells us in his *Historical and Critical Dictionary* (1697), could not constitute a true unity; it must be united to the inward spirit of the autonomous human being.[27] The philosopher Gottfried Wilhelm Leibniz wrote in 1695 that the soul is inseparably united with the organism in which God had placed it.[28] The presumed unity of man and nature meant that anthropologists like Georges Louis Leclerc de Buffon in his famous *Natural History of Man* (1778) had to step outside the discussion of purely material forces that were supposedly the domain of science and write instead that "our existence is organization of matter with spirit."[29] Though he sought to remain within the purely physical when he defined spirituality as the reaction of nerves, he did feel obliged to argue that physical appearance denotes character. The Enlightenment ideal entailed the unity of body and soul, which meant that the body was no longer merely an inanimate receptacle.

Johann Kaspar Lavater's theory of the human physiognomy exemplified this unity and at the same time the great importance of the visual in the modern age when he introduced a new way of seeing men and women: not according to the clothes they wore but through their physical profile—the shape of the nose, the color of the eyes, and bodily structure. These expressed true character. The new science, which he put forward in his *Essai sur la Physiognomy* (Essays on Physiognomy, 1781), was based upon "the ability to recognize the hidden character of a human being through his outward appearance"[30] (Figure 2.1). J. J. Winckelmann, to whom we shall turn presently, provided him with the standard by which such appearance could be measured: the Greeks exemplified the ideal of human beauty, and such beauty, in turn, symbolized the proper moral posture. The Greeks, so Lavater declared, echoing Winckelmann, were better and more beautiful than the present generation.[31]

Although Lavater was a committed Christian, a believer in miracles, men of the Enlightenment enthusiastically furthered this new science, and it was Johann Wolfgang Goethe himself who helped in getting Lavater's more extensive work on physiognomy published.[32] And even if Goethe later on broke with Lavater precisely because of his Christianity and irrationalism, the widespread acceptance of his theory shows that it served a purpose. Here was a certain pragmatism, an emphasis on the material, combined with concern for the proper morality. As Lavater expressed it: the more virtuous, the greater the beauty of any human being; the less virtuous, the uglier his appearance.[33]

Physiognomy is important for the construction of modern mas-

2.1 Lavater analyzes the face of the Swiss historian, poet, and critic Johann Jacob Bodmer (1698–1783). The text accompanying the picture reads in part: "Among a thousand blockheads where will you find this eye, this forehead? Whoever resembles this figure, certainly, possesses a perception of the natural, the beautiful, and the useful. . . . True wisdom is in the nose; and over the lips hovers all the simplicity of Attic wit." (Johann Caspar Lavater, *Essays on Physiognomy: For the Promotion of the Knowledge and the Love of Mankind* [London: C. Whittingham, 1804].)

culinity because in an obvious manner it reflected the linkage of body and soul, of morality and bodily structure. Just so, Lavater was explicit about the kind of morality that makes man physically beautiful: love of work, moderation, and cleanliness are conducive to bodily health and clean-cut limbs.[34] This was a middle-class definition of virtue that accompanied modern masculinity, just as the harmony of bodily and moral beauty that Lavater extols would characterize the ideal male stereotype. The very fact that Lavater's combination of beauty, body, and soul was implicit in other new eighteenth-century sciences, such as anthropology, and the enthusiastic reception of his rather simplistic theory show that we are entering the modern age with its preoccupation with beauty, with the human body, and with a morality that in the end owed little to an aristocratic past.

Medicine, too, encouraged the linkage between spiritual and bodily characteristics. Disease was now seen as making its mark not only upon the body but upon the human character as well. A previously invisible state was thus readily identifiable.[35] André David Tissot, for example, in his much read work *L'Onanisme* (1760) asserted that those who practiced the vice of masturbation would bear its mark not only upon their bodies—pale, effeminate, and devoid of energy—but also upon their spirit, which would become melancholy, lacking willpower and self-control.[36] Whether practitioners of the new eighteenth-century sciences of physiognomy, anthropology, or modern medicine, these men of the Enlightenment passed rather easily from an analysis of bodily structures to judgment upon character. The Roman slogan "a healthy mind in a healthy body," eventually inscribed on many a school gymnasium throughout Europe, sums up this linkage, which was to prove ready-made for the creation of a masculine stereotype. Jean-Jacques Rousseau advised the tutor in his educational tract *Émile* (1762) to keep his pupil "in constant bodily exercise; bring him up robust and healthy, to make him reasonable and wise. . . . Once make him a man in vigor, and he will soon become a man in understanding."[37]

Both John Locke and Rousseau thought that a physically fit body was essential for a proper moral posture. They popularized this linkage through their theories of education and human nature: outward appearance became a symbol of inner worth, a sign for all to see and to judge. For example, during the French Revolution, as part of its self-representation,[38] the structure of the male body itself became a symbol of a healthy nation and society. Indeed, as we shall see throughout this book, the male body continued to perform this function until it became in the twentieth century one of the most powerful means of national and even socialist self-representation.

Lavater had not made any gender distinction in his physiognomy; he wrote about humanity as a whole, and this in spite of his low opinion of women's capabilities.[39] For Wilhelm von Humboldt, a decade later, manly and womanly beauty complemented each other as symbolic of all of humanity. True beauty transcended the particularities of gender.[40] Throughout much of the eighteenth century, gender differences were not a neat axis ordering all of human thought, but they did become ever more clearly defined. Woman was often no longer regarded as merely the mother and educator of children; she was now an overt object of male desire and domination.[41] "Woman," so Rousseau wrote, "was especially made to please man."[42] Or as it appeared in Article 213 of the Code Napoléon (1804), which remained law in much of Europe: "the man owes his wife protection, she owes him obedience." Masculine and feminine beauty were usually by mid–eighteenth century no longer perceived as complementary but as distinct and separate without any connection between them, narrowing the ideal of human beauty. However, our concern is not the tender and tempting beauty of women but the masculine beauty that came to symbolize a healthy and progressive society. At the end of this chapter, we return to the specific function such gender differences played in the construction of modern masculinity.

As the male body assumed ever-more importance as symbolic of true masculinity, greater attention had to be paid to its development, as well as to setting a specific standard of masculine beauty. The development of the male body and the standard to which it was to be held are interrelated, for the manner in which the body was developed depended upon the perception of how outward appearance might reflect inner worth. That the ideal of masculinity should be held to a definite set standard that determined its bodily structure was new. But what, then, was the standard to which the male body should aspire—an ideal of masculine strength and beauty that would vary surprisingly little during the next century and a half?

The ideal of masculine beauty took its inspiration from Greece; it must stand as one of the chief examples of the influence that ancient Greece exercised over European thought. Wilhelm von Humboldt articulated this ideal and at the same time exemplified the search for stereotypes when he wrote in 1795 that only the Greeks had succeeded in transforming the individual into an abstract ideal.[43] The abstract ideal of human beauty was based upon a newly-found consciousness of the beauty of Greek sculpture, which could be seen in famous collections and, more important, was made available through descriptions and engravings. Thus a general principle was derived from concrete examples. Von Humboldt's praise of the Greeks can give us a hint as to why the

Greek revival in the second half of the eighteenth century had such an immense impact upon European intellectuals, and why its popularizer, J. J. Winckelmann, became one of the most quoted and discussed writers of the times.

Johann Joachim Winckelmann (1717–1768), archeologist and art historian, was from his youth onward obsessed with the need to rediscover the beauty of Greek sculpture, an art form that had been neglected for centuries. He earned his living as a librarian in Saxony, and then, fulfilling his life's dream of living in Rome, in 1759 entered the service of Cardinal Albani in order to catalogue his art collection. The chief pieces of Greek sculpture then known were in Rome, principally at the Vatican. Here Winckelmann wrote his works that through a mixture of scholarly research, pithy phrases, and aesthetic judgment not only popularized the beauty of Greek sculpture but, through the meaning that he gave it, made it relevant to the times.

In his most influential works, *Reflections on the Painting and Sculpture of the Greeks* (1755) and the well-illustrated *History of Ancient Art* (1764), Winckelmann sought to present a generally valid ideal of beauty through a description of Greek sculpture. Here he confirmed the primacy of sculpture over the other arts. As Winckelmann's contemporary, the famous philosopher Johann Gottfried von Herder, would write, echoing Winckelmann: only sculpture could represent multidimensional truth; painting merely offered a narration suffused by magic.[44] Indeed, the detailed structure of the male body and face, vital for the construction of the stereotype of male beauty, sprang alive solely through sculptural representation.

The sculptures that Winckelmann analyzed as the paradigm were mostly those of young athletes who through the structure of their bodies and their comportment exemplified power and virility, and also harmony, proportion, and self-control (Figures 2.2 and 2.3). His much-repeated phrase regarding their "noble simplicity and quiet grandeur" summed up the perception of these youths. Winckelmann's style, which described Greek beauty in memorable phrases, added to his effectiveness. The male bodies that he described were always lithe, without any surplus fat, and no feature of the body or face disturbed their noble proportions (he tells us that Alcibiades refused to play the flute out of fear that it might distort his face, and he warned against undue laughter for the same reason).[45] The ideal body projected both strength and restraint, the balance that Lavater had also praised, here exemplified by

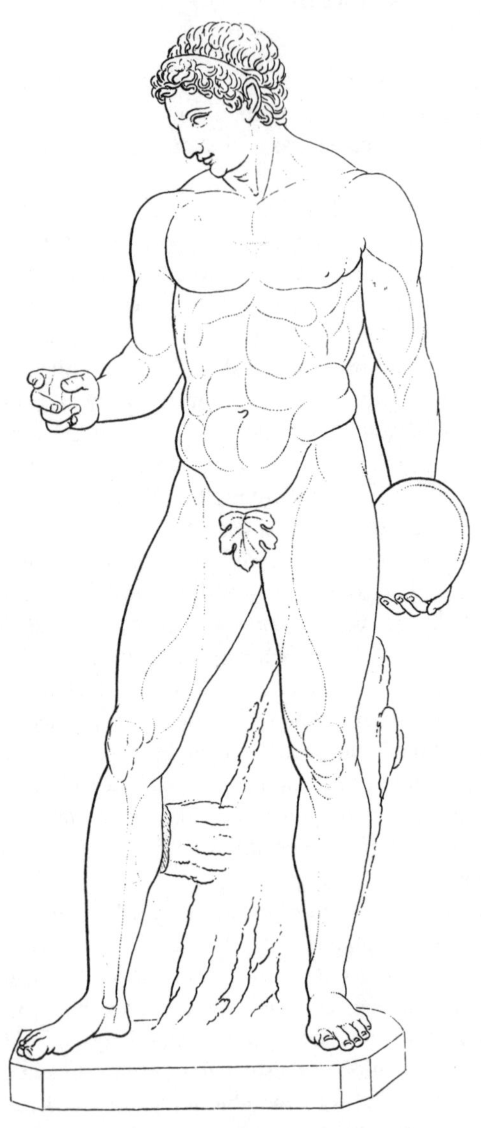

2.2 *The Discobulus in Repose* by Naucydes, pupil of Polycletus (n.d.). (J. J. Winckelmann, *Geschichte des Altertums* [History of Ancient Art] [Dresden: Walthers Verlag, 1764], plate VII.)

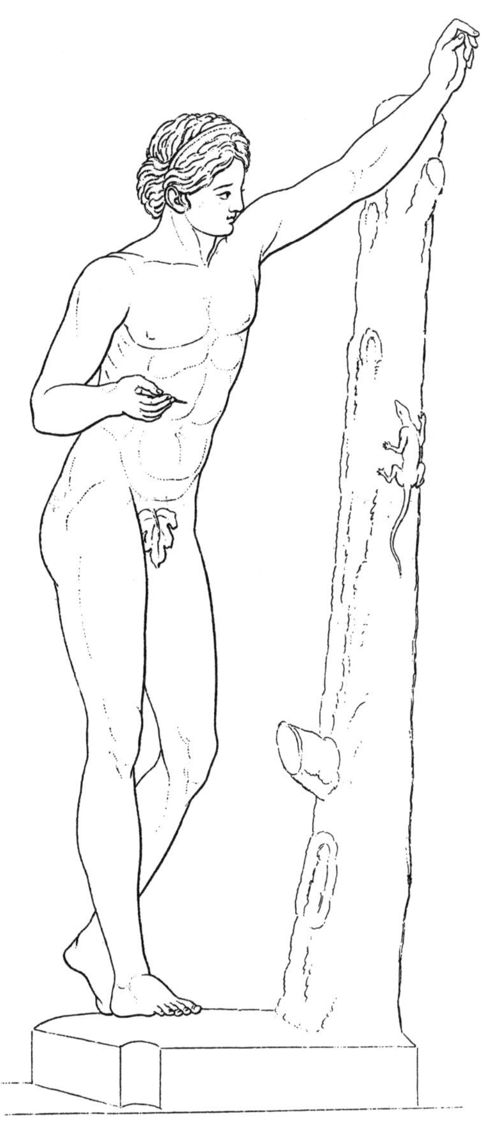

2.3 *Untitled Youth* (J. J. Winckelmann, *Geschichte des Altertums* [History of Ancient Art] [Dresden: Walthers Verlag, 1764], plate XV.

Apollo of Belvedere, the most beautiful of the young Gods. As Goethe was to write in 1771, "Apollo of Belvedere, why do you show yourself to us in all your nakedness, making us ashamed of our own?"[46]

The group of Laocoön and his sons strangled by snakes had been rediscovered in the sixteenth century, and Winckelmann, in a famous passage, described Laocoön's pain, which informed all the muscles of his body and yet did not lead to any sign of rage, which might have marked his face or determined his posture. Instead, the pain of the body and the greatness of the soul are in balance and seem to cancel each other.[47] Moreover, pain and suffering are distributed equally over the entire figure.[48] Laocoön and his sons came to symbolize self-control as part of true male heroism.[49] Winckelmann used an image to characterize Laocoön that became a commonplace, cited again and again: "Just as the depth of the ocean remains tranquil even if a storm rages above, just so the expression of the Greeks in spite of their passions indicates a great and tranquil soul."[50]

Winckelmann described his Greek statues as seen through the build of their bodies. Here the male body is deified, purged as he put it, of the dross humanity.[51] It is not astonishing in this context that when Winckelmann mentions Greeks who have accomplished extraordinary things, these are apt to be victors in athletic competitions. Just so, the noble soul of each youth manifests itself through the harmonious position of his naked body during gymnastic exercises,[52] foreshadowing the important role that gymnastics will play in shaping modern manhood. Typically enough, apart from athletes, Winckelmann mentions only artists as a profession among the Greeks.[53] This love for the body beautiful would continue to inform modern manliness: it would characterize the masculine stereotype. Indeed, the continuities are startling, as when, for example, over a century and a half later, Adolf Hitler traces what he calls the immortality of the Greek ideal of beauty to the combination of singular bodily beauty, a radiating spirit, and a noble soul. He goes on to establish the precedence of the beautiful body when he asserts that a rotten body cannot be beautified even by the most radiant spirit.[54] Winckelmann's own homosexuality is not irrelevant in this regard; whatever the evolution of the male stereotype, a homoerotic sensibility stood at the start of an image that was to inform the ideal of normative masculinity such as the clean-cut Englishman or the all-American boy.

Yet no one who has ever seen the statue of Laocoön in the Vatican Museum could in all honesty agree with Winckelmann's description: the rage seems dominant. Not only Laocoön's facial expression but even the actual proportions of the athletic Greek youths did not always correspond to the ideal Winckelmann projected. It is possible to read Winckelmann's *History of Ancient Art* as a book suffused by tension between the stillness that defines sublime beauty and the violence that informs sculptures such as Laocoön.[55] But Winckelmann was important for setting a standard of masculine beauty precisely because he seemed to resolve this tension; thus for Goethe, to give one example, Winckelmann controlled masculine strength through beauty of form. Even though it might seem that some of Winckelmann's well-proportioned youths could easily be stirred into a raging fury,[56] the point is that they were meant to control their passions.

Why did Winckelmann define his ideal of beauty through balance, proportion, and moderation, three attributes that for him equated a great and a tranquil soul? Perhaps he was under the spell of the "cosmopolitan harmony" advocated by the Enlightenment. We also know that he was impressed by Bayle's *Dictionary*, which has much to say about unity and proportion. Personal factors may have played a predominant part, perhaps Greek sculpture was meant to provide order to his own chaotic life; certainly, as we mentioned, his homosexuality may well have determined his focus on the almost-sensuous beauty of Greek youths in the first place.[57] At any rate, he admitted freely that it was his own contemplation of the sculptures, his "inner calling," that together with intensive study determined his judgment of their beauty.[58]

However important the personal factors in determining Winckelmann's judgment may have been, he struck a general chord at the time that accounts for his influence. He viewed these sculptures as projecting an ideal beauty; he saw them in abstract terms. As he himself put it, the absence of any individual or accidental traits was essential to the beauty of Greek sculpture.[59] Such a concept of beauty robbed the Greek youths of any sexuality and made their nudity acceptable.[60] But it was also in tune with the notion, voiced, for example, at roughly the same time by the English painter Sir Joshua Reynolds: that the ideal of beauty must be reduced to its general principles, that beauty is superior to individual nature.[61]

Here the important place that the concept of beauty occupied in an ever more visually oriented age is important, how it informed the symbols of private and public life. Though the ancient Greeks had already privileged sight over other senses,[62] and the Baroque had transformed the world into a stage, now the visual register was secularized and extended, becoming part of the rhythm of daily and political life. Winckelmann's preoccupation with manly beauty was abreast of his times. As Winckelmann was rediscovering Greek sculpture, artistic endeavor and the cult of beauty gained a new status among the bourgeoisie. For example, public buildings were decorated with frescoes symbolizing the virtues of city or nation, and still more important, works of art became accessible from the start of the nineteenth century onward as museums were built in most European cities. The quest for beauty became an integral part of middle-class life, and the search for a masculine beauty, the worship of Greece, must be seen within this general framework, and this, in turn, was set within the changes produced by the industrial revolution. The "beautiful, the true and the holy" reconciled, and redeemed, united they became a kind of salvation.[63] Here the ideal that Winckelmann projected acted as part of that quest for certainty and uplift that was a part of the modern age.

Typically enough, Winckelmann was praised as the rediscoverer of the "realm of beauty" at a university celebration in mid–nineteenth century honoring his birthday—at a time when the sense of beauty and the appreciation of true art had been shrouded in darkness, so it was said, he was singled out as the giver of light.[64] Winckelmann's birthday was celebrated yearly in many German universities, and their themes were, no doubt, similar. Here Winckelmann's ideal of beauty and manliness, which were irrevocably linked, underwent a process of institutionalization in which the secondary schools joined.

But it was not only because Winckelmann put forward an idea of beauty that was well suited to become a paradigm that so many of his contemporaries came under his influence, helping to transmit his construction of masculinity to future generations. Winckelmann also defined an aesthetic ideal of manliness that corresponded to one of the deepest needs of modernizing society. The new speed with which Europe was being transformed into an industrialized modern society frightened many people at the beginning of the nineteenth century, just as it seemed to threaten chaos at the century's end. Modern society needed order, but it needed a certain dynamic as well. Social hierarchies were being challenged by the new forces unleashed by the industrial revolution with its new opportunities for commerce and manufacture, its new speed of communications. Here order and movement had to be reconciled, and the "noble simplicity and quiet greatness"[65] of Winckelmann's figures allowed for virility—a certain dynamic—as well as for the harnessing of any untoward movement through bodily harmony and proportion. The figure of Laocoön provided a good example once more. Movement is indicated through his outstretched arm and in the lines of his face, but it is restrained, like pain and suffering—harmoniously distributed over the whole body. Just so, for Winckelmann himself, the steeling of the muscles through physical exercise was an integral part of the sculpture's beauty; it signified virility while posture and expression projected harmony.[66] The male stereotype represented a principle of beauty removed from individual considerations, even while it addressed the need to reconcile the two opposing forces that seemed to pull society apart.

Winckelmann's relevance to contemporary concerns, indeed to those of the new century, explains his influence. To be sure, those who popularized his interpretation of masculinity could have gone to the ancients themselves for inspiration, to form their own view of figures like Hercules or Laocoön. But the past is always mediated by the present, and Winckelmann's contemporaries and their successors thought that he had captured Greek reality and that it suited their own concerns. Here, as always in the pursuit of history, in order to understand later attitudes it may not always be relevant to ask how the past actually saw itself but, instead, what contemporaries took to be the truth about a bygone age.

Women, significantly enough, were excluded from the principles of beauty we have discussed and therefore from what beauty symbolized for society's self-image. Supreme beauty for Winckelmann was male rather than female.[67] Examples of supreme beauty such as the Apollo of Belvedere, Antonius, or Laocoön are never androgynous but are "real men" because female influences are excluded.[68] This idea of male beauty was an unusual one in modern culture, where beauty had traditionally been the domain of women and the association of a clearly defined timeless beauty with the activist male role might have sufficed to give masculinity a new dimension. But here, as we saw, in addition, virility was endowed with the precise virtues modern society treasured. Women retained a monopoly on their particular sensuous beauty, but that of men, newly discovered, was made to perform different and dynamic functions.

Men destined to much greater fame than Winckelmann himself came under his influence. Johann Gottfried von Herder, for example, saw Winckelmann as a Greek who rose from the ashes of his people in order to illuminate his age.[69] But he also believed in 1781, the precise time at which he wrote Winckelmann's eulogy, that ancient art had ceased to be in fashion.[70] Herder may have been correct, but the Greek revival continued to describe an appealing male stereotype. Goethe, for example, put his enormous prestige at Winckelmann's disposal. He wrote copiously about Winckelmann, in whose aesthetic he found confirmation of his ideal of the autonomous human being who must educate himself through art to a greater humanity.[71] Winckelmann's ideals became part of the process of *Bildung*, that middle-class urge to self-education and character building that in central Europe was meant to create good citizens. This was a powerful association, strengthened still further by Goethe's belief that Winckelmann himself exemplified all that according to nature a man should represent. The beautiful human being was said to be the end product of nature.[72] For these men of the Enlightenment, the manly beauty of Greek youths not only provided an example for those who sought *Bildung* but was a part of nature and nature's laws, a steady base in a rapidly changing world.

Even those who criticized Winckelmann admired him. Friedrich Schiller thought Winckelmann's descriptions too abstract; he himself saw Greek sculpture filled with color and form. And yet Schiller illustrates how the standard of beauty, the aesthetics, that Winckelmann advocated served to furnish a sense of stability in that age of Napoleonic Wars, revolution, and social change: art has preserved man's dignity, he wrote in 1795, and must remain beyond the reach of human interference.[73] Art provides the absolute standard of judgment. Karl Philip Moritz, the eighteenth-century writer and philosopher, may have been near the mark when he criticized Winckelmann's disembodied beauty and held that art should penetrate the beauty of the living body. Yet there was no real contradiction here; after all, Winckelmann's ideal of beauty was destined to guide the bodily development of living men. Moreover, Moritz showed no understanding of the attraction such an abstraction exercised when it was embodied in the familiar human form; it was a goal to be aimed at independent of government or politics.[74]

Winckelmann's influence radiated beyond the German-speaking lands. He was received enthusiastically in France, for example, even though his "noble simplicity and quiet grandeur" had native roots in the thought of the so-called ancients nearly a century earlier. Winckelmann's ideas had penetrated the France of the Enlightenment less than two years after he was first translated in 1755, and the *Encyclopèdie*, that great manifesto of the times, praised him for having proved that the Greeks had created the ideal beauty.[75] Ever since the French Revolution he was seen as a bridge between contemporary France and France as the rightful heir of the ideals of the ancients according to Winckelmann's interpretation.[76] Through his assertion that the Greek ideal of freedom was a prerequisite for the flourishing of Greek art, his *History of Ancient Art* became a focus of the political as well as artistic debates taking place in France at that time.[77]

It is not surprising, therefore, that Jacques-Louis David, the most important painter during the French Revolution, who himself influenced ideals of manhood, greatly admired Winckelmann. He was inspired by Winckelmann's copies of classical figures in painting some of his warriors, and these in turn exemplified quiet, thoughtful characters, the "*soldat calme*" who in his *Léonidas at Thermopylae* (1814; Figure 2.4) contemplated the promise of eternity before going into battle.[78] David joined heroism and calm to moral beauty, and in paintings such as his famous *Oath of the Horatians* (1784) opposed these manly qualities to female weakness and passion: the Horatians, father and sons, swear to sacrifice themselves for Rome while the women sit by, cry, and lament.[79] However indirectly, Winckelmann may have influenced the French: the standard of manly beauty and comportment he and they proclaimed were similar.

Yet Winckelmann's ideas, if never fundamentally changed, were revised during the nineteenth century. Walter Pater, in England, for example, writing in 1867, saw in the elegance and restfulness of Winckelmann's Greek sculptures that date from the fourth century B.C. an "archaic immobility." He had excluded from his vision the "bolder type of art," which was closer to the reality of life.[80] A few years earlier Robert Knox, the famous Scottish anatomist, had continued to see in Greek figures a mixture of robustness, energy, and vitality, characteristics, so he thought, inherited by the northern race.[81] However, the manly ideal in England, while still influenced by Winckelmann's Apollo of Belvedere was eventually joined to that of the Elgin Marbles, which were put on public display in London in 1807. These figures, even when in repose, use their arms, talk, and turn toward one another. Two criticisms of Winckelmann stand out by the end of the nineteenth century: that his Greeks are too passive, and that they are not close enough to the reality of life. Sir Charles Bell, medical man and surgeon, summarized the latter criticism in exaggerated fashion when in 1844 he

2.4 "The Serene Soldier"; *Léonidas at Thermopylae* by Jacques-Louis David, 1813–1814. Leonidas, chief of the Spartans, was killed in this battle. (395cm × 531cm; Louvre, Paris. By permission.)

rejected Winckelmann's assertion that Greek beauty represented divinity; for Bell, beauty had material causes dependent on the proper functioning of the nerves and muscles.[82]

Such criticism reflected an age of accelerating social and economic change, when a new romanticism craved greater sentimentality expressed through bodily gestures and movement, and at the same time the abstract must find concrete embodiment. The emphasis on materialism, the self-sufficiency of the figures, also points to a new scientific spirit that intended to bring the Greek ideal down to earth, to assert that the male body, however beautiful, was after all a biological construct. Pater wrote about the naturalness of Greek figures as well, and he had high praise for a Greek artist who had fashioned a Greek youth in that moment of rest that lies between two opposite motions: the backward swing of the right arm and the forward motion of the left foot.[83] But in spite of these attempts to bring movement into the ideal sculpture, the essentials of Winckelmann's male ideal remained intact, even when it was no longer considered a direct emanation of the divine, and if its quiet repose was invaded by gentle motion.

The emphasis on proportion, on the character of the whole figure, remained and passion was kept in check. According to Walter Pater, the beautiful male features must show no anger, desire, or surprise, and although he desired some motion on the part of the Greek paradigm, it must not be abrupt.[84] Robert Knox would have agreed with Pater's description of the ideal of Greek beauty as "rest in motion."[85] Winckelmann was modernized; his quiet repose and ideal manliness given a bolder, more severe, and less divine cast but without changing the basic principles of masculine beauty.

A standard for male beauty had been set by the second half of the eighteenth century that prevailed and was to be co-opted by those stressing national or racial peculiarities without realizing that rival nations and races shared much the same male ideal. Thus, for example, German advocates of an Aryan race believed that in their trek from their place of origin in the Far East, the Aryans had passed through Greece and co-opted what was best in the ancient world. Sometimes color was added to Winckelmann's ideal of male beauty. He had thought—mistakenly—that Greek sculptures were without color, but Carl Gustav Caro in his *Symbolik der menschlichen gestalt* (Symbolism of the Human Form, 1853) proclaimed that blond coloring derived from the sun was an additional mark of superior peoples.[86] Nevertheless, for Caro, the bodily structure of Greek sculpture was superior to all others. To be sure, there were those in Germany toward the fin de siècle who thought that irregular features reflected the inwardness of the German, his peculiar stubbornness.[87] But such Aryans were usually pictured as old and gnarled; the young measured up to a Greek standard of beauty. The Nazis at the height of modern nationalism, as we shall see, seemed to have an inkling that they shared this male ideal with others.[88] Throughout this book we point out such parallels in order to illustrate the depth of this male concept of beauty.

3

GETTING THERE

The standard of male beauty had now been set, but how was that standard to be reached? Winckelmann himself had written about the Greek gymnasium where gymnastic exercises demonstrate the manly contours and sublime beauty of the naked male body.[1] The rise of gymnastics as a means of steeling the human body was a vital step in the perfection of the male stereotype and came to play a leading role. The fit body, well sculpted, was to balance the intellect, and such a balance was thought to be a prerequisite for the proper moral as well as physical comportment. Upstanding youth should be "the straightest of limb, the keenest of brain," as an oft-repeated English saying has it. Gymnastics did not come into its own solely through Winckelmann's inspiration or even through Greek examples. Throughout much of the eighteenth century, it was seen as a component of personal hygiene, as André David Tissot put it in 1780: "Gymnastics is that part of medicine which teaches maintenance or restoration of health by means of exercise."[2] Tissot in his *Avis au peuple sur la santée* (The People's Handbook of Health, 1761), written around the same time that Winckelmann's most important writings were published, refers not to the Greeks but to primitive peoples close to nature as exemplars of a wholesome masculine physique. Even so, gymnastics was said to control unlawful passions as the moral imperative gained ever-greater importance in discussions about physical exercise. The identity of body and soul, to which we have referred earlier, was basic to athletics as part of the construction of modern masculinity. Thus for Rousseau, bodily exercise was no longer inferior to the spirit, but both were an integral part of life lived according to nature.[3] J. F. C. Guts Muth's *Gymnastik für die Jugend* (Gymnastics for Youth, 1793) was the basic text of modern gymnastics, even though a discussion about the usefulness of physical exercise for the education of youth had started in Germany a few years earlier,[4] and it was edited and reedited throughout the nineteenth century. Guts Muth, together with Friedrich Ludwig Jahn—who a few years later, at the beginning of the nineteenth century, became the energetic popularizer of gymnastics in Germany—founded a tradition that, as we shall see, influenced central Europe and touched France as well.[5] Admiration for Greece informs Guts Muth's book, though it does not dominate. Although Guts Muth repeats that body and spirit are dependent upon each other, he emphasizes the primacy of the body. Physical awkwardness, weakness of nerves, and ill health in a person mean that his awareness of world is distorted because it is transmitted from the body to the mind.[6] Nothing will benefit the man who is a weakling, prone to illness, and spoiled.[7] So far Guts Muth's justification for gymnastics is straightforward. It is when he emphasizes that his practical instructions brook no interference from aesthetics that he contradicts himself, for the ideal of beauty does play a role in his gymnastics for youth, where physical beauty is said to affect beauty of spirit.[8] The balanced proportions and the harmony of all parts of the body, as well as the proper posture, are important, for "who would not be impressed by the letter of recommendation beauty provides?"[9] Male beauty sets, once more, the standard of manliness, a symbol of strength and spirit. Guts Muth goes so far as to write that ugliness disheartens even the most barbaric nations.[10] Such a statement assumes a consensus about the nature of beauty, for, as we saw in chapter 2, a standard of beauty and ugliness had been set and was about to become normative.

Manly beauty was a sign of moral worth. Moral health and mental robustness, Guts Muth tells us, are more often than not the consequences of bodily strength.[11] The male body, beauty, and morals are linked once more; together they symbolize "manly courage" and a "manly spirit." The human examples Guts Muth cites to document his manly ideal are natural man, the Apollo of Belvedere, and Indian warriors, an odd mixture of Enlightenment ideals of the noble savage and the Greek.[12] This was no exhortation to resort to force. On the contrary, the moderation that enters here was typical of the longing for harmony running throughout the construction of the new masculine stereotype, just as it informed middle-class society as a whole. Manly courage, Guts Muth holds, must find a middle way between foolhardiness and cowardice. He defines manly courage largely as chivalry, which meant protecting the weak and speaking the truth, as well as saving the victims of fire or accidents.[13] Like Friedrich Ludwig Jahn, Guts Muth's younger contemporary who eclipsed him in fame, he saw in modern manliness the continuation of some of the chivalric tradition. Indeed, fencing did become a part of gymnastics, and Ernst Eiselen, one of the collaborators of Jahn in Germany, wrote manuals on both gymnastics and fencing. Jahn himself regarded fencing as one of the principal exercises completing gymnastic training.[14] But patriot that he was, he traced the tradition of fencing back not to the Middle Ages but to the ancient Germans.

For Guts Muth, this chivalric tradition was not just an aid to patriotism; neither considerations of national consciousness nor a warrior tradition played a part in his treatise written before the Napoleonic Wars had engulfed central Europe. Here the compassionate, moral side of the chivalric tradition was transmitted into the new century, rather than its more aggressive tendencies, which, as we saw in chapter 2, were to dominate the duel in Germany. Guts Muth's use of the concept of chivalry was a typical example of the adjustment of the chivalric ideal to bourgeois sensibilities: the compassion and uprightness it exemplified when it was integrated with the bodily and moral qualities that a modern man was supposed to possess.

Eventually, however, Guts Muth himself took advantage of the reaction to the French Revolution in order to get the Prussian authorities to accept gymnastics as part of the ongoing reform of the schools, which was, in part, designed to educate Prussian patriots. Guts Muth now argued for physical education as a necessary part of military training, an argument that was well received.[15] He followed this up after the Napoleonic Wars with his *Turnbuch für die Söhne des Vaterlands* (Manual of Gymnastics for the Sons of the Fatherland, 1817), and here he introduced military exercises and the use of rifles. Still, he did so reluctantly, and unlike Jahn or Per-Henrik Ling of Sweden (the third of the three founders of modern gymnastics), he wanted to keep military gymnastics separate from the gymnastics that he had advocated in his most famous book.

Military gymnastics meant gymnastics as part of military exercises, and not the so-called war games that Guts Muth proposed as part of the relaxation of body and soul. These were harmless games, usually the storming of some imaginary fortress or taking prisoners, where a staff was used as substitute for a sword, and where shoving or fighting to obtain this staff from an "enemy soldier" was strictly prohibited. Whoever lost his staff was either a prisoner or out of the game. Still, these were war games and there was an enemy whose flag must be thrown over the wall of the conquered fortress.[16] However mildly and indirectly, here manhood and war were linked and such war games were played in German boarding schools at least until the Second World War.

Both Ling and Jahn took over Guts Muth's basic propositions about manliness, and yet Jahn is still regarded by many as the founder of modern gymnastics, perhaps because he gave gymnastics an openly patriotic cast that he added to Guts Muth's ideal of manliness. He called gymnastic exercise the "lifeline of the German people" because it alone would lead to youthfulness and manliness, to a community of Germans without regard to religion, region, and caste.[17] Jahn, unlike Guts Muth, from the very first saw gymnastics as shaping true manliness and also as a preparation for military skills, and he never tired of reiterating this purpose of gymnastics from the German Wars of Liberation until mid-century.[18] Jahn viewed gymnastics as a public and communal activity, creating an esprit de corps for a future German elite. Seeing groups of athletes exercising on the Berlin meadow called the Hasenheide popularized gymnastics from 1811 onward in a manner that a mere book of exercises could not rival.

Jahn himself termed Guts Muth one of his predecessors and made use of his book.[19] By the time Jahn wrote his own *Deutsche Turnkunst* (German Gymnastics, 1816), however, the French occupation of Prussia had ended, Napoleon had been defeated, and yet the goal of German unity to which he was committed was not within reach. His emphasis upon a communal spirit among gymnasts, endurance, and selflessness[20] was meant to create German patriots ready and able to fight in Germany's cause at a moment's notice. Jahn stressed that gymnasts themselves must be "chaste, pure, capable, fearless, truthful and ready to bear arms."[21] These specific qualities need emphasis, for they will accompany us throughout the modern construction of manliness. Guts Muth had shared most of them, and they expressed the need for both a dynamic and order that, as we have mentioned, society needed as it entered the modern age. But Jahn did not neglect the aesthetics of true masculinity, so important for the masculine stereotype. Thus he gave the highest office among the first gymnasts to one in particular, Friedrich Fries, who exemplified, in his words, "youth, beauty of body and soul."[22]

Jahn's definition of gymnastics was all-encompassing. It took in not only fencing but also swimming, dancing, skating, riding, and the martial arts. These are athletics as opposed to team sports, an important distinction. The male body had to be sculpted in order to approach the male ideal, and here team sports were thought to be useless. Such sports, moreover, meant competition, but patriotism required solidarity. Jahn's gymnastic exercises were not only meant to form healthy and beautiful bodies that would express a proper morality but were designed in fact to create new Germans. He wrote that it was the most sacred duty of German boys to become true German men.[23] Training in manliness was always his aim. What he called "German gymnastics" were performed as a group, though individual accomplishment was recognized. To symbolize the purpose of these exercises, he changed the Latin word *gymnastic* to the supposedly German word *Turnen*.[24] The gymnasts wore identical attire suitable for exercise and that in addition made their bodily contours visible (protruding stomachs were not tolerated). The *Turnplatz*—the field on which gymnastics took place—was likened to a public sanctuary where, so one tract has it, legends about Germanic heroes sprang to life and the past informed the future.[25]

A messianic element was introduced into the formation of the male body, never to leave it entirely. The notion that a true man must serve a higher ideal became in the end an integral part of what could be called the militarization of masculinity. Though Jahn himself was a patriot, he had no use for either marching or military uniforms; they constricted the body and its movements. Even when he referred to Prussian military training,[26] he had in mind volunteers or freebooters who had fought in the wars of liberation but not as professional soldiers under strict military discipline. Nevertheless, from the French Revolution onward the connection between gymnastics and the military became an established fact. Gymnastics spread from Germany, Switzerland, and Austria to countries such as Italy and France through the example of Guts Muth and Jahn, and there it was supported above all by the military. Universal military service had just been introduced, and the health and fitness of individual recruits was a serious concern. But general medical considerations also played their part: for example, in France, Colonel Francois Amoros's *Manuel de l'éducation physique et morale* (Manual for Physical and Moral Education, 1830) advocated gymnastics for medical, military, and moral reasons, but the military purpose predominated.[27]

In both France and in Italy gymnastics got off to a slow, sputtering start, and did not really take hold until mid–nineteenth century, or even toward its end, when it finally became part of the school curriculum. German or Swiss influence was always important as an inspiration; thus Rudolf Obermann, who founded the first Italian gymnastic society in Turin (1844) and became the dominant force in Italian gymnastics, was of Swiss origin and inspired by German examples. The Italian military institutionalized gymnastics through its training program.[28] No matter how varied the reception throughout these nations, gymnastics was considered a means to attain the proper standard of masculinity, a means that, whatever its goal, both affirmed and reenforced the male stereotype through its emphasis upon bodily structure and comportment.

Not only Guts Muth but also his successors in France and Italy emphasized the moral consequences of gymnastic exercises: that a fit and beautiful body indicates a noble soul. Rudolf Obermann, for example, wrote that physical strength denotes moral courage.[29] At the same time he stresses that everything possible must be done to make youth virile, to save it from what he calls a hermaphrodism, which would leave only the appearance of the male intact while endowing him with the slackness of women. Gymnastics, as Obermann has it, prevents effeminacy and creates "manly men"—disciplined, industrious, modest, and persevering.[30] This litany of virtues reads like a commentary on Winckelmann's "quiet strength." The contrast between manly and effeminate men was present throughout the construction of modern manliness. The arguments on behalf of virility and manly beauty implied the existence of their opposite, and indeed Lavater had spent as much time on the ugly as the beautiful face. The new bourgeois society that was coming into being defined itself partly against its supposed opposite, and the ideal of manliness had the unmanly man as its foil.

As the nineteenth century progressed, gymnastics became a social hygiene that might even serve to transform feckless proletarians into virtuous citizens and eventually keep socialism, internationalism, and nihilism at bay.[31] In 1895 Walter Pater summed up the all-encompassing function of gymnastics in helping to sculpt the masculine ideal when he referred to the Greek enthusiasm for gymnastics as a matter partly of character and of the soul, of the balanced proportion between soul and body. Gymnastics, as in Greece, develops the physical perfection of the youthful form.[32]

England was the exception, in spite of Pater's paean to gymnastics; there team sport was regarded as education in manliness. When the public schools—boarding schools that educated the English elite—were reformed during the 1830s, "godliness and good learning" were supposed to prevail, and education to virtue was a matter of the chapel rather than the playing field. The strong evangelical spirit in the first half of the nineteenth century meant that a boy had to prove himself in the fight against sin; it was the outcome of that struggle that supposedly left its mark on his face.[33] He was supposed to fight a fair fight, but there was as yet no organized athletic activity to encourage fair play. But between 1850 and 1880 organized sport gradually took over all training in manliness: "a truly chivalrous football player . . . was never guilty of lying, or deceit or meanness, whether of word or action."[34] Here sport and morality were once again joined. Typically enough, the saying that the Battle of Waterloo was won on the playing fields of Eton dates from 1889 and not from the time of Napoleon.[35]

The predominance of games in these schools was due to the decline in evangelic fervor and the need for discipline in a boarding school. Fair play was now taught through proper behavior on the playing field, the chivalry that became part of the definition of an English gentleman. Team sports such as cricket were considered a training in manliness and also analogous to an imaginary, chivalrous field of battle, perceptions that distinguished England from the rest of Europe. Nevertheless, the virtues team sport instilled were much the same as those gymnastics furthered as well, with the exception of the emphasis on fair play, which was rare among the virtues attached to physical exercise in France, Germany, or Italy. Perhaps emphasis on fair play was regarded as necessary in the nation with an economy that, although the most advanced in Europe, could easily degenerate into a war of one against all. But in addition to such virtues, good breeding defined the English gentleman, meaning the proper manners (which Burke had thought so important in contrast to those of the Jacobins), simplicity, and tenderness. He must observe a balance in all things, never appear ostentatious or immoderate—but then, these were virtues that were part of a general consensus about the proper manly behavior.

The steeling of the male body had a significance far beyond health and hygiene or acquiring strength and motor skills. It created manly beauty and character, it forged a stereotype. Gymnastics and sport would retain this function throughout modern times. Even today, sport in the popular imagination remains a creator of manly virtue, though unbridled competition, typical for the mid–twentieth century, has made team sports such as football the focus of aggression rather than an educator in what had traditionally been regarded as masculine virtue.

The creation of a steeled and pleasing body was part of a general education in virtue that encompassed those qualities we have mentioned so often, such as moderation and quiet strength. The male aesthetic symbolized the virtues that society prized; male beauty was, as it were, transparent, displaying the ingredients essential to modern masculinity. And yet, fashioning a proper male body did not suffice. Willpower was needed to create the ideal type. Gymnasts were apt to assert that physical exercise not merely benefits bodily health but steels the human will as well.[36] The idea that the human will can be educated to manliness was widespread and not confined to gymnastic exercise. Instilling self-confidence in children, teaching them perseverance and courage were goals followed by German educators in the quest for willpower.[37]

As a rule, a physical element played a role in the training of the will, even if there was some confusion whether a proper moral attitude was not at the very least of equal importance. Thus in his *Die Erziehung zum Mute durch Tunnen, Spiel und Sport* (Education for Courage through Gymnastics, Games and Sport, 1900), Konrad Koch, a teacher at a German gymnasium, praised gymnastics as essential for training the will but at the same time located the roots of true willpower both in Christianity and in love of the fatherland. Physical courage always provided a test of the will, but passing this test assumed the existence of those manly virtues we have mentioned so often—without the proper morality neither manly courage nor, for that matter, the body beautiful could exist.

The high road to the construction of modern masculinity ran through the sculpting of the male body, which entailed a commitment to normative social attitudes and behavior, the virtues that modern society prized so much. But even in a secularizing society these were for the most part thought to rest on Christian foundations as well as upon the Greeks.

Some in the nineteenth century believed that the Greeks hand in hand with the Jews prepared the coming of Christ; the writer George Eliot found men educated at Rugby, an English public school, "supposing that Christ spoke Greek."[38] Many writers usually described self-control, moderation, and harmony not just as Greek but also as Christian virtues, and the influence of Christianity in creating true manliness must not be underrated. This was especially the case in Protestant Germany, with its strong Pietistic tradition, and in England, where, for example, in elite boarding schools the chapel, if no longer dominant, was at least supposed to equal the playing field. Morality could also be set on Enlightenment foundations, and there the development of reason was believed to be essential for an education in manliness.[39] But this was a distinctly minority position. Christianity still governed morality, even if it was often merely a metaphor for those rules of comportment society considered essential.

Many of the attributes a true man was supposed to possess had already played a large part in the Pietistic and Evangelical revivals of the eighteenth century—indeed, they could perhaps be traced back to Calvin's reformation. Control over one's passions, moderation, and sexual and mental purity had all been strong demands of Protestantism long before Winckelmann saw them personified in pagan youth. To be sure, these qualities had not, as a rule, been anchored in the appearance of the male body, and just such actualization was of prime importance in the construction of the male stereotype. Even so, a connection was forged from time to time, though the physical was always subordinated to the moral imperative.

Johann Kaspar Lavater, for example, whose reading of the human face we discussed in chapter 2, was a Pietist for whom man's encounter with God through Christ contributed toward perfecting the human body.[40] The emphasis must be on "perfecting" the human body, for nothing human could be perfect in a sinful world. Thus in an English Evangelical child's manual called *The Fairchild Family* (1818), the parents tell their little children (five, eight, and ten years old) that by nature they are fitted only for everlasting punishment and that no actions on their part, only trust in Jesus, can save them. The contrast with Winckelmann's belief in the autonomy of man symbolized by the beauty of Greek youths could not have been greater. But this difference also explains why the Greek model with its concrete and unchanging standard of beauty was indispensable in the fashioning of an ideal male stereotype.

Pietism itself was concerned with the problem of masculinity. God had made man of a robust nature, strong in body and mind, fit to protect and defend. Yet, as Philip Greven has pointed out, Evangelical men were uncomfortable with their masculinity, for man was supposed to be a bridegroom of Christ, and this meant total reliance upon the strength of Christ and an admission of one's own impotence.[41] Moreover, tenderness was considered both a Christian and a male virtue, and here Evangelical manhood came close to accepting so-called feminine attributes.[42] English Evangelicals were often on the defensive because they were attacked as weaklings and milksops, tender-hearted men who wept in public at a time when such a show of emotion—common enough in the eighteenth century—was thought decidedly unmanly. Evangelical Christianity did serve in this instance to modify normative manliness: showing tenderness and affection in public became respectable in such circles, even if by no means accepted by society at large. Still, in the long run even this kind of Christianity did not put forward an alternative masculinity because the basic manly virtues were kept intact, and were even reenforced as far as self-control, activism, and the status of men as rulers of the family were concerned. Nevertheless, Evangelicalism in England and Protestantism in Germany, by smoothing the rough edges, helped to adjust masculinity to middle-class sensibilities.

However, neither the emphasis on tenderness and compassion nor that upon original sin prevented the emergence within the English Evangelical movement in mid–nineteenth century of an aggressive, robust, and activist masculinity. "Muscular Christianity," as it was called, translated the belief in a robust body and mind into a battle cry against all sinfulness, and against those who stood in the way of England's greatness. The battle was joined on behalf of "the great calling of the English nation," as the Evangelical minister and novelist Charles Kingsley called it in *Westward Ho!* (which underwent forty editions between 1855, when it was published, and the end of the century)—a book dedicated to "that type of English virtue, at once manful and Godly." Self-control was essential, the "boldness of man against himself,"[43] but so were ideas of chivalry that mitigated a Christianity that in the name of masculinity sometimes came close to the worship of force. Thomas Hughes, an important propagandist for "Muscular Christianity," told

English boys in 1857 that if they fought, they had to fight to the end—it was neither godly nor honest to give in while one could still stand and see.[44]

Godliness and manliness were joined, but it was the so-called manly qualities that counted. David Newsome has called the phrase "I act, therefore I am" as good a slogan for the early Victorian conception of manliness as we can hope to find.[45] Muscular Christianity attempted to set the by-now traditional ideals of manhood upon Christian Evangelical rather than pagan Greek foundations. But these two roots of masculine morality could, as we have seen, exist in tandem; the morality itself could be called Christian, but masculinity as a living symbol was informed by the aesthetic taste of Greece. Typically enough, outward appearance played a somewhat less clearly defined role when real masculinity was said to result from Christian Evangelical belief. The true Christian man, however, was also physically well developed, even if the details of looks and appearance were not fully worked out. The stereotype of the clean-cut young Englishman—tall and strong—informed this masculinity. The countertype represented the very opposite, and in this case effeminacy was the principal enemy of masculinity characterizing, for example, Papists, Spaniards, and the French (all considered England's traditional enemies).

Will power and courage were essential masculine attributes for Christians fighting the good fight, and indeed the pietistic and Evangelical thrust of modern manliness differed only in emphasis from that discussed earlier. The standards by which masculinity must be judged could be reached by fashioning the male body through physical exercise as a transparent sign of moral worth or, to a much more limited extent in England, through the practice of Evangelical Christianity.

Whether Christian or Greek, or both, military virtues were usually present: after all, the masculine stereotype was created during a period of revolution and war. Heroism, death, and sacrifice became associated with manliness, as did the discipline that had encouraged the military to advocate the introduction of gymnastics into the school curriculum. The new citizen army of the French Revolution was in itself a school for manliness. At first, the French Revolution had relied on volunteers for its defense, but in 1793 the Legislative Assembly proclaimed the levy of the whole of the male population capable of bearing arms. This was a new departure, the end of mercenaries who had fought for money or adventure. Now soldiers were conscripted in a noble cause that itself would inspire their struggle. Here soldiering could become part of the training in manliness whereas earlier mercenaries had lacked interest in, or provided poor material for, education in manly virtue.

The soldiers of the French Revolution, just as the volunteers fighting in the Prussian army against the French, came from all classes of the population. The ideals of manliness viewed through the prism of war penetrated into the general population, a feat that the medieval knight had never managed or even wanted to accomplish. The so-called soldierly ideals themselves were disseminated by the literate and educated, officers for the most part, who came from the upper or middle classes. The modern warrior now joined the Greek youth and the athlete as a model of masculinity. When Friedrich Pockels, a prolific German author of books on man, woman, and society, in 1813 came to write on proper social behavior, he felt bound to include a section on the armed forces because, as he put it, they had attained a size and importance that they had lacked before. Moreover, a spirit of camaraderie reigned among them—they were all soldiers—regardless of rank.[46] And indeed, the soldier was now your son or your neighbor and not some mercenary whom you feared and shunned.

Heroism, death, and sacrifice on behalf of a higher purpose in life became set attributes of manliness. The revolutionaries in France had praised "heroic stoicism and dignity," and these were the subject of visual representations as well, just as Winckelmann's Laocoön in his agony had symbolized "quiet strength." Jacques-Louis David painted such heroes, and in the innumerable festivals staged during the Revolution in order to honor its martyrs, death, sacrifice, and heroism were inexorably linked. The physical description of revolutionary heroes in pamphlets and pictures was an integral element of the representation of their status. Thus an imprisoned young Girondin deputy, shortly to be guillotined by the Jacobins, was described by an admirer as holding his head high even in prison. Moreover, his character had left its mark on this face of a "virile and manly beauty."[47] Alex Potts has told us how the neoclassicism that dominated revolutionary art made male beauty more vivid through the body's violent encounter with death.[48] What has been called the revolutionary's love for pictorial representations of the athletic male body's encounter with death was certainly part of the new *ésprit militaire*.[49]

However, death and sacrifice were joined to the idea of freedom, whether it was liberty, equality, and fraternity, or as in the German Wars of Liberation, the quest for national unity. The freedom with which such heroes were associated was freedom in the service of a higher cause, not individual freedom but that of the nation or of the new French Republic. Friedrich Schiller's famous "cavalry song" (1797) defined that freedom: only the soldier is free because he has discarded the anxieties of daily life, faces his fate boldly, and looks death in the eye. Freedom here is an integral part of sacrificial death, which, as the poem has it, if it does not strike the soldier today, will strike him tomorrow. Indeed, freedom stands side by side with conformity: the heroes and martyrs were stereotypes exemplifying the manly ideal.

Commitment to an impersonal cause sanctified the life and death of the individual; it was the prerequisite for heroic manhood. Thomas Carlyle's heroes, for example, must be sincere and earnest but, above all, as he writes in his *Heroes and Hero Worship* (1841), they must be serious about ideas. He praised Rousseau because "ideas possessed him like demons."[50] What Carlyle in his much-read work calls ideas constitute a higher cause, something beyond the individual that defined his heroes. The proper moral comportment was the other essential component of true heroism; here, once more, virtue replaced the older aristocratic concept of honor. The hero must be all of one cloth: his courage should manifest itself in the words he utters, in his opinions no less than in his posture and facial expression.[51] The totality of manliness is reaffirmed. The hero thus focuses and incorporates all the factors that constitute the ideal of masculinity.

English ideas of heroism in particular were informed by a moral imperative that overshadows physical endowment. Thus when much later, in the twentieth century, John Buchan, like Carlyle an advocate of hero worship, wrote that Caesar and Nelson had something of womanish delicacy and courtesy in their faces, it was meant not as weakness but as praise for their spirituality.[52] Yet moral courage was the chief attribute of Buchan's heroes, a masculine courage that, as he put it, owed nothing to women.[53] The "higher purpose" to which the hero was devoted must be based on the proper morality. This left ample room for the cause to which most heroes were, in fact, dedicated, that of their respective nations. The construction of modern masculinity took place not only against the background of middle-class society but also in concert with the rise of a new national consciousness. The nation coopted the ideal of manliness as its own: French revolutionary heroes fought to defend *La Patrie*; Jahn put his gymnasts at the disposal of the

German quest for national unity. "Parents whose children died the glorious death for the fatherland are to be envied," we are told during the German wars of liberation; "among the various kinds of death we are bound to meet sooner or later, the death for the fatherland is the most enviable."[54] Here death, sacrifice, and fatherland are joined, a triad that will remain in place as a test of true manhood.

Indeed, for Joseph de Maistre, the conservative French political theorist, writing in 1797, the noblest ideals of manly virtue are realized in war, just as nations were said to reach the greatness of which they are capable only after long and bloody conflict.[55] Not only in Germany but also in France nationalists supported and were the principal transmitters of an aggressive masculinity. Death in war taught a lesson in virtue to the living. From this time onward, manliness and patriotism were closely associated, though later, as we shall see, socialists also co-opted ideals of masculinity. Nevertheless, it was always nationalism that exalted the male stereotype as one of its means of self-representation. The relative newness of such an association, and of the warrior element in the composition of modern masculinity, may explain the constant emphasis upon manliness found in contemporary writing during the German wars of liberation.

One vital ingredient is all but missing up to this point in our discussion of the building blocks of modern masculinity. Men cannot be seen in isolation; women are always present in men's own self-image. Jacques-Louis David's *Oath of the Horatii* (1785), to which we referred in chapter 2, was typical in this respect, with its heroic men and frightened women. Indeed, throughout the period of the French Revolution and Napoleon, women often lament, especially so in literature associated with war. The contrast between warriors and weak women is, for example, brought out in sharp relief in Wilhelm von Humboldt's poem "The Amazons" (1831). There Amazons rush into battle driven by their fate. And yet, unlike men, they knew no joy in battle, no certainty of victory; for them, love and longing must suffice.[56] That von Humboldt was no chauvinist but one of the great humanists of his time makes this statement all the more telling. Small wonder, that the accusation of effeminacy was supposed to deprive men of their manhood. The ideal female body conveyed a sensuous, sexual beauty as opposed to the heroic body of the ideal male.

The warrior projected a heightened image of masculinity, but the division between the sexes also took on a more absolute character. In

1795, von Humboldt, as we mentioned earlier, for example, still believed that beauty, as an expression of a noble humanity, united "pure womanhood and pure manhood." Yet at the same time, and typical for the view of masculinity we have discussed, he wrote that the construction of the male body, with its strictness of form, expresses what nature had wanted to achieve with the human body in general. The body of woman, with its voluptuous and rounded forms, had a more specific and restricted sexual function.[57] Eventually, as in describing the Amazons, von Humboldt dropped the ideal of a composite beauty and gave to each sex its own particular aesthetic.[58]

The separation between men and women was total in all its aspects. In a popular work on the female sex, for example, Friedrich Pockels asserted in 1797 that if woman was endowed with manly strength, manly courage, and a manly spirit, all her charm would vanish.[59] Women were often pictured surrounded by flowers and children, such as Charlotte in Goethe's *Werther* (1774) (see Figure 1.1) or in Max von Schenkendorf's poem of 1814, "Where is the flowering rose garden, where is the sweet maid?" While women did participate in the festivals of the French Revolution, the selection of a Goddess of Reason at times took on the appearance of a beauty pageant.[60] The Code Napoléon, while being generous to a formerly persecuted minority such as the Jews, was singularly restrictive for women; they were, as we indicated in an earlier chapter, deprived of all rights and became all but chattel to their husbands; it set the seal upon a time when the division between the sexes was finalized. The basic reasons for this sharpened gender division, which cannot be addressed at any length, are to be found in the establishment of the nuclear family, the changing economic structure that excluded women from the workplace, and the needs of the new bourgeois society that we have mentioned so often with its requirement for dynamic and order symbolized by a masculine ideal. Women had, of course, always been largely excluded from the active world of men, but now their place in society was set, at least until the challenge by the woman's rights movements toward the end of the nineteenth century.

In 1796 Johann Gottlieb Fichte summed up the difference between the status of men and women in a manner that illustrates how contemporaries could rationalize the abandonment of the quest for unity centered, for example, on a shared concept of beauty. There had to be a clear division between the sexes, Fichte writes, for if they were in constant flux, it would mean an eternal becoming and the inability to settle upon a determinate mental and bodily form.[61] At the same time, the female was a step below the male, for in the process of conception, woman was an object of male power. Man once again was said to incorporate all of humanity;[62] divine unity was no longer exemplified, as it had been, by the androgyne—part man and part woman—but had been co-opted by man alone.Fichte's ideas about gender are typical, and we hear similar sentiments throughout the next century. "Woman," in Friedrich Pockels's phrase, was "the indulgent friend of man."[63] The words of one right-wing agitator toward the end of the nineteenth century merely summed up a more general feeling, shared by Fichte in a more philosophical mode: "The more female the woman and the more male the man, . . . the healthier society and the state."[64]

Those who did not fit the set pattern laid down for men and women were the enemies of society; they were considered the foil of true masculinity. The building blocks of modern manliness did not stand in isolation; they were constantly reinforced not only through the status of women but also through the presence of enemies apparently bent upon masculinity's destruction. Here, once more, masculinity mirrored the imperatives of society, for modern society also needed enemies to sustain itself, to give it additional focus and coherence. War, as we saw, strengthened the male stereotype, and the enemies of masculinity provided its foil: for the Germans fighting Napoleon, the French were decadent and effeminate, and although the French did not think the Germans especially decadent, they were seen as lacking those virtues necessary for the attainment of true masculinity. The enemies hidden inside the nation were perhaps a greater, certainly a more permanent menace: a reminder of a failed manhood that threatened the established order. Who were these enemies within, and how did their character and appearance relate to the construction of modern masculinity? The countertype they represented is vital for an understanding of the ideal itself, and both were inseparably linked in an unholy alliance.

4

THE COUNTERTYPE

The construction of masculinity had fashioned a stereotype that in its "quiet grandeur" and self-control reflected the view society liked to have of itself. It was relatively easy to identify with such an unambiguous symbol whose external appearance reflected the moral universe, a normalcy that set the standard for an acceptable way of life. But this ideal of masculinity, indeed modern society as a whole, needed an image against which it could define itself. Those who stood outside or were marginalized by society provided a countertype that reflected, as in a convex mirror, the reverse of the social norm. Such outsiders were either those whose origins, religion, or language were different from the rest of the population or those who were perceived as asocial because they failed to conform to the social norms. For those so marginalized, the search for an identity proved difficult and painful. However, not all outsiders faced the same problems, though basically their options were limited to a denial of their identity or its co-optation by the acceptable norm, until—in the last decades of the nineteenth century—these choices were increased by acts of self-emancipation.

What exactly were some of the characteristics of the groups marginalized by modern society? Those who were said to be unsettled, without roots, were usually considered outsiders:

Gypsies, vagrants, and Jews, who, being without territory of their own, were placed into this category by their enemies. Habitual criminals, the insane, and so-called sexual deviants must be added to this list. The marginalization of these groups was not new; they had existed at the fringes of society during the Middle Ages and early modern times, but now their exclusion was systematized as modern society became more structured and more sharply defined. The same systemization that, as we saw, informed the masculine stereotype was now applied to its countertype. The outsider symbolized physical and moral disorder, and popular German novels of the nineteenth century liked to contrast a settled bourgeois life to an unsteady, rootless existence. Here the Jews were a prime target, for unlike Gypsies or vagrants, they were a menacing presence as competitors and, more important in this period, an emancipated minority in the process of assimilation. Thus Gustav Freytag in his popular *Soll und Haben* (Debit and Credit, 1855) pitted a virtuous German merchant house, rooted in its locality, against a Jewish merchant house, always on the move, shifty and dishonest. Similarly, Friedrich Hackländer's *Handel und Wandel* (Trade and Change, 1850) derided frequent travel as leading to insanity, as well as commercial speculation and risk taking over against so-called honest work. These are perhaps extreme examples of trying to slow down modernity and to get a hold on the new speed of time.

Typically enough, the legend of the "wandering Jew," which took its modern form in the seventeenth century, obtained a new lease on life. Gustav Doré, famous as an illustrator of the Bible, in 1852 made a woodcut of the Wandering Jew with a red cross on his forehead, spindly legs and arms, huge nose and blowing hair, and staff in hand that popularized this image (Figure 4.1). This image was now co-opted by anti-Semitic propaganda, whereas originally he had moved with some dignity.[1] The legend itself concerns a Jew who refused to shelter Christ on his way to Golgotha and was condemned to wander about for all eternity. The anti-Semites in nineteenth-century Germany called him the "eternal Jew," emphasizing restlessness as the punishment for sin—the Jew as an eternal vagrant. (The Nazis made a film and staged an exhibition using "the eternal Jew" as its title.)

The specific factors that went into the making of the countertype to modern masculinity were identical with those that had informed the creation of modern masculinity in the first place. Anthropologists in the eighteenth century began to use aesthetic criteria in judging the differ-

4.1 *The Wandering Jew* by Gustav Doré (1852). Doré was mainly famous for his Bible illustrations. (Eduard Fuchs, *Die Juden in der Karikatur* [Munich: Albert Langen Verlag, 1921].)

ence between whites and so-called primitive peoples, and through the so-called scientific methods of cranial comparisons and facial measurements, they exalted the "physically beautiful" as an attribute of superior European species. Moreover, in the 1790s an influential classifier of races such as Peter Camper—in an age much taken with classification—used Winckelmann's ideal of beauty as his principal standard.[2] Other anthropologists and physiognomists followed suit. As we saw, the standard of human beauty was set both in aesthetic perception and in the science of man.

What, then, was the normative standard of ugliness? The standard of beauty determined society's judgment of those who differed from the accepted norm. And as the ideal of beauty reflected the needs of society, so ugliness served to characterize its enemies. The standard of manly beauty was built upon the concept of harmony and measured movement, but also upon the absence of anything accidental; every part of the body must fit into place. Mankind must seek its perfection through beauty.[3] How deeply, therefore, mankind must fall through ugliness—especially if as a practical matter we remember the role that beauty was destined to play in the life of the so-called cultured middle classes as uplift, as a lay religion, as symbolizing the sacred. Ugliness was the reverse of beauty: it was accidental, without harmony, nothing was in its place. Bodily structure lacked firm contours, and the face was marred by a "movable physiognomy." Ugliness was the obverse of the principle of beauty we have described; and just as that principle was objectified by the ideal of true manhood, so ugliness was symbolized by the outsider. His bodily structure differed in every detail from that of the ideal type. Schiller and his contemporaries stressed the importance of form for the perception of beauty, meaning clear lines and harmonious proportions with no tolerance for excess. Not only restlessness, perpetual movement, but also formlessness characterized the outsider; there was no moderation here, no sense of the golden mean that Schiller praised[4] and that corresponded so well to the social ideals of the times.

However, ugliness referred not only to bodily but also to mental characteristics, and here, once more, the outward symbolized inward man. A person's disordered outward appearance signaled a mind that lacked control over the passions, where male honor had become cowardice, honesty was unknown, and lustfulness had taken the place of sexual purity. In short, virtue had been transformed into the practice of vice. Whenever they saw the caricature of the Wandering Jew in all his ugliness, for example, people assumed that he was without morals, a warning against the awful consequences of straying from the accepted norm. And, in this case, the legend of the Wandering Jew had been conceived as a cautionary tale from the beginning. Clearly, ugliness signified in its bodily and mental characteristics the exact opposite of the ideals that beauty symbolized.

The linkage of body and soul was solidified and sharpened by the role that medicine played in designating and defining the so-called outsider. Medicine made its contribution to the construction of modern masculinity through its assertion that a healthy mind and a healthy body are inseparable, a view whose function parallels that which gymnastics and physical exercise fulfilled in sculpting the male body. Beyond this, however, physicians set about defining as diseased those who did not fit into settled society; physical sickness became a menace to society's own well-being. André David Tissot's *L'Onanisme* (Masturbation), cited earlier,[5] provides a good early example of how this was accomplished, the more so as *L'Onanisme* was an influential work that set the tone for the perception of masturbation throughout the next century and a half—and masturbation was thought to be a critical sickness causing other so-called debilitating diseases, including insanity and homosexuality, leading to the nervousness that characterized all outsiders. Outsiderdom left its mark upon the body and mind; in addition, it was part of a whole chain of diseases, one leading to another. The outsider was hedged in on all sides. Even though masturbation, according to Tissot, was accompanied by some real bodily pain, such as headaches, stomach pains, and rheumatism, it was the damage done to the nerves, along with the overall weakness of the body, that posed the chief threat.[6]

Nervousness had been considered a sickness long before this, linked to the condition of the body. Robustness was a barrier against such a disease, and therefore, as Thomas Sydenham, the famed English physician, wrote in 1682, women, because of their delicate constitution, were more prone to nervousness and mental diseases than men.[7] Sick and diseased men had ruined their nerves, which not only threatened to make them effeminate—a point to which we will return—but, through the state of their bodies and mind, documented their lack of manliness. Here everything was accidental, without a fixed place: body, face, and mind were in constant motion. The word *disorder* characterized a state that could end in chaos.

The fascination with nervous disorder throughout the nineteenth century was encouraged by the eighteenth-century cult of sensibility, as well as by Romanticism, but basically it was a response to the rapid pace of social, political, and economic change. The outsider, such as the Jew, came to symbolize change and what it might portend. Shattered nerves were associated with modernity; they were to blame for the degeneration of culture and politics. Typically enough, it was only by the eighteenth century that one could be said to be "nervous,"[8] at a time when toward 1752 physicians such as Albrecht von Haller began research into the sensibility of the nervous system. Here the muscles that induced abrupt bodily movements expressed the diseased state of the nerves. Illnesses that had been ascribed to foul vapors or bad humors were now apt to be blamed upon the nervous system. Nervousness was first of all a mental illness, but it took in all of the body through its muscular contortions. This equation of ugliness and disease, so opposed to the masculine ideal, was spread abroad through words and pictures. The stereotype of the nervous outsider has remained astonishingly stable, just as that of true manliness underwent no fundamental change. But, then, one mirrored the other. Nervousness was destined to remain a principal foe of manliness well into the twentieth century, and for perhaps the majority of the adult population up to our own time.

Tissot thought that the cure for masturbation was cold baths and exercise, by which he meant walking and riding, for gymnastics had not yet made its mark. But there was another cure that did not involve the body directly but came from the mind: the reining in of man's fantasies, passions, and imagination. Pierre-Jean-Georges Cabanis, one of the most influential physicians during the age of the French Revolution, believed that it was the special mission of medicine to integrate the physical and mental into a science of man, and though he regarded the physical condition as basic to health, he was much disturbed by men's passions and misguided flights of the imagination. The "invisible reins of human nature" have to be seized and disciplined.[9] Writing at the end of the eighteenth century, much later than Tissot, he thought that physical exercise and changes in physical habits could change men's character through fashioning new senses.[10] That physical exercise could help stem unwarranted flights of the imagination was a subtext for many advocates of gymnastics and most English supporters of sports in schools.

The German educator Christian Gotthelf Salzmann wrote in 1787 that disorders of the body led to an overheated imagination that should be kept in check by strengthening the human physique.[11] Fanciful imagination, such men believed, could be the harbinger of severe illness. Men's uncontrolled drives lead to excesses that distort body and mind, the very opposite of the manly ideal that had to be devoid of surplus bodily or mental fat.

The strongest drive was thought to be the sex drive, which, when not kept in check, led, for example, to masturbation, with all the consequences Tissot described so graphically. However, not only so-called self-abuse but also an excess of lust in the marriage bed led to dire results. Thus a German guide to all that a man regardless of age has to know, published in 1838, asserted that if marriage partners did not practice moderation in their sexual relations, they might waste away and an early death might result.[12] The aim of this and other manuals of the time was, evidently, to ennoble the sex drive, and as far as this particular manual was concerned, only those perfect in body and mind should have intercourse. If they sleep together before such perfection has been achieved, the body will be destroyed.[13] The unrestrained use of passion and the undue use of the imagination, like nervousness, was thought to destroy the normative stereotype. These were attributes of those marginalized by a society that looked with suspicion upon any exaggeration, whatever form it might take. Just as normative masculinity reflected the ideals of an active, working society, so the outsiders constituted its countertype.

Health and sickness were always considerations close to the concern of men and women living in constant fear of disease and early death. Modern medicine was in its infancy, and already the medicalization of the outsider supported the prejudices of modern society. The physician was about to become an important arbiter of manners and morals in the quest by the medical profession for status, aided by society's awareness of the connection between hygiene and health. Disease was equated with vice, especially by those physicians who helped the courts of law identify deviant sexuality, punishable in all European nations.[14] Health and sickness became conditions that distinguished insider from outsider, easily recognized signs written upon their bodies. The outsider, after all, looked the same as Tissot's masturbator—nervous, feeble, prematurely aged, apparently close to death—and the insider in body and mind expressed that balance for which the Greeks had provided the model. The medical concepts of health and sickness were like the tip of an iceberg that contained all that we have discussed: the state of body and mind, the restlessness in a society where everything must have its place. Small wonder, that an encyclopedia of 1788 could write that he who neglects his health insults the society of which he is a member.[15]

The ideal of beauty so important in the construction of modern masculinity was reversed. Jews, for example, were regarded by many as the inverse of Germans in every respect and were sometimes reviled as subhuman. But this did not mean that they were regarded as nonhuman even by National Socialists; the difference could not be so absolute.[16] The "subhuman" had to be concretized, to be made familiar if it was to pose a believable threat. Jews and the other outsiders were stereotyped as evil kinds of men but nevertheless still recognizable as men even if they reversed traditional values.

Such outsiders, whether Jew or homosexual, could have no honor, which, as we saw, was regarded as an integral part of manhood. As we mentioned earlier, in Germany toward the end of the century an increasing number of student fraternities refused to give Jews the satisfaction of dueling, while Nationalist fraternities in Austria had excluded all Jews from the duel in 1896 because they could not understand the nature of German honor.[17] Whether or not Jewish challenges to a duel were accepted was one barometer to measure the state of anti-Semitism, given the manly qualities of courage and sangfroid that had to be tested. The supposed cowardice of Jews was a staple not only of anti-Semitic literature but also of popular farce; in Germany ever since the mid–nineteenth century, the supposed funk of Jews in the face of the duel and military service was a frequent target.[18] Actors specializing in such characters helped to popularize the Jewish stereotype. It hardly needs emphasis that anti-Semites read the Jew out of all the qualities associated with masculinity; he was at best half a man.

Once again, the external mirrored the internal; the structure of the Jewish body was thought to be different from that of normal men, as Sander Gilman has explained so well,[19] and that difference was made manifest through precisely those parts of the body that command most attention: nose, feet, neck, and coloration. All of these bodily features project ugliness as opposed to the standard of manly looks. The so-called Jewish nose, bent at the top, jutting hawklike from the face, existed already as a caricature in the sixteenth century (after all, the nose is one of the most prominent features of the face). It became firmly established as a so-called Jewish trademark only by the mid–eighteenth century, however, and soon became a foil for the straight nose of Greek beauty (Figure 4.2). Winckelmann himself had not explicitly condemned the Jewish nose, which he described as similar to a hawk's nose, and instead singled out the squashed nose usually attributed to blacks as the obverse of the straight and pointed nose with which he had endowed the Greeks.[20] Nevertheless, the Jewish nose, which had a longer European tradition behind it, came to symbolize an untrustworthy, immoral, and suspicious character.[21] However, not only the nose but his whole body identified the Jew, through the same kind of totality, taking in body and mind, that informed the manly ideal of beauty. Except here beauty was turned on its head: the flat feet, the waddling gait (opposed to the manly stride), the neckless body, the big ears, and the swarthy color. Moreover, young Jews are an exception in nineteenth century literature. Jews are usually pictured as worn and aged at a time when youth was highly prized.

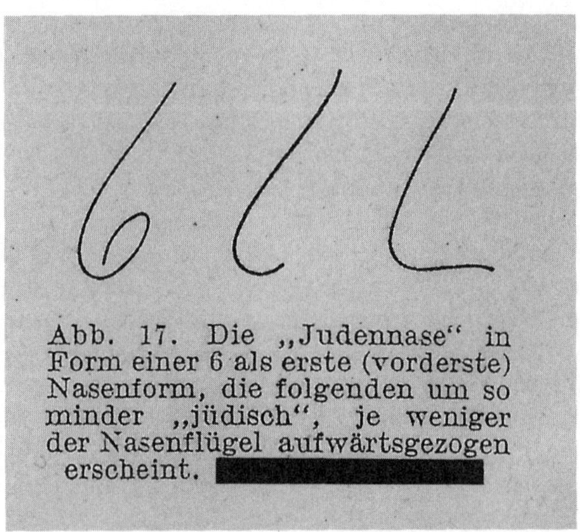

4.2 The Jewish Nose. The text reads: “The Jewish nose first and foremost resembles a figure 6 as in the first sketch, the nose becomes less Jewish the more the nostrils are pulled upwards, as in the other two sketches.” Hans Leicher, a physician and ear, nose, and throat specialist, as well as a lecturer at the University of Frankfurt, was the author of both this sketch and the text. (*Die Vererbung Anatomischer Variationen der Nase, Ihrer Nebenhöhlen und des Gehörorgans* [Munich: J. F. Bergmann Verlag, 1928].)

These telltale signs by which the Jew could be recognized also documented his sickness. At a time when hygiene was becoming part of medicine, the Jew was said to lack all cleanliness and to neglect his body. The phrase "dirty Jew" came to sum up the Jewish stereotype, meaning ugliness, filth, and disease. Indeed, Jews were sometimes accused of transmitting the most dreaded disease of the century, syphilis, and the Jewish nose itself was at times attributed to the ravages of that disease, as was the Jews' supposed swarthiness. Clearly, a countertype was being constructed against the background of a growing consensus on what constituted true beauty, health, and manliness.

The depth of this stereotype is illustrated in exemplary fashion by no less a person than Henri Baptiste Grégoire, the champion of Jewish emancipation during the French Revolution. Even while introducing his measure for the emancipation of the Jews into the constituent assembly (1789), he held that Jews in general had sallow complexions, hooked noses, hollow eyes, and prominent chins, and that they aged prematurely. Moreover, Jews were chronic masturbators, testifying to a nervous disposition.[22] The attempt was made to see the Jew in his entirety, and that in an age when the quest for totality occupied many thinkers. Grégoire, typically enough, entitled his pathbreaking tract advocating Jewish emancipation *Essai sur la régénération physique, morale et politique des juifs* (An Essay about the Physical, Moral and Political Regeneration of the Jews, 1785). This title leaves no characteristics of the Jew unexplored—making a perfect stereotype—and all of them were found wanting and would have to be reformed. That the physical comes first in this title may well be significant; after all, the outward supposedly told the story of the inner man.

The salient features of the Jew as stereotype that Grégoire lists were shared in some measure by all outsiders whether Gypsies, homosexuals, blacks, habitual criminals, or the insane. All of them were as stereotypes ugly, ill-proportioned, and fidgety. Blacks were not as visible in Europe as the Jews; otherwise, they would also have served as a principal foil of normative manliness. Even so, the Nazis arrested and killed most of the eight hundred or so offspring of mixed unions between German women and the black French soldiers who had occupied the Rhineland between 1921 and 1924. The Jews had brought the blacks into the Rhineland, as far as Adolf Hitler was concerned, with the clear aim of ruining the white race (once again, the Jews were the root of all evil, the archetypal countertype).[23] Blacks were obviously strong and fit, but this itself was turned against them: their strength was barbaric, without order or direction, displaced into an overflowing sexual energy menacing white women. Physical power, however healthy, was dangerous unless paired with self-control and moderation.

The outsiders were constantly homogenized, made into an evil fraternity that confronted the norm. Jews were associated with blacks through the supposed swarthy color of their skin; indeed, for some racists, the physiognomy of the Jew was like that of the black: Jews and blacks—the two inferior races—had intermixed. The strongest bond between blacks and Jews according to National Socialists may well have been their hysteria, their love of violent motion, symbolized by what the German political right called "nigger music," once more said to have been introduced into Germany by the Jews in order to further the degeneration of the German people. Joseph Goebbels did his best to aryanize jazz, for, as one Nazi publication has it, "Negro tribes do not march."[24]

Jews were also, if to a lesser degree, associated with homosexuals and eventually as perpetual wanderers with the Gypsies as well. The physiognomy of the Jew was, in turn, closely related to that of the insane and habitual criminals, in the latter case especially through the large ears, which according to criminologists like Cesare Lombroso, at the end of the nineteenth century, were supposed to be the criminal's trademark. The outsider in general was locked into place by the ideals of beauty and manliness, and the choice of how he could be represented was therefore limited, as any comparison of modern illustrations, especially caricature, shows.

The true nature of a stereotype can be seen in its proper perspective only if both the ideal and its antithesis are put side by side, one reenforcing the other. This contrast came alive, for example, at the time of the German occupation, in the 1941 Paris exhibition "The Jews of France," where a larger-than-life-size statue of a nude male called "the perfect athlete" was placed in the center of the display in order to document the contrast between an ideal manhood and the moral and physical inferiority of the Jews.[25]

It was the so-called unmanly men, however, who provoked perhaps the deepest anxiety among those who were part of normative society, and who, while possessing all the traits of the outsiders, in addition seemed to have crossed the barrier of gender. We have seen how in times of insecurity strong lines of demarcation between genders were considered essential; blurring the division between them seemed to conjure up the specter of anarchy. Homosexuality, or sodomy, as it was then known, was threatening, and though like anti-Semitism it had roots far back into history, it was also stereotyped in the eighteenth century. Fear of sodomy and catastrophe were linked,[26] thus, for example, the Napoleonic Wars unleashed a wave of sodomy persecutions in England. And yet, as Paul Derks has shown, in the eighteenth century there was a certain tolerance of homosexuality that would be unthinkable in the next century.[27] Tolerance then did not mean acceptance of homosexuality but an ability to ignore it, provided it did not become too visible. However, by the new century, as in gender division, clear lines had been drawn that must not be crossed.

In his essays on Winckelmann (1805), for example, Goethe wrote that nature had provided him with everything that makes and graces a man, and this in spite of the fact that he knew full well about Winckelmann's homosexuality.[28] What Goethe as a worshipper of Greek beauty could not stand were effeminate men and manly women.[29] Here tacit acceptance of homosexuality could coexist with a strict division between the sexes. The greater openness shown by Goethe and others of his Weimar circle was not due to any approval of homosexuality but to admiration for Winckelmann's concept of manly beauty—the manly body that, in Wilhelm von Humboldt's words, symbolizes our hopes for the human body in general.[30] But this tolerance did not last, for the homosexual was soon endowed with a body that in its ugliness matched that of the Jewish stereotype. Though it was conceded that he might be tall and could even seem well proportioned, his beauty must needs be incomplete. Thus a biography of the historian Johannes von Müller, a known homosexual, written in 1810, described the lower part of his body as destined for a man of considerable height, yet nature did not fully execute its plan, and the upper part of his body remained small. His nose and forehead signaled strength and daring, but the eyes were clouded and the lower part of his face was that of a feckless youth.[31] Even if a homosexual approached the manly idea of beauty, he was bound to fall short. And in 1816 one opponent of Jewish assimilation asserted that if a Jew seemed beautiful, something was bound to be missing.[32] The emphasis placed on beauty in this context meant that those who stood at the beginning of the construction of modern masculinity realized its importance as a test that manliness had to pass, and that it had to be denied to those who were destined to be the foil of masculinity. The line between modern masculinity and its enemies had to be sharply drawn in order that manliness as the symbol of a healthy society might gain strength from this contrast.

The homosexual countertype to masculinity in all its implications was summed up in exemplary fashion by the anonymous *Getroffene Bilder aus dem Leben vornehmer Knabenschänder und andere Scenen aus unserer Zeit und herlichkeit* (Scenes from the Life of an Aristocratic Pederast, 1833), published in Germany. Its antihero, Don Pederasto, was an aristocrat in accordance with the middle-class belief that it was among that corrupt class that homosexuality was especially rampant, and his opulent and magnificent lifestyle provided the proper background for his perverse personality. Don Pederasto's toast "Long live Greece!" and his founding of a society for the dissemination of Greek ideas served as a front for the debauchery of young men. Peasant youths emerged from this so-called circle of friends broken in body and soul; they had been healthy, and now they were sick. Moreover, Don Pederasto's society was part of a general homosexual conspiracy to take over Spain.[33]

Conspiracy theories haunted outsiders. Whether directed by homosexuals or the world Jewish conspiracy, their methods and end were, by and large, the same. The phalanx of healthy men representing normative society confronted an equally coherent opposition, but while society was cemented by high ideals and led by men of courage and probity, those who sought to destroy it worked by devious means. They attempted to create a countersociety directed by men who subverted the accepted standards of masculinity. Thus when Don Pederasto is challenged to fight a duel, his soft, sponge-like, womanly body trembles with fear, and he begs forgiveness.[34] The "outsider" can have no honor.

Jews were at times accused of being homosexual, and in the twentieth century two of the most prominent Jews, Walter Rathenau, first wartime economic czar in Germany and then foreign minister of Weimar Germany, and Léon Blum, prime minister of the French popular front (1936–1937), were all but openly accused of such deviance by their enemies. The image of the Jew and the image of the homosexual ran parallel to each other by the end of the century.[35] There was no doubt a certain hesitation, except for the most fanatical anti-Semites, to make overt use even for polemical purposes of a love that dared not speak its name. Respectable people were not supposed to know about such sexual practices.

The gender-bending of the Jews could equally well be documented through their feminization (thus Léon Blum was, for example, pictured in drag; see Figure 4.3). Jews were generally accused of transgressing the divide between the genders not sexually but through their supposed effeminacy. They were often given a "soft weakness of form," and their passive, supposedly cowardly and devious behavior added to such a characterization. But it was Otto Weiniger's famous and perversely popular book *Geschlecht und Charakter* (Sex and Character, 1903) that proved to be the most important source book for the feminization of the Jews. Here Jews and women were equated as creatures of passion and emotions, lacking true creativity; both were without any individuality, devoid of self-worth.[36] The supposed passivity of the countertype

4.3 The French Jewish socialist Prime Minister Léon Blum: the Wandering Jew as a transsexual from the French satirical journal *Le Charivari*, June 20, 1936.

reached a climax in this book. To be sure, Weininger distinguished between the individual Jew and Jewishness as a principle, but however he tried to abstract his anti-Semitism, the Jews were feminized in feeling and spirit on the basis of Weininger's negative view of women.

Woman with her uncontrolled passion was the embodiment of untrammeled sexuality, and for Weininger, "no true man of talent can exist who fails to see in sexual activity more than a swinish, animalistic act."[37] Weininger obviously had difficulty coming to terms with his own sexuality, and he himself may have been confused by the theory put forward in *Geschlecht und Charakter* that every human being has within something of both male and female. But the true man, unlike the Jew or homosexual, has overcome the female components of his nature, knows only platonic love, and leads a balanced life free from the hysteria associated, in Weininger's mind, with women, Jews, and homosexuals. He praised the manly qualities that by now were traditional; the unmanly as usual provide a countertype. The outsider is homogenized once more, this time infringing upon the space that was supposed to divide true men from women. Here masculinity was the principle that united all that was creative and great in spirit. Clarity of form was decisive as well: "Masculine thought is distinguished from the feminine through the need for clear and unambiguous form."[38]

Jews, then, were often "feminized," though for the most part they were pictured with their passions out of control, predators lusting after blond women. Indeed, this and the accusation of white slavery, that is, selling white women into prostitution, became anti-Semitic staples. Thus Edouard Drumont's *La France Juive* (1886), a veritable breviary of all the accusations leveled against the Jews during the nineteenth century, singles out their supposed creation of pornography with its pictures of nude women as evidence of Jewish opposition to Christianity.[39] Jews were once again seen as aged, weak, or effeminate, and their stereotyped bodies were different from those of homosexuals only in degree. Jews were given specific bodily features and measurements to demonstrate their difference from the norm; homosexuals were generally limp and thin, men in whom an unmanly posture rather than specifically ugly features predominated (see Figure 4.4). However, in the end, both were judged and condemned by the standards of masculine beauty.

Jews and homosexuals were not the only countertypes, but they were the most readily visible and frightening examples. They were frightening on the one hand precisely because they were stereotyped, but on the

4.4 *The Dainty Young Man*, an antigay caricature from the Parisian periodical *L'Assiette au Beurre*, no. 422, May 1909.

other, because they were assimilated, they could live unrecognized, hiding among the population. The Gypsies would not disguise themselves and had been considered a "plague" ever since the Middle Ages; they were often likened to robber bands that afflicted the countryside. A price was put on their heads and an attempt was made to press them into military service.[40] The French Revolution tried to suppress Gypsies altogether and began a period of severe persecution. Gypsies were sometimes also likened to Jews, for pious Jews also dressed differently from the norm and Jews often appeared as itinerant hawkers. Moreover, both were accused of spreading disease, as well as being dirty, shifty, and dishonest. Gypsies because of their way of life were mostly seen as "descendants of vagabonds, swindlers and thieves" as the Nazi expert on Gypsies was to put it. Theirs was exclusively "the blood of vagrants,"[41] and although Jews were often seen as robbers and vagrants as well, Jewish evil was more far-reaching, undermining the very foundation of society and the nation. Interesting enough, there seems as far as we know to have been no specific preoccupation with the Gypsies' bodily structure, such as we found with Jews and homosexuals. Gypsies, of course, were much more mobile than Jews, and because there was no move to assimilate them, they played merely a minor role as a masculine countertype: unlike Jews or homosexuals, they lived totally apart from society, kept to themselves, and for much of their history seemed largely to be taken for granted—until National Socialist racism decreed their extermination.

The insane and habitual criminals were relatively more important as outsiders, made to represent the reverse of society's ideals. The insane exemplified the consequences of shattered nerves, and we saw how masturbators through destroying their nerves could become insane.[42] Jews, however, were also endowed with an oversensitive nervous system and, as we shall see, thought apt to sink into insanity as well. The contortions and grimaces of the insane constituted the quintessence of ugliness; they could never be still. Habitual criminals, during the second half of the nineteenth century, were also said to possess a unique bodily structure: big ears, thick necks, or some other mark of Cain. In his book *The Criminal* (1912), Havelock Ellis, for example, like Lombroso in Italy, wrote that the projecting ears of criminals have usually been considered atavistic in character, as found in apes and some of the lower races.[43] Habitual criminals were said to be a throwback supposedly to more primitive times and large ears gave them away—this in contrast to the small and well-formed ears of Greek manhood.

Vagrants should be added to the list of outsiders, unkempt and dirty, and usually shown with ugly features. They upset all norms of bourgeois society: they had no work or place of residence and therefore were not integrated into any community. Moreover, they had no family. Vagrants or vagabonds, as they were sometimes called, were considered a "classe déclassée," not just in France but all over Europe.[44] Vagrants and other outsiders were later designated as "asocial," that is to say, opposed to productive work and all ordered society. Every one of these putative enemies of society would face the threat of physical extermination in Nazi Germany.

Modern society, as we have pointed out repeatedly, apparently needs a countertype against which to define itself and that will serve to shore up its self-esteem. But then, in the first place, outsiders were thought incapable of forming a community, a settled society. This accusation may well have been one of the most portentous leveled in particular against the Jews, a part of their supposedly destructive nature. The creation of societies and states was a masculine task, and those like the Jews, at best "half men, half women"—as one French book written shortly after the First World War put it—could have no part in this enterprise.[45] That is why many anti-Semites were to ridicule the Zionist movement as bound to fail, and eventually, during the Nazi period, Jews and asocials were lumped together once more as "*gemeinschafts-unfähig*"—a German word coined in order to describe the inherited inability to sustain social life. The Nazis were to make much of this accusation, and not only against the Jews. When Jews were being exterminated, an attempt was made in 1943 to formulate a comprehensive law that would deal with all of those incapable of creating or being part of a community. This law was directed against those permanently dissatisfied (*querulanten*), vagrants, beggars, those who shunned work, the mentally impaired, and homosexuals. The list of asocials, which, as we saw, originated at an earlier date, was kept intact, encompassing all those thought to be useless to society.[46]

The social role of the outsider in all its ramifications, encompassing morality as well as aesthetics, is perhaps the chief reason that the stereotype of the outsider has remained constant over such a long period of time. But then, despite its often shifting power relationships, the basic contours of modern society have not yet undergone any fundamental change comparable to that which occurred from early modern to modern times and that stood at the birth of the modern construction of masculinity. To be sure, habitual criminals and the insane are no longer stereotyped in the same manner today as earlier in the century because our concept of illness has changed; in some aspects it has become less moral and more pragmatic. But present-day caricatures of Jews and homosexuals are still those of the countertype to modern masculinity;

here ideas of sickness and health have not changed, nor, for that matter, have ideas of beauty and ugliness.

Women, of course, were not outsiders; they had their fixed place in society. In 1810 Madame de Staël, in her book about Germany, put it succinctly: it is right to exclude women from politics and civic affairs but in return women can expect scrupulous marital fidelity. Competing with men is contrary to women's natural vocation.[47] Marriage was the institution that assigned to men and women their respective places in society, and the ease with which divorce could be obtained in Germany threatened—for Madame de Staël—to introduce anarchy into the family relationships.[48] Madame de Staël was no bluestocking but—rare for women of her time—a lively and public participant in French intellectual life. Her testimony on gender division is all the more impressive for that reason. Widespread fear of "sexual anarchy" had to wait until the last decades of the century, when the women's rights movement challenged the exclusion of women from civic affairs.

Yet already there were signs that all was not well, that woman might indeed become an enemy of man and thus threaten society. For example, the new Bavarian Law Code early in the nineteenth century recognized that men could be victimized and threatened in their sexuality by women.[49] The Romantic movement seemed to confirm the division between the sexes, with its idealizing of woman as pure, chaste, and tender, removed from reality, appealing to the highest instincts of humanity. But at the same time, Romantics were fascinated by woman the temptress who massacres in the morning the lovers with whom she has passed the night—the *femme fatale*, who seduces men only to destroy them: Cleopatra was considered one of her first Romantic incarnations.[50] Romanticism helped to keep woman in her place through idolizing her, but at the same time the *femme fatale* pointed ahead, to the end of the century, when some women would be regarded with the same suspicion as outsiders, as a menace to masculinity.

Yet even if woman was not an outsider, the perceived difference between men and women did help to boost the ideal of masculinity. In his novel *Lucinde* (1799), Friedrich Schlegel, for example, held that only the love of an understanding woman can spur man on to true manliness.[51] Man needs woman to become conscious of his own masculinity, however rough-hewn it might be, but the woman who fulfills this essential function must remain truly feminine. Just so, for Fichte, woman reenforces man's strength of character and his courage, and she herself must obey man's law.[52] Woman had a definite function in the building of modern masculinity that is not merely negative, even if man was considered her superior in intellect and status.

The cult of womanly beauty had defined the ideal of beauty for centuries, but now men could claim a beauty of their own. Once a standard for male beauty had been established, as we saw in chapter 3, male beauty tried to assert itself as a superior beauty. Goethe, for example, believed that manly beauty was more perfect than womanly beauty. Such perfection was exemplified by antiquity, and it was male sculpture—figures such as Apollo of Belvedere—that according to Winckelmann, set the standard for the ideal of modern and ancient beauty.[53] Sexuality was involved here as well: the constant refrain that for men sexuality was incidental while it absorbed women was part of the exultation of male beauty, its chastity and restraint. *Männerbibliothek, oder Handbuch aller Kentnisse welche der Mann in jedem Alter . . . zu wissen nötig hat* (A Library for Men, or The Guide to All a Man, Regardless of Age, Needs to Know, 1838), contrasted manly youth to insatiable woman. Man must be continent and chaste; if he is not, he may inflame a woman's lust and find himself unable to still her appetite. Man was, as we saw, in control of his passions, devoted to harmony of body and mind that excluded sudden movements either of the body or soul. Woman's sensuousness had no place here, and her sensuousness was for the most part regarded as an integral part of her own particular beauty.

Strictness of form, which Weininger among others had praised, was missing from womanly beauty as well. It is this lack that made Wilhelm von Humboldt write, as we cited earlier, that the construction of the male body was a model for the expectations aroused by the ideal human form.[54] Strictness of form meant, to quote Friedrich von Schlegel, a smooth body, tight and firm like marble.[55] Once again, we face a classical ideal popularized throughout the nineteenth century. The differing ideals of beauty became part of the division between the genders, which, as we have seen, was made more absolute around the close of the eighteenth century. Carl Friedrich Pockels in his multivolume attempt to characterize the female sex (1797), wrote that woman clings to man and through her helplessness appeals to his compassion.[56] Such a view of woman was in tune with the new popularity of Raphael's *Madonna* at the beginning of the nineteenth century, or the Madonna hairstyle fashionable among English women at the time.[57] To summarize points made earlier as well, the construction of modern masculinity defined itself partly in contrast to woman, who was a subordinate yet essential partner, with her quite different beauty and fundamentally passive nature. The demands she made upon man, moreover, were thought to strengthen his masculinity.

Yet, Romanticism did know women as heroes who, while remaining intensely feminine, were endowed with the so-called masculine qualities of willpower and courage. Sir Walter Scott's Rebecca in *Ivanhoe* (1820) is the most famous, intrepid in facing her enemies, defending herself with spirit and indomitable courage. Yet she is womanly in her beauty and chastity. More important, she is a Jewess, an exotic stranger, described as oriental—and therefore standing outside the confines of normative society. At the same time, even apart from the novelist's imagination, Jewish women such as Rahel von Varnhagen played a central role in Berlin intellectual—and masculine—society, which was off limits to Christian women. The so-called masculine virtues such women possessed were granted to them as outsiders, and therefore they were not seen as challenging masculine privilege.

From the middle of the eighteenth century to the first decades of the nineteenth, the stage had been set for the rise of modern masculinity and its dominance. The standards for the ideal of manliness had been put in place and its countertype designated against the background of the rise of bourgeois society with its demands, hopes, and fears. Modern masculinity as an ideal type was popularized in words and pictures, and men attempted to attain its standards through steeling their bodies, passing the test of war, defending their honor, and molding their character accordingly. The manly stereotype remained astonishingly constant from its beginning into recent times. Yet modern masculinity did have to pass new tests that while strengthening the normative ideal also seemed to provide alternative definitions of manhood. New political and social movements, like socialism, attempted a different version of manhood, and those who were considered the enemies of masculinity forged ahead, seeking to make a distorted mirror into a true mirror, flaunting their unmanly attributes. Modern masculinity was put to the test toward the end of the nineteenth century, its second great crisis since that which stood at its birth. The consequences of accelerated change produced a new restlessness aggravated by men and women in rebellion against the established order. Chaos seemed to threaten once again.

5

MASCULINITY IN CRISIS: THE DECADENCE

I

The stereotype of modern manliness has now been established as it built upon an ideal of bodily beauty, symbolizing the attributes that a true man ought to possess. At the same time, the means of reaching true manliness, of "getting there," were made explicit. The imagined presence of a countertype reinforced and further clarified the manly ideal. The stereotype of manliness, once popularized by Winckelmann's Greek youths, remained singularly stable, surmounting all challenges, defining normative masculinity for the nineteenth century and during most of the twentieth. Many contemporary men will have recognized their own ideal of masculinity as it emerged from the preceding pages.

We have already addressed one of the principal reasons for this continuity in the perception of modern masculinity, and in the means required to reach it. The manly ideal corresponded to modern society's felt need for order and progress, and for a countertype that would serve to increase its self-confidence as it emerged into the modern age. Moreover, from its beginning, the manly ideal was co-opted by modern nationalism, giving it an additional powerful base. But the process of stereotyping itself was also responsible for this astonishing continuity.

Stereotypes are difficult to change, and the process of stereotyping, with its emphasis upon set looks and comportment forms a mental picture that cuts deep. Typically enough, thinking in stereotypes received additional respectability and continuity through its association with modern science in an age that equated science and progress. Thus medical men, as we have mentioned already and as we shall see shortly, encouraged the creation of stereotypes through the way in which they defined sickness and health as not only clinical categories but moral judgments as well. Germans, with their penchant for systematization, at the beginning of the twentieth century even reinvented what seemed to some a new scientific theory of stereotypes based upon the belief that visual perception could lead to a human typology—a theory that, as we saw, Johann Kaspar Lavater had already proclaimed over a century earlier in his instructions on how to read a human face. Now such stereotypes were called "eidetic images," defined as especially clear and detailed pictures that remain fixed in the mind.[1] This seems a telling reaffirmation of the unchanging nature of a stereotype, including that of masculinity and its countertype.

The needs of society, nationalism, and the process of stereotyping all contributed to the fact that despite its challenges the history of modern masculinity lacks dramatic tension. Nevertheless, there were certain distinct turning points in that history, even if they did not fundamentally affect the male ideal. The fin de siècle was one such period: the years roughly from the 1870s to the Great War gave a new impetus to both masculinity and its countertype. On the face of it, that age was one of great stability: "proud of their science and their law, and buoyed up by their newly acquired wealth, the Middle Class emerged from the old social framework."[2] But in reality this very society was on the offensive against new challenges that questioned some of the most important presuppositions on which it was based and threatened the image it had of itself. The enemies of modern, normative masculinity seemed everywhere on the attack: women were attempting to break out of their traditional role; "unmanly" men and "unwomanly" women, whom we mentioned in chapter 4, were becoming ever more visible. They and the movement for women's rights threatened that gender division so crucial to the construction of modern masculinity. At the same time this opposition to the norms of society found support in a literary and artistic avant-garde, itself in rebellion against the establishment, as well as in the new mass media, which provided them with a public forum, however hostile.

Moreover, labor unrest, the rise of the socialist movement, prolonged economic crises, and new technologies that once more seemed to speed up time itself added to the anxieties of the upper and middle classes by the end of the century. Other factors must be taken into consideration as well: the fear of depopulation, strong in most western and central European nations, and especially so in France following the defeat by Germany in 1871. Just as important, such threats to individual health as syphilis, tuberculosis, and hysteria were becoming a general obsession that made it easy to apply the categories of health and sickness to society and its enemies. Under such circumstances the ideal of masculinity, symbolizing as it did the ideals of society had to be defended more strongly.

Manliness, already fully formed, was now discussed and defended often in medical terms that spoke to the deep anxieties about the diseases we have mentioned. Here a new and more public preoccupation with sexuality was destined to play an important role as well. The very challenges to manhood at the fin de siècle helped to bring on a greater openness in the discussion, and therefore in the consciousness of sexuality, and here concern with so-called sexual deviancy and malfunction often stood in the foreground.[3] The emergence of the science of sexology as a branch of psychology was a sign of the times. Typically enough, the most famous sexologists, such as the Austrian Richard von Krafft-Ebing, were concerned with so-called deviant sexuality. The official repression of the public mention of sexuality had not ended, but physicians wrote about sexuality with greater openness, and the literary and artistic avant-garde seemed to have dropped all shame. Discussions of masculinity in terms of health and sickness often took place without addressing sexuality outright, but it was always close to the surface in the ongoing debate about the deplorable state of manners and morals.

Disease and the practice of vice had been associated since the beginning of the nineteenth century, just as health and virtue had been equated. Masculinity stood for the image society liked to have of itself, but it also, as we have seen, symbolized the moral universe of the middle classes with its emphasis upon chastity, earnestness, and self-control. The practice of vice was much more readily understood than the scientific medical ideas used to describe it. Those who were loose-living, without the proper moral standards, cut at the roots of society, threatening to destroy its tender fabric. Moral sickness and physical sickness were thought to be identical, for moral sickness left its imprint on the body and face, as Oscar Wilde sought to demonstrate so dramatically in *The Picture of Dorian Grey* (1890). The avant-garde, which openly attacked the morals and manners of society, was seen in this light, as were all the others who menaced the settled order of things. Physicians took the initiative in ratifying the equation between morality, health, and sickness, partly because this was expected of them and partly because they themselves gained status as the arbiters of established norms. Physicians lent their medical authority to the creation of the moral and physical stereotype of the outsider, whether it be the so-called racially inferior, emancipated women, Jews, or homosexuals. Modern masculinity symbolized the norm, and its enemies were assumed to be the enemies of established society.

The corruption of the purity and chastity of manhood stood for the sickness and dissolution of society. Already in 1847 Thomas Couture's painting, *The Romans of the Decadence*, exhibited in Paris, had set the tone (Figure 5.1). There austere Greek heroes standing tall at the back of the painting provide a startling contrast to the orgy taking place at

5.1 *Les Romains ou la Décadence* by Thomas Couture (1847). (Musée d'Orsay, Paris. By permission.)

their feet: men and women in poses of sexual abandon, and in the background, barely visible, two men are holding hands. As late as 1917 this painting was praised as a work directed against selfishness and immorality.[4] It foreshadowed the key role that the concept of decadence played toward the end of the century in defining the enemies against which manliness and society measured itself. Benedict Augustin Morel in his famous *Traité des dégénérescences physiques, intellectuelles et morale de l'espèce humaine* (Treatise on Physical, Intellectual and Moral Degeneracies of the Human Species, 1857) expressed it well: "The incessant progression in Europe, not only of insanity, but of all the abnormal states which have a special relation to the existence of physical and moral evil in society struck my attention."[5]

Degeneration is a medical term that must be distinguished from *decadence*, a term used by poets such as Baudelaire and writers such as J.-K. Huysmans, for whom, for example—writing in the second half of the century—*decadence* meant a new sensibility, a refinement of the nerves and the senses that was not always seen in a negative light. Here it was the androgyne who was often featured, rather than true manhood. And yet, *degeneration* and *decadence* were often confused; in the end they were used interchangeably for the most part. After all, decadence as understood by writers and artist was itself considered degenerate by the defenders of normative society.

The supposed decadence of the age was frequently likened to that of Rome at its fall, but just as often it was cast in medical vocabulary. The causes of degeneration according to Morel, himself a physician, were diverse, such as alcoholism (a much-discussed problem at the time), bad personal habits, and social conditions. But, above all, degeneration was thought to be hereditary. The German novelist Arnold Zweig's *Aufzeichnungen über eine Familie Klopfer und das Kind* (Notes About the Family Klopfer with Child, 1911) can stand as exemplary of the general view of degeneration. The father is beset by phobias; one of his sons dies in infancy; the other, only nineteen, shoots himself, leaving behind letters and diaries that tell of his homosexuality; a sister lives in self-enforced isolation, unable to face life. The family tree ends here, for at the end of decadence stands extinction.[6]

At the same time, descriptions of disease by medical men at the turn of the century were often filled with references to social conditions as signs or even causes of illness. This was especially true for physicians concerned with mental health, a term that was said to encompass the entire human personality. For example, Oswald Bumke, an important German psychiatrist and professor at several prestigious German universities, active from the turn of the century until after the Second World War, maintained that mental health equaled the movements of the human soul.[7] He demonstrated quite clearly how physicians, through the medicalization of morality, attempted to co-opt what had once been a clerical monopoly.

They were seconded by others who were not doctors themselves; thus, a woman writer in the English *Fortnightly Review* of 1895 held that it was up to the physician, not the moralist, to define the meaning of the fin de siècle, with its immorality and contempt for tradition and the established order. After all, he was an expert in the two diseases most responsible for this condition: degeneration and hysteria.[8] Physicians in turn considered the problems of modernity as symptoms to be taken into account when making a medical diagnosis, attempting to stop or at least to mitigate the rush of time. For example, Max Nordau, himself a physician, argued in his famous *Degeneration* (1892) that the constant vibrations undergone in railway travel were partly to blame for the shattering of men's nerves, typical of the havoc wrought by the approaching end of the established order.[9] At much the same time, J.-M. Charcot, the famous French psychiatrist, saw the railway as the dramatic setting for nervous breakdowns.[10] Clearly, the new speed of time, a result of rapid technological progress, had become a pressing medical concern. Nordau, who popularized the term *degeneration* believed that rapid and apparently uncontrolled bodily movement and restlessness were indications of shattered nerves, sure signs of decadence.

Nervousness and hysteria were of central importance here, whether symbolized by the lack of personal restraint that, so it was said, had led to the fall of the Roman Empire, or by the weakness and sterility brought about by "physical and moral poison," such as alcoholism, the use of opium, or debilitating disease. Oswald Bumke was typical of many of his contemporaries when he asserted that the human soul could not function properly without a healthy nervous system, the material foundation of its very existence.[11]

Degeneration and decadence, as physicians defined them, were now said to characterize all outsiders at the very moment in which they achieved greater visibility. We saw in chapter 4 how, without the visible presence of a countertype, society itself found it difficult to project its own image of strength and stability. The traditional outsider, the stranger or social misfit, had been cast in that role: Jews, Gypsies, or asocials. But now, at the turn of the century, they were joined by those who by rights should have been part of the mainstream, otherwise respectable middle-class men who could not live up to the manly ideal because in some manner they were considered sick or unmanly. They seemed to narrow the gap between true masculinity and its foil in a dangerous way. Here the growing awareness of the existence of men with a weak constitution was typical. It can be illustrated through advertisements printed in German newspapers toward the year 1900: "Men with weak nerves, here is a guaranteed cure"; "The sickness of male nerves, its prevention and radical cure"; or, simply, "Weak men! Here is a special kind of electricity that has cured thousands!"[12] (See Figure 5.2.)

Effeminacy seemed especially troubling in this context. To be sure, most effeminate men could be labeled as homosexual, and therefore stigmatized as outsiders, but there were others whose supposed effeminacy was stigmatized as a sickness by medical men even though they were heterosexual. Here it was medical men who tried to safeguard the masculine ideal by setting pale-faced and effeminate men needing treatment apart from robust and healthy manhood. French physicians wrote during the 1880s that because of effeminate men's "irritable" weakness, any sexual act performed by them would end in profound exhaustion and sterility.[13] Degeneration was at work here, leading once more to sterility and extinction.

Still more troubling, science itself seemed to lessen the space that was supposed to exist between manliness and its foil. Hysteria had previously been confined to women as a sign of their tender nerves and barely controllable passions. Nervousness, after all, was the very opposite of the image of masculinity. Now, toward the end of the century, the words *nervous* and *nervousness*, which in Germany had been confined to some medical texts, became part of the general vocabulary.[14] Hysteria, in turn, was considered the most serious disease of the nervous system,[15] its symptoms being mental instability, bodily contortions, and abrupt movements. These became familiar not just through the many literary descriptions but also through the use of medical photography, which was pioneered by the Salpetrière, the famous hospital for the insane in Paris, in order to document the disease. Such familiarity must have contributed to the contempt with which people looked at those stricken with that illness; it was constantly used as an argument to keep women from taking control over their own lives, and it produced an

Gegen die vorzeitige

Neurasthenie bei Herren

Die neurasthenischen Leiden gehören heute zu den weitverbreitetsten und ihre Folgen fügen dem davon Betroffenen ganz empfindliche Schädigungen zu. Die häufigsten Erscheinungen der Neurasthenie sind Angstzustände, durch Neurasthenie hervorgerufene Schlaflosigkeit, Gedankenflucht, Kopfdruck, Gedächtnisschwäche, Appetits- und Verdauungsstörungen, Wallungen, Zittern, Erregbarkeit, nervöse Depressionen, Kopfschmerzen, Schwindel, Mattigkeit, Abgespanntheit etc.

Besonders erwähnenswert ist die sexuelle Neurasthenie bei Herren, welche durch Verwendung des bekannten Kräftigungsmittels Muiracithin äußerst günstig beeinflußt wird. Zahlreiche Professoren und bekannte Ärzte haben das Muiracithin erprobt und als wirksam befunden. Die erschienene umfangreiche Literatur wird auf Wunsch gratis und franko zugesandt.

Fabrik: Kontor chem. Präparate, Berlin SO 16/20.

Muiracithin ist in allen Apotheken zu Mk. 6.—, 10.— und 15.— erhältlich.

Depots: Bellevue-Apotheke, **Berlin,** Potzdamerplatz; Engel-Apotheke, Dr. E. Mylius, **Leipzig.**
General-Depot für die österr.-ungarische Monarchie: Hirschen-Apotheke, **Wien VII,** Westbahnstraße 19.

• „JUGEND" Bezug zu nehmen.

5.2 German advertisement for curing "Neurasthenia in Men" from the periodical *Jugend.* The text reads in part: "Neurasthenic diseases are among the most common diseases today . . . sexual neurasthenia in men deserves special attention." (*Jugend: Münchner illustrierte Wochenschrift für Kunst und Leben* [1914].)

effect opposite to the quiet strength and self-control that masculinity represented.

Jean-Marie Charcot, a famed physician at the Salpetrière (1862–1893), seemed therefore to strike a serious blow at normative masculinity when he extended the definition of hysteria from women to men. During one of his Tuesday lessons at the Salpetrière in 1872–1873,

Charcot asserted that some men subject to hysteria lacked all feminine traits; they were to all appearances robust men. However, such men can become hysterical, "just like a woman," and this "is something that has never entered the imagination of some people".[16] Charcot seized every opportunity, Marc S. Micale tells us, to establish the masculine nature of the "hystérie virile,"[17] and yet he also made attempts at safeguarding the male ideal itself: for in men all the phenomena associated with hysterical nervousness were never complete. In the same breath, however, he went on to describe virtually identical cases of male and female hysteria.[18] Moreover, although in men hysteria as a rule developed following a physical trauma, usually at the workplace, women "went hysterical" thanks to an overpowering emotional experience.[19] Micale has calculated that in the sixty-one case histories of male hysteria among Charcot's patients that he examined, there were only two instances of an adult man crying.[20] Apparently some attributes of manliness were retained even in hysteria. Indeed, the few male cases of hysteria that came to the courts were less likely to benefit from judicial indulgence than those of women. (Ruth Harris found only two such recorded French cases.)[21] Even so, the courts showed a certain incredulity that male hysteria could be considered a legitimate illness.

However ambivalent Charcot's position as the chief proponent of male hysteria may have been, male hysteria now became a subject of considerable scientific interest. Books were published about it, and the young Sigmund Freud made his debut at the Vienna medical society in 1886 with a paper that included a discussion of male hysteria. The hysterical male, he told a discomfited audience, is not a rare or peculiar case but an ordinary case of frequent occurrence.[22] Here also the manly ideal was under attack.

Social causes were always important to the diagnosis of nervous disease within the framework of the decadence. Richard von Krafft-Ebing, for example, in his much-used *Lehrbuch der Gerichtlichen Psychopathologie* (Manual of Forensic Psychopathology, 1879), thought that lack of success in social life was a vital cause of mental illness.[23] At the same time older religious ideas continued to make themselves felt, now equated with medical concepts. Thus Benedict-Augustin Morel held that evil and illness coincide as a consequence of original sin, departing from the basic human type created in the image of God.[24] Here, too, however, the normal male could be safeguarded from nervousness or hysteria that might place him in dangerous proximity to degeneration or to the passive attributes women were said to possess. Man, after all, was supposed to shape society and to protect women from its dangers, according to Bumke, because both faced social conditions that might lead to degeneration.[25]

Control over sexual drives was usually considered a sign of mental health, and lack of control indicated mental illness. It is necessary—according to Krafft-Ebing, writing in 1886—that the civilized human being keep his sexual drives within the limits set by the community. A sense of modesty and shame must prevail. Without such normalcy the family and the state as the foundations of a legitimate and moral order would cease to exist.[26] For Krafft-Ebing, the man has the advantage over the woman in keeping his sexuality under control. As he wrote in his *Psychopathia Sexualis* (1886), for man, the love of a woman is just one among many other interests; for woman, life is dominated by biological concerns—she cannot quench her thirst in one embrace.[27] The famous sexologist merely, as it were, dresses up a normative stereotype. The male ideal once more predominates as exemplary of the normalcy that provides a counterweight to nervousness and decadence—symbolized in this instance through the control of sexual passion.

II

The ideal of masculinity and what it represented were challenged as part of the decadence not only by sickness but by the increased assertiveness of unmanly men and unwomanly women. From the 1890s onward such "degenerates" provided an ever more visible presence and, however small their number, a continuous challenge to normative masculinity. These were not simply normal men with effeminate manners or appearance but so-called abnormal men and women who flaunted their sexual deviance, their own unorthodox woman- or manhood.

The emergence of lesbians and homosexuals into the light of day started slowly in the 1860s and peaked in the last decade of the century. To be sure, they had obtained some visibility long before, but as criminals to be condemned rather than in their own right. Friedrich Engels had acted with abhorrence and fear when in 1869 Karl Marx sent him one of the first calls for homosexual rights published that same year and written by Karl Heinrich Ulrichs, a one-time German civil servant and journalist: "The Pederasts are starting to take stock," Engels wrote, "and to find that they constitute a power in the state. As yet, an organization is missing," he continued, "even though secretly it exists already. . . . [I]t is lucky that we ourselves are too old to witness the victory of their cause and to pay the price with our own bodies."[28]

The fear of a homosexual conspiracy must have been still greater two decades later among those who observed how some homosexuals now openly challenged normalcy. Thus at the opening in London of Oscar Wilde's play *Lady Windermere's Fan* (1892), the author and his friends, for the first but not the last time, each wore a green carnation in his lapel. It was an emblem that, as Wilde had it, in individuals was a sign of a subtle artistic temperament; in nations, of laxity, if not a decadence of morals.[29] Yet many saw in its artificiality a symbol not only of decadence but also of homosexuality. Thus Robert Hichens—himself once a member of Wilde's circle of young men—in 1894 associated the green carnation with the gay stereotype: "[A]ll the men who wore them looked the same. They had the same walk, or rather waggle, the same coyly conscious expression, the same wavy motion of the head."[30] The *Ladies Pictorial* in 1892 denounced the green carnation as unmanly.[31] At the same time *The Artist and Journal of Home Culture* printed Uranian (that is, homoerotic) poetry among weighty reviews of the arts.

Men and women living in Paris during the last decade of the century seemed in the forefront of the public defense of homosexuality and lesbianism. They did so in books; in journals such as the very successful *Chat Noir*, affiliated to one of Paris's famous cabarets;[32] and, equally important, through their public lifestyles. Some examples from around the year 1900 must suffice to document a much more extensive and visible "coming out" than that found, for example, in England. Jean Lorrain was a prolific novelist and publicist who wrote openly about pederasty, just as he glorified prostitutes and androgynes (but not lesbians, whom, as Amazons, he accused of wanting to do away with men).[33] Here the linking of such outsiders, all supposedly decadents given to vice, led to a specific affirmation of homosexuality. Lorrain took his stand without apology such as referral to ancient Greece, which was supposed to provide homosexuality with a respectable historical past. He was called, not without justice, "the Ambassador from Sodom."[34]

Robert de Montesquiou is better known, for he was, in all probability, the chief model for Marcel Proust's homosexual Baron Charlus, though some of Proust's own self-hate determined this unflattering portrait. He himself congratulated Proust for having in his *Sodom et*

Gomorrhe for the first time openly addressed homosexual love.[35] With his companion, Gabriel Yturri, he moved at the turn of the century in the homosexual underworld but at the same time frequented the best of Paris society through his own famous and elaborate festivals, and the salons where he was a welcome visitor. Both Jean Lorrain and Robert de Montesquiou flaunted their decadence, taking advantage of it in order to construct their own full-blown homosexual lifestyle in full view of the public. Both wore rouge, eyeshades, and gaudy clothes, and were not afraid to appear effeminate (see Figure 5.3). They may well have thought their provocative stance their best defense, though Lorrain got into constant brawls because of his looks and behavior. For all that, their openness about their homosexuality may have been viewed by others as a rather exotic but harmless eccentricity. Nevertheless, these men and others like them, and, as we shall see, lesbians as well, found heterosexual friends and admirers because of a general fascination with the decadence among a certain upper stratum of society. Such mixing took place here probably for the first time and, once more, highlighted the danger of the decadence to the respectable community.

Oscar Wilde's spirited defense of male love during his trial in 1895 fell on deaf ears at the time, and that in a society whose elite lived most of their lives in a male-oriented community. However, here too attempts to give greater legitimacy to love between men increased, though it was stripped of sexual connotations and given a respectable ancestry through invoking Greek homosexual practices, a past to which not only Lorrain but also Wilde refused to appeal, substituting the modern notion of the primacy of personal identity.[36] However, groups, such as that in Oxford of which Walter Pater was a member in the 1890s, used Plato and the Winckelmann tradition of masculinity in order to praise a so-called deviant morality. They took their inspiration from Plato's lines (which could have been written by Winckelmann), that "it is only when he discerns beauty itself, through what makes it visible, that a man will be quickened with . . . true virtue."[37] The masculine stereotype was used as a weapon against normative masculinity. Still, there was less openness about homosexuality in London, Oxford, or Cambridge than there was in Paris, and that despite the momentary publicity of Oscar Wilde's trial.

Lesbians occupied a prominent place in the life of Robert de Montesquiou, and certain lesbian groups in Paris at the fin de siècle seemed much more vital in their openness than their homosexual counterparts.

5.3 *Le Comte Robert de Montesquiou* by Giovanni Boldini (1897). (Musée d'Orsay, Paris. By permission.)

Here there was a great deal of mixing with heterosexuals but also, concurrently, frankness about sexuality. Thus Nataly Barney defended lesbianism in her writings and took no pains to hide her various lesbian love affairs, while at the same time, at the beginning of the new century, presiding over one of the most successful literary salons of Paris. Looking back in old age over her long life, she proudly quoted Walt Whitman, "I have never conformed, and nevertheless I exist."[38] Lilian de Pougy, the most celebrated courtesan of her day, wrote *Idylle-Saphique* (1901), which consists of a series of lesbian seduction scenes.[39] Decadent themes weave in and out of the writings and the lifestyle of this circle, best described in retrospect by Colette in *The Pure and the Impure* (1931).

Such openness and visibility challenged normative society, as did to an even greater extent the ever more visible homosexual subculture in the big cities. Magnus Hirschfeld, the German sexologist, listed more than twenty homosexual bars in the Berlin of 1904 (by 1914 there were thirty-eight such places), and the so-called Urningsbälle, dances that were held regularly, attracted some eight hundred people and became one of Berlin's tourist attractions.[40] When the French popular playwright Oscar Méténier visited Berlin in 1904, he found a society much more open to homosexuality than that of Paris. He was astounded by the serenity and unself-consciousness of the homosexuals he met at various dances.[41] The difference between the relative visibility of homosexuality in Berlin and Paris was summarized very well, and roughly contemporaneously, by two French observers of Germany: Paris had its homosexual "happenings" that were public during Mardi Gras or in some establishments during Lent, but otherwise homosexuals met in private. Here, unlike Germany, one did not often meet "these effeminate persons" in public.[42] They seemed to have ignored the homosexuals just mentioned, but, then, they were concerned with larger subcultures and not individuals. Even London, where so-called sexual deviance was under tighter control than on most of the Continent, men dressed up as women at public dances that took place during the last decades of the century. Moreover, homosexuals held their own dances, a custom that was becoming increasingly public all over Europe.[43] Whether in Paris, Berlin, or even in London, so-called unmanly men and unwomanly women had attained a new visibility.

As a further example of how the existence of homosexuality was penetrating public consciousness, some 320 publications about homosexuality appeared between 1895 and 1905 in Germany alone[44]—not to mention the increasing number of caricatures of homosexuals in journals such as the German *Simplicissimus*, or the English *Punch*, or the French *L'Assiette au Beurre* (Figure 4.4). The homosexual scandals at the fin de siècle involving the highest levels of society, such as the Eulenburg affair in Germany or the Cleveland Street scandal in England, were taken up greedily by the new mass media. That such scandals involved, above all, members of the aristocracy fueled the fears of the middle classes that decadence had successfully infiltrated the core of government and society.

Homosexuals themselves were aware of the opportunity to redefine masculinity that the decadence provided—not those who attempted to assimilate to normative masculinity but men and women such as Jean Lorraine and Nataly Barney, who were proud to take the label decadence as their own and to exploit it as much as possible. Oscar Wilde provides another example, refusing, as we saw, to clothe himself in the respectable mantle of the Greek tradition, summoning instead a so-called higher philosophy to his defense. This has been aptly paraphrased by one who knew Wilde well as "dare to live as one wishes to live, not as the middle classes wish one to live; to have the courage of one's desires, instead of only the cowardice of other people."[45] Such sentiments were repeated among those Parisian homosexuals and lesbians who equated decadence with individual freedom.

The increasing visibility of "unmanly" men and lesbians frightened even men like the German socialist August Bebel, who otherwise supported the emancipation of homosexuals. Others began to pay increasing attention as well, some on the political Right seeing in the new visibility the hand of a Jewish conspiracy, linking the two outsiders once more.[46] Yet this visibility and assertiveness must not be exaggerated: for example, when Magnus Hirschfeld in 1897 founded an organization to fight for the abolition of legal discrimination against homosexuals, it never attained more than five hundred members at its height,[47] and even so the organization declared that it was not homosexual but acted only in the interests of science (which its title, Wissenschaftlich-Humanitäres Kommitee, reflected). However, this organization and the petitions it presented to the Reichstag did further the public discussion of homosexuality.

In this situation, the rigid division between the sexes that modern masculinity symbolized proved an almost insurmountable obstacle to the acceptance of sexual deviance. Instead, homosexuals and lesbians met in their admiration of the androgyne, who combined, in Oscar Wilde's words, the grace of Adonis with the beauty of Helen[48] or—more commonly—who saw the soul of one gender imprisoned in the body of another. If before 1850 the androgyne had been a symbol of fraternity and solidarity, by the end of the century it had been transformed into a symbol of vice and sexual perversity.[49] This transformation documents the increasing importance attached to the clear-cut division between the sexes during the course of the nineteenth century. As one sexologist wrote in 1903, however, the androgyne ideal of perfect harmony was still alive among many artists, and especially among those who were homosexuals. Here the ideal of a youthful, delicate, girl-like, feminized body was said to combine with male genitals representing the active masculine force.[50] The grace and beauty associated with the androgyne distinguished it from the hermaphrodite, regarded either as a freak of nature or subject of medical study. Although the androgyne could at times be represented as a freakish monster, and Aubrey Beardsley painted such androgynes, usually at the fin de siècle the androgyne was seen as a young Ephebe with a woman's breasts and a boy's penis. He was supposed to present a fleeting moment where beauty could still be regarded as fluid.[51] The androgyne stood for boyish youth, grace, and beauty in the service of a constantly shifting sexual identity.

To be sure, the image of the androgyne and the hermaphrodite could be fused, as, for example, in Magnus Hirschfeld's journal dedicated to the study of deviant sexualities; there, in conformity with the usual image of the hermaphrodite, the androgyne was disharmonious, its bodily malformation due to the malfunctioning of its sex glands.[52] Yet this was not the view of androgyneity among the so-called decadents, and it was certainly a popular literary topic in the milieu in which homosexual and lesbian writers moved; indeed, as Mario Praz has written, the androgyne ideal became an obsession of the decadence movement.[53] As we have seen, both Lorrain and even Montesquiou affected an androgynous appearance, and all her life Nataly Barney longed "for a past age which made its Apollo effeminate and its goddesses virile, leading to the triumph of the androgyne."[54] Androgyny now served to legitimize so-called sexual deviance as well as attacks upon normative masculinity and femininity.

At the end of the nineteenth century, the androgyne could bridge the division between the sexes through the worship of beauty; this was a theme that would attract many so-called decadents. Thus Louis Couperus, the foremost Dutch novelist at the turn of the century, in his *De Berg van Licht* (The Mountain of Light, 1905–1906) wrote about the young Roman emperor Heliogabal, a man-woman of surpassing grace and beauty. Couperus delights in the description of beautiful objects but also in the details of sensuous and cruel orgies that in the end lead to the death of the feminized boy-emperor and his beloved male husband. Charles Kain-Jackson's article on the "new chivalry" (1894) provides a telling English example of the importance of beauty as opposed to gender. "The more spiritual types of English manhood," he wrote, "already look to beauty first."[55] Gender does not matter; human beauty must form the basis of all intimate human relationships.

This was a different beauty from that which informed the masculine stereotype; soft rather than hard, it did not project energy but languor instead—that state of near-exhaustion that in opposition to normative manliness symbolized true sensitivity. Moreover, this was no sexless beauty; it expressed itself through vivid colors, appealing to the senses. Although the androgyne's legendary cruelty and uncontrolled passion were present, for example, in Couperus's boy-emperor, the androgyne at the turn of the century fulfilled a liberating function opposed to gender stereotypes. Here was an alternative to the normative ideal of masculinity, one that we will meet again some seventy to eighty years later, in the 1970s and 1980s, when modern masculinity finally showed signs of erosion. There was good reason that Wilde's contemporary and enemy William Ernest Henley condemned the "effete and romantic yearning for the hermaphrodite asexuality."[56] Sexuality here is defined in strictly "normal," heterosexual terms; contrary to Henley, for many so-called decadents, the androgyne was strongly sexed. Thus for the French writer Colette, the seduction emanating from a person of uncertain or dissimulated sex was a powerful force.[57] But then, the newly found visibility of lesbians and homosexuals, as well as their lifestyles and ideals, must have seemed sterile and destructive to normal manhood.

The frightening visibility of such men and women at the turn of the century coincided with the onslaught upon social norms of a young literary and artistic avant-garde. It castigated the philistinism of its elders, the restrictions that were put upon the free expression of men's and women's emotions as well as their sexuality. These were the moderns, the degenerates, whom Max Nordau wrote about in his book

Degeneration: artists and writers whose nerves he believed had been shattered and their vision impaired. And indeed, it was the outsiders, the prostitute of Baudelaire's poems or those who said no to gentility in the early stories of Thomas Mann,[58] who were exalted in such decadent literature and art. The conflict between generations preoccupied others: plays in which adolescents rebelled against their parents and exposed parental manners and morals, parental respectability, as hypocritical.

Frank Wedekind's *Frühlings Erwachen* (Spring's Awakening, 1891), for example, portrays schoolboys facing punishment (one commits suicide) because they embrace what is only natural, satisfying their sexual curiosity, and society punishes men for such acts. As one schoolboy says to another in the flush of their first manhood: "We can do anything. . . . We can deplore youth that takes its timidity for idealism and age that dies of a broken heart rather than surrender its superiority."[59] Jarry's *Ubu Roi* (1896)—the title derives from a children's toy—looks at the distorted and frightening world and the sexuality of adults through the eyes of a child. The avant-garde revolt against bourgeois culture cut a wide swath, and movements such as Expressionism and a new primitivism in painting (for example, Gauguin's seminude natives) challenged accepted morality.

Normative manliness was under attack here as well, not all of it in this case but the central ideal of restraint and self-control, the concept of manly beauty. Yet there remained a certain emphasis upon decisiveness and willpower, even on the part of the avant-garde; after all, the firm boundaries of permitted human behavior had to be overthrown. As the central figure of the Viennese Robert Musil's novel *Die Verwirrung Des Zöglings Törless* (Young Törless, 1906) remarks somewhere in the novel, the external world is stubborn but there have been people who have succeeded in bending it to their will. The cruelty of the German Expressionists, their exultation of force and even war, was an antidote to what seemed a stagnant, boring society. But then, unlike the other challengers of bourgeois morals, these men and women considered themselves in active revolt; they wanted to obtain not only freedom of expression but the overthrow of traditional manners and morals. They added to the fin de siècle challenges to modern masculinity, for although their emphasis on willpower and aggression was certainly manly, they wanted to give free reign to their own emotions.

The apparent challenge to normative masculinity as part of settled society, however, was not always straightforward. Bourgeois society, which had adopted the masculine ideal, could be challenged, and the ideal itself nevertheless affirmed. The German Youth Movement provided an excellent example of normative masculinity idealized against rather than within important existing social norms. The movement, ever since its founding in 1901, had been divided into various groups of young boys who roamed the German countryside without supervision by older adults, creating a "natural" subculture of their own. They sang songs, camped out, held discussions, and played games—and many of them were patriots and proud of their manhood as well.

Their journals often put forward a masculine ideal type, effectively summed up by Hermann Popert's *Helmut Harringa* (1910), a novel about the Youth Movement widely read at the time. The hero's appearance, his blond hair, broad chest, energy, and decisiveness should not astonish us, for he represents once again the normative ideal of manhood, nor does it come as a surprise that when Helmut Harringa has been accused of cheating, a judge declares that someone with the defendant's good looks could not possibly be a criminal.[60] Helmut's looks, his abstinence, chastity, and physical endurance stand in contrast to the illicit love, alcoholism, and syphilitic frames of his brothers—the degenerate "countertypes."[61] By and large the Youth Movement's protest against society was centered upon independence from adult tutelage and only rarely transgressed the bounds of normal manhood and respectability. Nevertheless, there were times when the Greek example of manhood was resurrected together with its homoeroticism, as for example, in 1911 when one small segment of the movement was rocked by a homosexual scandal. But this was a fringe phenomenon. By and large the Youth Movement transmitted the normative ideal of masculinity even while considering itself a movement of protest likening normative society to a packhorse facing a sports car going by at lightning speed.[62]

Hermann Popert devoted the cover of his journal *Vortrupp* to depictions of semi-nude males with perfect bodies (Figure 5.4), and indeed as far as the Youth Movement was concerned, nudity played a large part in the representation of the masculine ideal type, as it had for Winckelmann earlier. But here such nudity rarely referred to the Greek example; it referred nearly always to nature. The so-called turn-of-the-century rediscovery of the human body, as it has been called, was part of the search for the genuine as opposed to the artificiality of modern life, for unspoiled nature embattled against modernity. Not only the Youth Movement but various nudist movements, which had their origin in this

5.4 The journal *Der Vortrupp* was closely linked to the German youth movement and attempted to regenerate German youth by stressing the Germanic spirit, teetotalism, and sexual abstinence. (*Der Vortrupp: Deutsche Zeitschrift für das Menschentum unsere Zeit* 7, no. 24 [December 2, 1919].)

period, and persons interested in physical education, shed their clothes in order to regenerate their bodies. Sun, light, and unspoiled nature were supposed to steel the body and to give it health and strength. Physical exercise as a road to manly beauty was not necessarily neglected, but above all, these groups—mainly in Germany—indulged in nature worship. Here, once again, nudity without sensuality was the aim. Nudity was acceptable only, so we are told, when seen in an unspoiled natural setting (Figure 5.5). The nude body—whether male or female in this case—was supposed to be one beautiful object among others, such as meadows, gardens, the sea, or the rising sun. The male body still exemplified harmony and virility, now framed by symbols of the genuine and the eternal.

Male nudity would continue to present a problem to respectability. Winckelmann's solution, praising smooth and transparent bodies as lacking all sensuality, would be used often in order to make nudity respectable, and when framed by nature, the nude body seemed even less threatening still. Nevertheless, such nudity would not have presented a challenge if it had remained abstract, as did the statues of Greek youths, but now it was practiced by youth groups and nudists—living contemporaries as it were—and thus threatened to challenge the image of masculinity as symbolizing respectable society. Neither the youth movement nor nudism was as direct a challenge to masculinity as, for example, nervous diseases and the unmanly, unambiguous symbols of degeneration. Still, they added to the feeling that morality was dissolving under the pressures of modernity, and we saw earlier the impor-

5.5 Women in nature. A scene from the German educational film *Wege zur Kraft und Schönheit* (1925); its motto was "the Ancient Greeks and Modern Times." The film was meant to encourage physical exercise in order to sculpt a beautiful body.

tant role that the maintenance of a proper morality played in the construction of modern masculinity. The masculine ideal was in crisis at the fin de siècle even when its basic contours remained intact. The so-called decadents seemed to forge ahead even while society struck back, attempting to protect itself and its normative manly ideal.

III

The strengthening of masculinity at the fin de siècle must be discussed against these challenges of the real or supposed decadence, which, however isolated and literary at first, were seen as confirming the corruption of existing society. Symptoms of decadence did not exist in isolation but heightened the fear of modernity that we have mentioned. It is no coincidence that from the last decades of the century onward homosexuality was more actively and publicly persecuted. For example, in England, the so-called criminal law amendment act of 1885, punished all private homosexual acts as "gross indecencies," and the Netherlands in 1911, for the first time, passed a law directed against all intimate relations among men. Germany had possessed a nationwide antihomosexual law (the notorious paragraph 175) since 1871, and at the beginning of the new century the police opened a "pink file" containing names of homosexuals.[63] Finally, it is significant that the new medical science of sexology, which, as we noted, emerged in the 1890s, was concerned with clearly defining the pathological and the deviant. Here it bears mentioning as part of the atmosphere of the fin de siècle, that even as society sought to strengthen gender division, it contributed despite itself to the greater visibility of homosexuals. Sexologists needed live witnesses, and to this end they collected homosexual autobiographies, stories of suffering, frustration, and secret encounters that their patients had told them. Though these were supposed to be part of the specialized medical literature, they soon had a much wider readership.[64]

Christianity took up its traditional role once again. Ever since the end of the eighteenth century, it had played a crucial part in the establishment of respectability. If we take Germany as our example, Christian associations for the protection of morals (Sittlichkeitsvereine), so-called Purity Leagues, multiplied at the turn of the century, another sign of a heightened fear of decadence and social instability. Although the battle against prostitution was their specific aim, they opposed all sexual and moral nonconformity. What they wanted, as one of these associations put it in 1908, was to restore to the nation its moral health with the help of "true German men."[65] Protestant clergymen and schoolteachers predominated among the members of such associations. Not many physicians seemed to have joined the Purity Leagues, though German professors of medicine had issued a proclamation of their own even earlier in which they lamented the increase of indecency and called for restraint.[66] The central federation of the Purity Leagues in 1892 attacked Krafft-Ebing's *Psychopathia Sexualis* for demanding freedom from criminal prosecution for certain "abnormal" sexual acts. Homosexuality once again conjured up visions of the fall of the Roman Empire.[67] It was a physician, A. Roemer, who also in 1892, in an article entitled "The Moral Law before the Bar of a Medical Authority," published by a journal of the federation of German Purity Leagues, mounted the attack against Krafft-Ebing, and demanded that in this age of increasing nervousness the state must act in the name of self-preservation.[68]

Medical men possessed perhaps the greatest influence when it came to suggesting cures for so-called degenerate or abnormal behavior—after all, they had medicalized degeneration and thus brought it within their own healing function—always exempting hereditary degeneration, which was thought to be outside anyone's reach. Apart from the pressures of modernity, so-called bad habits were said to lie close to the root of nervous or abnormal sexual behavior. Krafft-Ebing was in agreement with most physicians in putting masturbation at the top of his list of personal habits that shattered the nerves and perverted the *vita sexualis*. Here nothing had changed since Tissot's work, well over a century before. The modern age was said to encourage masturbation, which stripped men of their manliness.

There is now a vast secondary literature on attitudes toward masturbation and its attempted cures, and little more needs to be added. Suffice it to say that masturbation continued to be regarded as the root cause of all loss of control, of abnormal passions. Masturbation was said to reflect an overheated imagination opposed to the moderation and "golden mean" that characterized the ideal of manhood as a symbol of settled society. Because one abnormality was widely thought to lead to another, masturbation was seen as opening the door to the practice of homosexuality. Masturbation, Krafft-Ebing wrote, resulted in "artificially produced pederasts."[69] Throughout the nineteenth century and the early twentieth, the most elaborate devices were designed to keep boys from this malevolent practice. But beyond the control and punishment of a specific sexual act judged debilitating or abnormal, it was once again the strength of willpower that was said to count in the end.

Willpower had been characteristic of modern masculinity, and the education of the will had been an important factor in reaching the masculine ideal, as we saw in chapter 2. But now—toward the end of the century—willpower became almost an obsession when it came to describing true manliness. The new challenges just discussed were important, but the influence of Nietzsche must not be underrated as encouraging this development, not merely in Germany but in other European nations as well. Nietzsche seemed to give voice to the temper of the times: "What is good?—All that heightened the feeling of power, the will to power, power itself in man."[70]

Many German intellectuals believed that Nietzsche had liberated their manliness and, like Thomas Mann, they praised the "colossal manhood of his soul."[71] They confused manhood with sheer willpower, resolve, or decisiveness and weakened the other manly virtues that had served to temper the masculine stereotype. If the will fails—so a medical dissertation for which Oswald Bumke was one of the examiners—a human being falls apart and remains incomplete in all that concerns his life. Strength of will was one of the distinguishing marks of the proper male ideal as opposed to so-called weak and womanly men.[72] Damaged willpower was said to lead to vice, and in 1908 the journal of one of the Purity Leagues called for gymnastics of the will, by which it meant strengthening male courage (*Mannesmut*) through sexual restraint and physical exercise.[73] Here, once more, the ideal of masculinity and sexuality were closely related.

Willpower was usually equated with courage, knowing how to face danger and pain. Steeling the body through sport was universally advocated as one of the best ways to accomplish this end. Angelo Mosso, a renowned Italian physiologist, in addition to praising gymnastics as a perfect way of perfecting the male body, also admired the manner in which English schools encouraged team sports. Sport, he held, develops individual energy, teaches the proper work habits as well as discipline, and in this manner completes the shaping of real men.[74] However, a German book about bravery, written by a physician in 1900, tells us that it is not physical prowess alone that wins victories but the qualities of the male character based upon courage.[75]

Courage and pain were linked, and this meant facing injury bravely;

indeed, the image of Laocoön seemed to serve as a model for the manner in which men were taught to deal with bodily pain, and service in war provided a glorious opportunity to put theory into practice. To bear pain without complaining was proof of manhood and showed strength of character, whether it was Tom Brown suffering the torture of the bully Flashman in Thomas Hughes's famed *Tom Brown's Schooldays* (1857) or the much-repeated German schoolboy's story of the Spartan boy who had stolen a fox and then, when called before a judge, refused to give himself away even though the fox hidden beneath his cloak was eating away at his body. Indeed, there was much cruelty, even sadism, in English Evangelicalism, as when in *The Fairchild Family*, a book we have quoted already, little Lady Augusta Noble is burned to death for disobeying her parents. And the caning practiced in Germany as well as in British schools gave boys plenty of opportunity to learn to bear pain like a man. Knowing how to cope with pain without showing distress was regarded as courageous, a preparation not only for normative manhood but also, as it turned out, for service in war. At that time, as we will see, suffering and sacrifice were glorified as signs of devotion to the nation and served as well to ennoble relationships between men. Men with willpower, courage, and capacity to deal with pain, confronted degeneration, just as the other strategies we have mentioned were designed to meet this challenge.

Physicians supported and provided much of the rationale for combating degeneration and the challenges to true manhood. From time to time other methods of control were added: thus marriage was thought a barrier to the practice of vice. A German tract on "manly honor" of 1889 reminded youths that one day they would be heads of families, raising the question of how one could rule others when one could not rule oneself.[76] The autonomy of the ideal male in contrast to women's dependency was a constant subtext in such admonitions. Personal cleanliness was also put forward as encouraging manliness, and so was the removal of all temptation—from the exposure of a nude body to the strict supervision of bathing places advocated almost passionately by Krafft-Ebing.[77]

The masculine ideal was considered a bulwark against decadence, representing in words, pictures, and stone an image of chaste manhood that had sunk deeply into modern consciousness. Thus, for example, even while the androgyne was becoming a significant image among some decadents, as we have seen, adventure novels praising manly deeds, and paintings of heroic classical gods, were becoming increasingly popular.[78] The "outsiders" considered a danger to society, whether homosexuals or lesbians, were always represented for what they were not rather than for what they were. The countertype, as we saw in chapter 4, was negative, the exact opposite in looks, appearance, and comportment of normative manhood.

The indissoluble link between insider and outsider, between the true man and the decadent, was much strengthened at the fin de siècle by the greater visibility of so-called decadents and the true men's reaction to their existence. Masculinity was the rock upon which bourgeois society built much of its own self-image, but abnormal sexuality was also tied to the idealized image of man that determined the counterimage it was made to represent.

IV

Women as a whole do not fit into the decadence as a challenge to men, though they shared some of the stereotype of the outsider, for example, the lack of robustness, a tendency to sickness and hysteria. However, women were not all *femmes fatales* or creatures of uncontrolled passion; unlike true "outsiders," in the main they had their solid place in fin de siècle society as mothers and educators, ruling children and servants, giving tenderness and affection. Woman in her own sphere was considered the equal of man. However, when woman left the place assigned to her in the division between the sexes, she became an outsider as well and presented one of the most serious and difficult challenges to modern masculinity.

This is not the place to write a history of feminism, but within our context it is important to indicate the growth of the women's movement, which threatened masculinity in spite of the fact that the vast majority of feminists did not want to shed their femininity or form a bridge between genders. Their demands were different from those of the challenges we have discussed: they were not primarily concerned with different lifestyles or in creating a world where expressions of sexuality would be determined merely by individual preference. Some feminists did sympathize with the so-called decadents, but on the whole they directed their energies into giving women a place in the public realm, a space that held little interest for those men and women considered marginal, whom we have discussed up to now.

The women's movement in Europe got a slow start during the last third of the nineteenth century, becoming a force to be reckoned with from roughly the 1890s onward. There were moderate and radical feminists, those who agitated for legal equality, those who agitated for suffrage, and those such as the Federation of German Women's Associations who in 1907 demanded the vote, equal pay, equal education, and equal promotion and job prospects.[79] Such a program was adopted in the end by most women's movements, and as far as masculinity itself was concerned, it mattered little if various feminists adopted only some points of this program in their struggle for parity and others took a more radical stand. For the first time in memory they challenged men's control over politics and over the direction that society should take. Not only was men's undisputed leadership put into question but with it their function as symbolizing the reconciliation of society's ideals of order and progress, a function that modern masculinity had fulfilled ever since the time of Winckelmann.

This crisis in masculine identity led Otto Weininger to write his *Geschlecht und Charakter* (Sex and Character, 1903), with its relentless hostility to women; in France, Paul Vogt in his *Le Sexe Faible* (The Feeble Sex, 1908) imitated Weininger. Moreover, Weininger found important admirers in Italy, such as the painter Giorgio de Chirico and the right-wing philosopher Julius Evola.[80] The image of the *femme fatale*, which had played a role in the Romantic movement, reached its climax during the decadence, and not only because of the love of the exotic. Female cruelty abounds in the works of male novelists in France and writers like Oscar Wilde in England, and, still more typical, the works of the Marquis de Sade and his cruel women were rediscovered in this period.[81] But it was Salomé as painted by Gustave Moreau in 1876 who was destined to symbolize the *femme fatale* popularized by Joris-Karl Huysmans's *A Rebours* (Against Nature, 1884) as "weird and superhuman," poisoning everything that approaches her, everything she touches.[82] Salomé dancing with the severed head of John the Baptist (as, for example, in Wilde's play) exercised perhaps the greatest attraction for writers and artists: "the symbolic incarnation of undying lust, the goddess of immortal hysteria, a beauty accursed."[83]

Women who wanted to be emancipated posed a threat that was even more powerful in its impact than that posed by the ever more visible countertype. Women, after all, not only attacked men's social functions but held an essential place in society—they were indispensable—and the outsiders we have discussed were just that, they could be reformed or dispensed with. Hostility to feminism varied, from conservatives to liberals and many socialists who were, as a whole, much more positive toward women's emancipation than were other groups of the population. Indeed, in the end, the Social Democrats proved the staunchest advocates of the political equality of women.

Nor did the relative strength of the women's movement seem to have made a difference in the reaction of men. For example, France, which had a relatively weak feminist movement (in 1901 only twenty thousand women were members of the National Council of French Women),[84] saw men frantically celebrating their superiority as an integral part of their manhood. This was perhaps not surprising in a Catholic country where men's control over women was part of the law of the land. Yet in England and Germany as well, many men reacted in panic to the new demands made by women. Yet, in fact, both feminists and many men met in the advocacy of moral reform exemplified by the Purity Leagues. Here the overwhelming majority of feminists were conservative, just as many of them wanted to strengthen and not to destroy the family and the fabric of married life. That a small radical branch of the women's movement, from the new century onward, was in favor of birth control, legal abortion, and sometimes even free love, tainted the whole movement in the eyes of most men already frightened by women's demands for political participation.

William Vogt, for example, likened women to Jews in their supposed adaptability, forwardness, and absence of reason. M. Prévost, in turn, was afraid that "*les vièrges fortes*" would remake the world.[85] Many more examples of the fear of feminists—"virile women" as they were sometimes called—could be given, and even Émile Zola, who asserted that women should be liberated, hastened to add, contradicting himself, that it was unnatural for women to try to assume the role of men.[86] The feminist movement at the turn of the century, together with the other challenges already discussed, strengthened manly self-consciousness.

To be sure, masculinity was on the defensive, but the challenges to gender division were not as yet so overwhelming nor the pressure of new lifestyles so great as to produce a compliant reaction. The ability of modern society to co-opt its challengers benefited the ideal of masculinity as well. Many examples of such a co-optation could be given; for example, the writers and artists challenging normative masculinity were not suppressed but classified as mere artists or dreamers who could be enjoyed without endangering settled society. The German Youth Movement, for all its challenge to adult society, retained the masculine ideal, and the challenge itself all but vanished as adventuresome boys became patriotic men. Most of those in the women's rights movement never wanted to leave respectable society in the first place. As long as respectability held, the manly ideal was sheltered, even though none of the challenges to normative manhood would vanish completely.

Sexual knowledge and the insights that derived from it had made advances even while the image of manliness at the fin de siècle confronted unmanly men and unruly women. Thus the notion that masculinity had to define itself in large part against femininity and homosexuality was modified by most sexologists. Even the sexuality of normal men might contain elements of other so-called lesser sexualities. Sigmund Freud was by no means the only advocate of this thesis. Nor were manly men chaste and pure because their willpower and self-control overcame all temptation; they were subject, instead, to hidden anxieties about their sex.[87] Though some efforts were made to confine any discussion about sexuality to the medical community, this proved impossible; increasingly, problems concerning normal and abnormal, male and female sexuality became part of the public discourse. Men and women were exposed to public discussion of sexual topics that they would not have encountered prior to the end of the century. Once more, it was sexuality as a topic of public discussion that mattered, and those who opposed this new openness, such as the Purity Leagues, greatly furthered the very visibility that they abhorred. Public discussion, however, led to efforts at suppression or co-optation as society attempted to defend itself.

Despite all challenges and the advance of knowledge about sexuality that tended to undermine clear divisions of gender, the ideal of masculinity and its social function remained intact. Indeed, as we shall see, it was furthered by the First World War and its aftermath. The Europe of the dictators would once more exalt the masculine ideal as the defender of society and the state. Then Josef Weinheber, a leading poet in Nazi Germany, would again sum up the meaning of true manhood, brushing aside all the insights gained through the science of sexology in the past half century—the myth, not reality, mattered, as it had throughout the construction of modern masculinity. This extract comes from a poem entitled "Youth," which was included in the 1940 edition of one of the most popular readers for German schools:

> Be hard against yourself,
> Chaste in the glow of your strength and the passion
> of your sexuality,
> Love and lust must be kept separate from one
> another
> Just as life and death are opposites
> Life and honor are one.[88]

6

WARRIORS AND SOCIALISTS

I

The warrior and the socialist seem opposites who should not be forced to coexist in the same chapter of one book. The warrior provides a climax to a concept of manliness inherent in much of the construction of modern masculinity, adding important features to a stereotype strengthened by the First World War. Some socialists, as we shall see, attempted to project a new kind of man who rejected the normative stereotype. And yet the very fate of this new man can throw new light upon the ideal of modern manliness, its strength and its failing. To pass from the glorification of the warrior and nation to this socialist man is like seeing a ray of light penetrating the surrounding darkness, even though it was extinguished at the time by a society that, when not at war, encouraged aggressive competitiveness and the good fight even in peace.

The crisis of masculinity at the fin de siècle had not changed but stiffened the ideal of normative manhood. Whatever challenge remained, it was temporarily drowned out by the August days of 1914 as European youth rushed to the colors. The Great War was a masculine event, in spite of the role it may have played in encouraging the greater independence of women. The men at the front saw women largely in a passive role as nurses or prostitutes. Marianne, for example, as she appeared during the war, did not march or fight among the *poilu* but floated above them, exhorting them to do battle.[1] The manner in which the war was waged on the western front encouraged the view of the war as dependent on a functioning male camaraderie as soldiers fought, lived together, and died together in the trenches.

Yet alternative ideals to the manhood discussed up to now remained alive, and gained importance in the postwar world. The warrior image did not obliterate the ideal of a different, gentler manhood that did not have to mimic the normative stereotype. Indeed, during the 1920s an alternative ideal of manhood was, for a moment, locked in unequal battle with traditional manliness. Socialists during the First World War had tried to put forward the stereotype of a more peaceful masculinity dependent on solidarity rather than struggle, but those who were disillusioned with the war also took stock of their manhood, and even if they were embittered by the carnage, nevertheless despite themselves, proved the strength of the normative stereotype. Much cited antiwar poets and writers, such as Siegfried Sassoon and Wilfred Owen in England, and Ludwig Renn in Germany, shared the consciousness of their masculinity with those who continued to support the war. They were apt to criticize the reason for fighting but not the fighting itself.[2] Renn, for example, in his antiwar novel *Krieg* (War, 1929) transformed one of his leading characters, though disillusioned and opposed to war, into an ideal soldier, courageous and severe, proud of his frontline service. And although he is no true patriot, he nevertheless stands his man. The most famous of all the pacifist novels, Erich Maria Remarque's *Im Westen nichts Neues* (All Quiet on the Western Front, 1929), gives Paul Bäumer, one of its central figures, the manly qualities of endurance and calmness in battle, though he considers himself lost.[3] Here the ideal of masculinity so closely linked to war even informed the attitudes of those who asserted their hatred of the military conflict.

The ideals of courage, sacrifice, and camaraderie—indeed the image of the warrior himself—were not touched by such criticism of this particular war. The more so because most of the volunteers considered the war a test of their manhood. After all, manliness in the definition long current, for example, in British and German schools, meant to do one's duty, to meet the demands made by any given situation, and to take the measure of the enemy. Just as in previous wars, such as the German Wars of Liberation, the obvious fact that the combatants were men was constantly used as a symbol and example for the physical and mental qualities of true masculinity.

The First World War added no new feature to the stereotype of modern manhood, but it deepened certain aspects on which we have touched in previous chapters. The association of militarism and masculinity had always been present—after all, the birth of modern masculinity had culminated in the Napoleonic Wars. The military, once universal conscription began, had co-opted the neoclassical ideal of the male body as formed, for example, through gymnastic exercise. Indeed, in its quiet strength and self-control this ideal of masculinity was ready-made for the kind of discipline the military needed. Masculinity and militarism, however, did not have to be so closely linked. Manliness symbolized society as a whole and not merely one part of it. The education to manliness was directed toward making boys hard, sculpting their bodies, and giving them a proper moral posture. Within the constant preoccupation of how to make boys into men, worries about immaturity counted for less than fears of effeminacy: the attainment of a certain standard physical and moral fitness.[4] Moral fitness based on virtues such as restraining the passions, leading a chaste life, and developing power of will did not require war in order to become effective. The "clean-cut Englishman," for example, went out to rule the empire but rarely joined the armed forces in peacetime, and although the "true German man" did become an officer of the reserves in Wilhelmian Germany, he also lived a civilian, quite unwarlike, daily existence.

However, the urge to serve in a cause higher than the individual, to put manliness in the service of an ideal, had also been part of the definition of masculinity from the very beginning. The nation fulfilled this requirement; it was a constant presence during the history of modern masculinity from the Napoleonic Wars onward to the Great War. But nationalism was a flexible ideology, it did not have to be aggressive but instead could give every nation its due without designs upon its territory. Even so, the search for a "national character" that had occupied nations ever since the Romantic age in the early nineteenth century took the creation of a virile manliness ready to defend the nation as one of its goals, even as it glorified sensuous and feminine women. However, once more, decisiveness about gender was not necessarily aggressive or even chauvinistic, as we saw in an earlier chapter when discussing the manly courage of the very feminine Rebecca in Sir Walter Scott's *Ivanhoe*.[5] Aggression was, however, latent in nationalism, even if it was not overt, through its ideal of exclusiveness. The First World War brought nationalism's aggressiveness into sharp focus, and made man as warrior the center of its search for a national character.

The First World War tied nationalism and masculinity together more closely than ever before and, as it did so, brought to a climax all those facets of masculinity that had merely been latent and that now got their due. Trench warfare freed aggression from restraint as men went over the top in order to take the enemy's trench. A famous passage from Ernst Jünger's German war diary, *In Stahlgewittern* (The Storm of Steel, 1920), was typical of this fighting spirit: trench warfare, he writes, is the bloodiest, wildest, and most brutal of all warfare, "yet it too has its advocates, men whom the call of the hour has raised up, anonymous foolhardy fighters." These German soldiers were the "princes of the trenches" who never retreated and knew no mercy.[6] Jünger's glorification of this type of warfare was extreme, but one can find similar statements in other nations as well, although none became so popular after the war.

The war for Jünger was a struggle for existence in which man's animal instincts were released, but so was his power of will, even while his courage was tested. His *Der Krieg als Inneres Erlebnis* (War as Inner Experience, 1922) praised the stunning energy that a wartime battle released. Yet hatred of the enemy was not part of this energy; there is very little chauvinism in Jünger (despite his reputation). Rather, in his view, war strips man down to his primordial instincts, enabling the best of men to fight not so much for a higher ideal as for discovery of their true nature as warriors. The general drift of his much-acclaimed wartime writings gave a heightened meaning to what it meant to be a man, a newfound joy in struggle without mercy as part of the maturation of the individual. To be sure, the reaction to the war by the vast majority of soldiers was that they were simply doing their duty—"their bit." And yet even among many of them what was regarded as true manliness gained a new dimension of brutality, not so much during the actual fighting, when soldiers had no time for introspection, as in retrospect, after the war. Reveling in his manhood, Robert Brasillach, the young French fascist, looking back at the interwar period, wrote that joy springs only from force used in the name of a pure race and nation.[7]

The release of such feelings of aggression was related not only to the reality of combat but also to a search for individual freedom from social imperatives, a freedom that, as we saw, had long been associated with modern warfare. For example, Friedrich Schiller's already-cited poem, the "Cavalry Song," held that only the soldier is free because he can look death in the face, in contrast to cowardly and false mankind among whom all freedom has vanished, which knows only masters and slaves.[8] The contrast here is telling, not unlike Jünger's praise for true men, foolhardy fighters, in contrast to the cowards at the base, behind the front. Such men were free because, in Jünger's eyes, they were on their own and had recaptured their individuality.

Even those frontline soldiers who became widely known as opponents of war savored not only their manhood but also the freedom that war apparently brought them. When in England Siegfried Sassoon wrote in his first war poem in 1915, "War is our scourge; / yet war has made us wise," and "Fighting for our freedom we are free," he was still in training and had not yet seen combat. The horror and the anger at the foe will pass, he goes on, but the happy legion of comrades and brothers remain.[9] When he had taken part in battle, his reaction was quite different from Jünger's, and he began to condemn trench warfare. But Adrien Caesar is nevertheless correct that both Sassoon and England's other famous antiwar poet, Wilfred Owen, continued to see in war an instrument of their personal freedom, not only through the shared male camaraderie in the trenches but also by making them feel that poets after all were no weaklings as their stereotype had it but could "take it like a man."[10]

The sense of having achieved the freedom "to be a man" through the instrumentality of war was widely shared. It did not have to lead to Jünger's brutalization but could serve to solve other dilemmas inherent in masculinity, such as being both a poet and yet a true man. The anxieties of Sassoon and Owen show how well the stereotype of normative masculinity had become established; here there was little room for artistic sensibility, for as we saw throughout our discussion, the aesthetic of masculinity was hard, stoic, and resolute. Passions had to be kept under control; a true man did not cry out in pain nor did he shed a tear even for fallen comrades. Indeed, so-called true men often suspected artists of homosexuality, and because both Sassoon and Owen were poets as well as homosexuals, they, no doubt, felt the need to be manly more deeply than many others.

Even here war was a symbol of masculinity, if different from that which Jünger erected once the conflict had ended. Sassoon and Owen emphasized purification through pain and suffering, a passive kind of heroism as opposed to Jünger's joy in battle. The suffering and horror endured by the troops ennobled them, and the fact that they tried to kill others is conveniently forgotten.[11] Both these poets' concept of heroism, as well as that of Jünger, glorified the male camaraderie of the trenches, and such comradeship did indeed serve to mitigate the brutality that rejoiced in killing. The frontline soldiers in the trenches, Richard Aldington wrote—looking back at the war—had every excuse for turning into brutes, but they did not do so because instead of hating they developed comradeship among themselves.[12] Indeed, most war literature and war diaries as well put the squad into the center of their narrative, the "little band of comrades" that fought and died together.

Still, one German officer, later killed in the war, wrote that he felt best when bullets surrounded him and cannons thundered; he experienced "voluptuousness even in pain."[13] Such feeling was related to that of Jünger, but also to the quest for purification through suffering that intensified the association of masculinity with the ability to bear pain stoically. As we have mentioned, the sense that true manhood must put itself into the service of a higher cause was always present. Sacrifice for a cause was now thought to be the highest virtue of which masculinity was capable, without replacing the other, by now traditional virtues.

Those who believed in some form of Christianity—as did Owen and Sassoon—may have thought of sacrifice and purification through war as analogous to Christ's sacrifice; both ideas were closely linked during the war and used in order to commemorate the fallen.[14] For Owen, as his war poems seem to teach us, there was no concept of sacrifice for the nation, only a pure sacrifice according to the Christian doctrine of endurance. After the war, however, the resurrection of the dead was symbolized by the crosses or chapels of resurrection in military cemeteries, and the graves in serried ranks were reminders of wartime camaraderie: "death had lost its meaning and the will to live was now in the custody of our nation."[15] Pain and suffering combined with the will to sacrifice counted toward an education in manliness.

This manliness was merely the old masculinity writ large, and indeed many who had stayed at home regarded the war as an instrument in their continuous fight against physical and moral degeneration. Some physicians, for example, believed that the war promised victory in this fight, begun, as we saw, during the crisis of masculinity at the fin de siècle. Paul Weindling has written about the so-called medical optimism in Germany during mobilization. Not only was military service glorified as healthier than urban life, the consumption of alcohol and tobacco (traditional causes of degeneration) was placed under strict control as threats to military efficiency.[16] The war was conceived as a therapeutic, even though the best and most fit would be killed in great numbers. The gap they created could easily be filled, however, if the survivors strengthened and purified through combat would produce more children. Meanwhile, the victorious nation would have acquired additional territory in order to provide homes and work.[17]

German racial hygienists dreamt such dreams, but they can be found in other nations as well. Henry de Montherlant in France asserted that war and sport, with their male camaraderie, were the antidote to degeneration.[18] Drieu La Rochelle, war veteran, writer, and essayist (later to become a fascist), held that to put an end to all forms of warfare would weaken man's élan vital and condemn him to decadence.[19] The European Right continued the fight against degeneration after the war, and here war was held up as the restorer of true manliness. And though this view was strongest on the political Right, to be codified eventually by European fascism, it was to a greater or lesser degree widely shared. And indeed, as we have seen so far, the war, even if it did not redefine masculinity, strengthened many factors that had gone into its making in the first place.

The spirit of adventure that was alive among some soldiers during and after the war is difficult to capture. It had been present from the very beginning of modern masculinity and had taken many forms: exploration of new lands, the creation and maintenance of empire, and enlistment in the armed forces. These are only a few examples, for this spirit was often present as a secondary concern, not always clearly expressed. The literature of adventure, of daring, had always been uncompromisingly masculine, and so it will remain, in spite of the accomplishments of women explorers, or even women as pioneers of empire—as, for example, Gertrude Bell in Arabia. Before and after the war, many boys rather than girls were raised on nineteenth-century adventure stories that, however, like those of G. A. Henty in England or Karl May in Germany, were not necessarily warlike. The ideal of chivalry was more often than not an important component of tales of adventure.[20] The spirit of adventure and manliness were considered all but identical.

Here was a quality that all true men must share but that was rarely listed among the so-called masculine virtues. Jünger certainly saw the

First World War both as an adventure and as a test of manliness. And another German right-wing author, looking back at the war, wrote, "Greatness derives from danger; ordinary life means strangulation."[21] The popular writer Saki (Hector Hugh Monroe), to give a British example, usually used words like *excitement* and *romance* when he wrote about war. He enlisted with enthusiasm, and though he had lost some of that spirit by the time he was killed, his stories of war, excitement, and adventure found a greater audience after his death than when he had been alive.[22]

Excitement blends with a spirit of adventure in the works of such authors, as well as in the writings of those who rushed to the colors in 1914. Even Erich Maria Remarque's *All Quiet on the Western Front*, in spite of its realistic descriptions of the horrors of war, contains the ingredients of a good adventure story, which may have helped to determine its popularity. The two young soldiers, the central characters of the novel, are, on the one hand, numbed by the horror that surrounds them and, on the other, play pranks and engage in what might be called schoolboy adventures. The absorbing way in which these adventures are told, despite the surrounding realism, made even a left-wing journal (*Die Weltbühne*), describe the book as "pacifist war propaganda."[23]

The manly sense of adventure is also clearly expressed in works such as T. E. Lawrence's *The Seven Pillars of Wisdom* (1926), which was not set in the confinements of the trenches but in the wide open spaces of Arabia as during the Great War England clashed with the Turks. Lawrence links masculine virtues and the spirit of adventure. The protagonists, Arabs or Englishmen, are real men—courageous, intrepid, and engaged in a great adventure. That is what made this book such a favorite of English schoolboys between the wars. The reality of war had, for the most part, put an end to the close association of war and adventure, but that linkage revived all the more strongly in the postwar world. For many too young to have fought, reading war stories and looking at picture books stripped of the horrors of war meant regret at having missed this great adventure and test of their manhood.

Yet, the spirit of adventure was thought to be entirely dependent upon willpower and courage as the preeminent masculine qualities. Many of the so-called war stories are primarily tales of courage and iron devotion to duty in which a spirit of adventure is also present. Nevertheless, masculinity from the very start was fascinated by adventure, even if this was not consciously expressed. The spirit of adventure was easily co-opted by governments once the war started, used by recruiting posters and war propaganda, or expressed by volunteers eager to serve their country.

Although the warrior image of masculinity had existed ever since the French Revolution and the Napoleonic Wars, the Great War further accentuated certain aspects of masculinity that of themselves did not have to be warlike but—like willpower, hardness, or perseverance—were qualities that peacetime society prized as well. There was, it must not be forgotten, a certain realism to the warrior aspects of masculinity: frontline soldiers had to be tough, had to have willpower and a certain aggressiveness in order to survive in the trenches. Nevertheless, qualities that might have been useful in battle remained operative in peacetime as well, giving a cutting edge to the already present masculine stereotype.

War as an educator in manliness was harsher than, for example, gymnastics or the defense of male honor, and those who believed that the war had made men out of boys were not necessarily mistaken. Thus, Siegfried Kracauer in Germany makes fun of the reckless enthusiasm of the soldiers he met when volunteering for war, "I find so much health strenuous," and yet he too believed that boys matured into men more quickly at the front.[24] But it was an altogether different matter when Adolf Hitler reminisced in *Mein Kampf* that he watched seventeen-year-olds who had fought at the battle of Langemarck (1914) marching from the field of battle looking no longer like boys but like true men.[25] Indeed, for Hitler himself, fighting this battle had steeled his own nerves and power of will. But unlike Kracauer, the left-liberal, Hitler immediately transformed this experience into a principle of politics: such maturation was a battle cry against all adversaries, a belief in force and conquest.

Whatever the reality behind the wartime myth of masculinity and the links between pre- and postwar man, a general feeling prevailed that a new type of man had emerged from the trenches. Jünger led the way, writing about the new race of men the war had produced: men of steel loaded with energy, ready for combat. Typically enough, their outward appearance was crucial: supple, lean, muscular bodies, striking faces with eyes that had seen a thousand deaths.[26] The German painter Fritz Erler created just such a man in 1917 for a war-loan poster (Figure 6.1). Here a soldier in battle dress stands against the background of barbed wire; a gas mask on his chest and two grenades in his pouch, he is perhaps about to go over the top. The picture concentrates on his face;

6.1 "Help us to be victorious." Poster designed by Fritz Erler for the German war loan of 1917.

most of his body is invisible. The face is blackened from the dirt of battle, but the luminous eyes draw all the attention: they speak of experiences that have made him hard. This—to Erler—was a "true German face."[27] The poster popularized a so-called new soldierly type, and the Nazis subsequently made the most of it. Then, in 1940, during the Second World War, Werner Picht's *Der soldatische Mensch* (The Soldierly Man) put forward a new and specific German type, in contrast to other lesser forms of manliness: the English gentleman or the French ideal said to derive from the Revolution. To be sure, Picht placed the origin of this new German type in the age of Frederick the Great, but his description was that of a fighter from the First World War.[28]

Perhaps the most striking example of all the qualities that such a new type of man should possess was not to be found on the ground but in the sky: the fighter pilot practiced a new profession, unknown before the First World War. He became the object of romantic longing, of the spirit of adventure, and at the same time conjured up memories of knightly combat, of a more civilized kind of warfare sadly absent in the trenches. Fighter planes, until fairly late in the war, flew in single combat against the adversary, and once an enemy had been shot down, actual gestures of chivalry were not unknown: captured pilots were entertained at officers' mess, and at times a wreath was dropped behind enemy lines to honor the fallen. The "knights of the sky" were a new race of men in their flying machines and, at the same time, embodied the traditions of male honor and chivalry.[29]

The very fact that they fought in the sky, "within timelessness," gave them a special aura; they were "spacemen" (*Raummenschen*), as one account has it, and even after the Second World War we are told that the fighter pilots like the gods and heroes of Germanic sagas fought it out in the sky. Modern fighter pilots were said to have put flesh and blood on the bones of the gods.[30] The heroes of the war in the sky were pictured as representatives of true manhood, its looks and its virtues. Thus Oswald Boelcke, Germany's most famous flying ace during the First World War, who died in battle, was said to be endowed with a "harmonious beauty," possessing a simple and modest character even while keeping his own strength under control—an interesting echo of the "quiet greatness" Winckelmann's Greek youths were said to possess. Such a representative of exemplary manhood had to be chivalric as well: "Oswald Boelcke does not shoot the defenseless."[31]

That pilots controlled the most up-to-date machinery no doubt reenforced the masculine ideal, though this image was immediately spiritualized: a German book published in 1936, laying down what it took to become a good pilot, asserts that the airplane was not a mere product of technology but must be part of the soul of the flyer, just as a rider is yoked to his horse.[32] This new hero heightened the manly qualities attributed to the soldierly ideal in general as it emerged from the First World War, but in addition, through the concept of chivalry and the setting in timelessness, the fighter pilot mediated between the individual and the perils of modernity.

Most of the examples cited in this chapter have been German, and indeed it is in Germany that this supposed new type of soldier had its strongest political impact as it was co-opted by the political right, while in Italy, shortly after the war, the "soldierly man" also became a fascist ideal.[33] However, even in England so-called soldierly men were reproduced on some war monuments. By and large, however, they were not considered new types which had emerged from the war but represented a normative manly ideal. Thus Tait McKenzie, who sculpted the figures of young men on several such monuments, tried to convey their "power, beauty and virility," their physical appearance as a symbol of their moral perfection, in tune with the accepted masculine ideal.[34] The youth upon whom, so he thought, England's future depended, had an alert, happy, and slightly quizzical expression, as on the Cambridge War Monument.[35] The German "soldierly man" as the true inheritor of the war experience, by contrast, was supposedly close to Jünger's description, deadly in earnest, dedicated, forceful, and disciplined.

The German soldierly type marching into the peace had a certain ruthlessness quite different from McKenzie's young man, a reminder that it was only with the Great War, the unjust peace, and the revolutions that followed that German politics became brutalized, aiding National Socialism's peaceful access to power. Manliness as distilled by the war certainly played an important role in that process of brutalization, and the idealized, aggressive, and disciplined male body became, as we shall see, a much-used symbol of National Socialism. But in Italy, for example, fascism also placed its hopes in such a rejuvenation of masculinity. Yet, inasmuch as the supposedly new soldierly man was in fact built upon normative views of manhood, the dangers of aggression and callousness that had always been latent in its construction now received full play. It is important to bear in mind, however, that what was latent did not necessarily have to become overt, that for the most part masculinity continued its measured pace, symbolizing a society that prized moderation, harmony, and quiet strength. Even here the heightened masculinity of the war years had its effect, in the stepped-up search for a "new man" who would renew a battered society and nation.

II

Before and even during the war, however, another and different ideal of manhood had emerged that would challenge for a brief time both the wartime image of masculinity and the bourgeois masculine ideal. Those disillusioned by the war might well have put forward a new, softer masculinity. Yet some, as we saw, accepted the warrior image. Still, there were those who with greater consistency rejected the accepted male stereotype. Leonhard Frank, for example, in *Der Mensch ist gut* (Man is Good, 1918), published in Germany, took as its hero a man who had become a pacifist, opposed to all use of force, leading a peaceful revolt against the war, proclaiming the solidarity of all peoples. He was guided by belief in personal freedom and love of all mankind. Most of those who were disillusioned with war tended to join left-wing movements, and if they became socialists they were apt not only to reject war but to question the manliness that had supported the conflict. The writer Ernst Toller, for example, who had enlisted believing in Germany's cause, became disgusted with war when he realized the senselessness of death at the front. The "simple fact" of the intrinsic worth of each man dawned upon him, and with it, the idea of the unity of mankind. At the same time, he advocated a change in the existing social order, and this would entail changing the hearts of men as well.[36] Toller became a socialist, embracing the ideal of a "new humanity." He joined the Munich revolution of 1918, and however reluctant to use force, did become the commander of its armed forces. Nevertheless, it was the socialist ideal of a "new man" that provided a counterpoint to many of the qualities of normative manhood: a masculinity based upon solidarity, the renunciation of all force, and the rejection of nationalism as an ideal that would serve to purify modern man. Such a new man could become reality only at a time when masculinity was no longer anchored in bourgeois society; only a socialist commonwealth would produce a new and radically changed manliness. And in perhaps the greatest break with the past, the very concept of masculinity would be subsumed under mankind as a whole—a common humanity that drew masculinity's sting.

Max Adler, the Austrian socialist, described this new masculinity at its best, so different from the generally accepted stereotype. His book, *Neue Menschen, Gedanken über sozialistische Erziehung* (A New Humanity: Thoughts About Socialist Education, 1923), dealt with the transformation of present-day men and women into new human beings, and here the much-discussed postwar renaissance of youth did not mean physical or soldierly renewal. Adler based his concept of a new humanity on a belief in human rationality, that one had only to explain the world in order to motivate change.[37] Creating new men was a purely educational enterprise in contrast to the role that gymnastics or war had played in the construction of normative masculinity. Here they were given no role, one reason that the new socialist man lacked the hardness of traditional manliness. Education in the philosophy of Kant and the spirit of the Enlightenment provided the key to the formation of Adler's new humanity, and at the same time, Marx's theories concerning the need for a classless society were fully accepted.

Marxism, combined with this spirit and philosophy, acquired a Kantian foundation; the moral imperative must not be lost from sight. Man as part of a new humanity, for example, still had to fulfill himself in the service of a cause, not of nationalism but of bringing into being a new more humane society.[38] But, even so, man would not be able to serve this cause without first having cultivated his own mind and character as a free, moral human being. The central European concept of *Bildung*, which refers to such a cultivation, and which as we saw in the first chapter that Winckelmann had already accepted, was used here; it had served to further the emancipation of the bourgeoisie and would now serve that of the workers as well. Always it was the spirit that counted; for example, education should be not utilitarian but directed toward creating the future society. Adler did not stand alone in projecting the image of such a new humanity. At the same time, Max Koref, the leader of the upper Austrian socialists, wrote that this new man within a new humanity should be informed by humanist thought—a good man, upright and free.[39]

The Austrian socialist ideal of masculinity opposed the warrior image dominant during the war that had just ended. Moreover, here the innate superiority of the male was denied and the equality between the sexes emphasized. Adler made no distinction between the qualities a man or a woman should possess. Both played an equal part in building the socialist society of the future; both were to receive the same education toward this end. Women, using their reason, were as capable as men of creating a new society. Indeed, these Austrian socialists believed that bobbed short hair on a woman—the so-called *Bubikopf*, usually thought to be an indicator of the perverted femininity associated with the so-called new woman—was a sign of woman's independence.[40] Women were not deprived of their reason or barred by their temperament from playing a role in public life—prejudices that, as we have seen, were common enough among men. The new man these socialists envisioned did not require such strict gender division in order to be conscious of his masculinity.

Here, then, was an alternative to that manhood which has filled this book. Yet for all the difference in the conception of masculinity, the identical ideal of moral purity united these socialists and those who believed in the normative ideal of manhood; both shared the view that the generally accepted standards of personal comportment and sexual behavior were crucial attributes of masculinity. The significant difference lay in the attitude toward political morality, in the acceptance or rejection of aggression and violence. The Austrian socialists we have discussed, moreover, did not as a rule mention outward appearance: the aesthetic of masculinity, so important in forming the male stereotype, played little or no role in their thought.

Max Adler and the socialists who followed his lead ignored the problems that most other socialists faced in attempting to construct a new man who could be the midwife of the new society of their dreams in which equality reigned and the individual could live up to his own potential. Socialists as a whole were confronted by social and political realities that had a direct bearing upon their concept of a new masculinity. Revolution and counterrevolution accompanied the transition from war to peace in the defeated nations after the Great War, and the new Soviet Union declared itself representative of a new civilization: the socialist society in action. Could the use of force, then, be rejected in this postwar world? Would the ongoing class war not require the same manly qualities that had stood nations in good stead during the Great War? And perhaps even more crucial because it concerned so many of the party's members, could the war experience that had shaped their lives be ignored or simply condemned in the name of antimilitarism and the moral imperative of creating a new man? Adler's message remained isolated, faced by grim reality. The socialists themselves drew ever more closely to an acceptance of normative masculinity.

The German Social Democrats had been instrumental in founding the Weimar Republic and now had to defend it against the onslaught of the Communists and the political Right. The organization that they created for this purpose, the Reichsbanner/Schwarz-Rot-Gold, taking the colors of the Republic as its standard, provides a good example of the conflict between pacifist ideals, humanistic inclinations, and political necessity.[41] The Reichsbanner was organized along military lines; it was supposed to utilize the war experience for the benefit of the beleaguered Republic. Paul Löbe, the Social Democratic president of the Reichstag, the German parliament, was apologetic: the use of militarism by the party was a political necessity in order not only to defend the Republic but also to tie youth more closely to its cause.[42] This was surely a surprising admission of the attraction of the war experience even for Republican youth. Yet members of the Reichsbanner were forbidden to march according to military rules and had to sing soldiers' songs, if at all, then nonaggressively. Moreover, wearing military decorations awarded in the First World War, if not forbidden outright, was certainly frowned upon. However, when in 1930 the Reichsbanner created special shock troops organized along military lines in order to aid the Republic under conditions that resembled a civil war, the title of "Führer" soon replaced that of the "president" of the troop. This example should demonstrate the ambivalence of the Social Democrats toward militarism, aggression, and the warrior type.

The Austrian Republikanischer Schutzbund was founded by the socialists in 1923 in order to protect the Austrian Republic against the onslaught of the Austrian political Right, as well as to protect the workers against their enemies. The Schutzbund at first witnessed a debate similar to that which had informed the Reichsbanner, if on different, more immediate terms, because of the seriousness of the political situation in Austria. The Republic seemed to be drifting toward civil war between the Socialists and the political Right allied with the Austrian government. Should the Schutzbund constitute itself as a guerilla force where personal initiative and individual judgment counted or should it be a militia organized along military lines? Those in favor of militarization won out within the Socialist Party: the Schutzbund became a paramilitary formation where obedience took the place of democratic discussion, and where the lines of command were clearly laid out.[43]

This was a large army, at times larger than the Austrian army itself; it counted some eighty thousand members at its height.[44] Yet when the Austrian civil war broke out in February, 1934, its resistance lasted only a few days because the Schutzbund was easily defeated by the Austrian army and the right-wing militias (Heimwehr). The Schutzbund had waged a purely defensive struggle, refusing to take the initiative, and its command structure disintegrated.[45] Perhaps in this defeat we can see a lasting unease with militarization, which found expression in the constant fear within the party that Schutzbund soldiers would lapse into military arrogance and a praetorian mentality.[46] The only socialist militia actually to fight in a military encounter between the world wars was handicapped by the same ideals that made it so difficult for German Social Democracy to face up to the ruthlessness of its right-wing adversaries.

The proposition of Austrian Socialists such as Max Adler that the will to power must be joined to knowledge and ethics—to the tradition of Schiller and Kant—was strong in German Social Democracy as well. Here, also, in theory, the emancipation of the individual must precede that of the people.[47] But such ideals were eroded, not only by the need to form organizations such as the Reichsbanner or the Schutzbund and to maintain party discipline but also by the adoption of a masculine aesthetic. Moreover, socialist attitudes toward women, even while proclaiming their emancipation, remained largely traditional. To be sure, all of these essentially bourgeois viewpoints were usually ambivalent, often taken in order to solve social problems that directly affected the working class. The aesthetic of masculinity found expression through concern for the workers' health and, perhaps even more important, as a counterweight to the way in which society often portrayed the workers: living in darkness, filth, and chaos. Socialists themselves cast their hopes for the future in the metaphor of rising from darkness to sunlight.[48] The metaphor of light as over against darkness was symbolized by the idealized figure of the worker as he was usually shown on posters, in publications, or on postcards (see Figure 6.2). He radiated manly strength that, though it was obviously related to manual labor, had some ties to the aesthetics of modern masculinity.

The workers' sport movement not astonishingly paid almost the same attention to the male body as the bourgeois gymnastic and sports movements. Gymnastics, so we read in an appeal made before the First World War to young German workers, creates a healthy body and awakens a

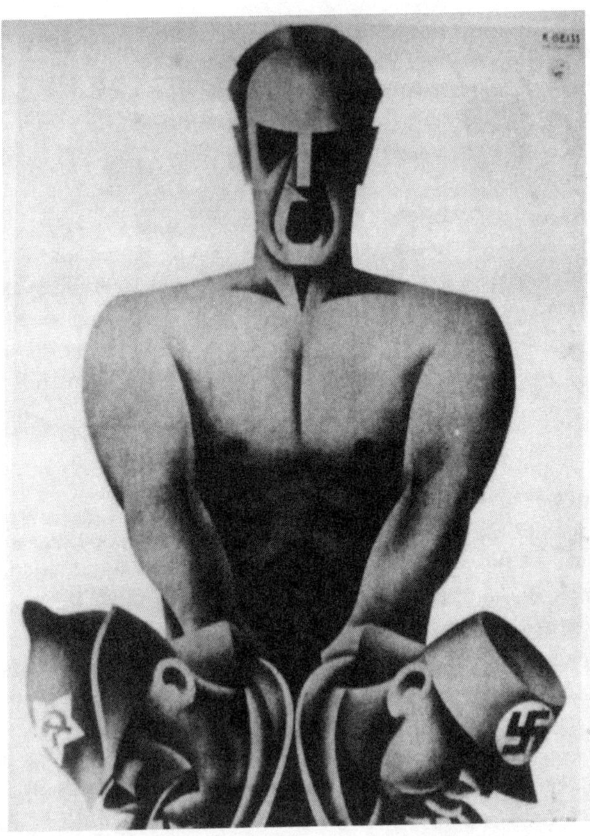

6.2 German SPD poster for the parliamentary election on November 6, 1932, directed against Nazis and Communists: "These are the two responsible for the gentlemen's club we have as a government." (Beth Lewis and Peter Paret, *Persuasive Images* [Princeton: Princeton University Press, 1992]. By permission. Original in Hoover Institution Archives, Poster Collection, GEXXX.)

desire for the noble and the beautiful.[49] After the war we continue to hear about the well-developed and steeled masculine body, the importance of a well-trained physique.[50] The director of the film made on behalf of the first German workers' olympics in 1925, in that same year directed the film *Paths to Strength and Beauty*, which focused on the strength and beauty of the male body in the setting of a Roman gymnasium.[51] Strength and beauty permeated the workers' film as well. Postcards and posters showing half-nude workers further document such concern, though in the workers' movement the male body never played the important symbolic role that it did for society at large. Thus, for example, an electoral poster for the German Social Democratic Party during the Weimar Republic shows a half-naked worker shoving aside both Nazis and Communists, but it is his strength and not his beauty that is emphasized (Figure 6.2).

Nevertheless, young socialists were exhorted to rediscover and to cultivate their bodies. The journal *Arbeiter-Jugend* (Young Workers), leaning toward the right wing of the socialist movement, even gave priority to physical exercise; for example, it told its readers in 1925 that "it is wonderful that mankind, which has become soft and debauched, . . . begins once again to discover the value of the beauty and strength of the body."[52] The contrast between weakness and debauchery on the one hand and the strong and beautiful body on the other is familiar as a commonplace during the growth of the gymnastics movement as well as during the decadence. If traditional masculinity did not assert itself in the socialist movement, it existed just beneath the surface.

Socialist youth must be trained in body and mind and possess the traditional sense of manly beauty. Gymnastics as a branch of the workers' sport movement seems to have fulfilled something of its traditional function, except that here team sport soon came to replace it in popularity. Was Ernst Fischer, a cultural editor of the Austrian *Arbeiter-Zeitung*, then correct when in 1931 he saw all the elements of capitalist ideology present in workers' sport: heroism, discipline, and subordination to the group. Where, then, was there room for a "new man" in this, by far the most popular working-class organization?[53]

Yet, for most of the interwar period, competition in sport was despised or hotly contested as a relic of capitalism opposed to socialist solidarity. Thus the program for a workers' sports festival tells us that sport was supposed to induce a feeling of community and respect for all that is human.[54] The workers' movement attempted to leave room for the education that would produce the new man of Adler's dreams, just as the Reichsbanner wanted to bend militarism in order to accommodate a nonaggressive spirit.

The differences in emphasis and the ambivalences that distinguished workers' sport and socialist attitudes toward militarism from those of normative bourgeois society did not carry over to manners and morals. The importance of the family was upheld and even if divorce was to be allowed, sexual permissiveness was deplored. Respectable behavior here, as in society at large, emphasized industry, sobriety, order, and self-cultivation. The end product was to be an orderly and decent family life.[55] Maintenance of an ordered, peaceful, and clean household was a sign of respectability, not just, for example, among the labor aristocracy of Vienna but among the working class as a whole, and a study of the prewar British working class has come to a similar conclusion.[56] Whether these attitudes were informed by a mimicking of the bourgeoisie or by the fear of descending into a brutish existence or simply by the desire for security is not important for our purposes. But a preference for a lifestyle similar to that of normative society would presumably mean openness to normative ideas about masculinity as well.

The division between the sexes held for the most part, despite efforts at woman's emancipation, or approval of the *Bubikopf*. Even Socialist Party members thought that girls knew enough when they had learned to knit and to mend socks, and such notions were shared by most working-class parents themselves. Many socialists called for the equality of women and championed women's education, but among the majority of the working class, and many party members as well, patriarchy was only slightly dented. As Otto Bauer, a colleague of Adler's in the leadership of Austrian socialism, put it, the wife was to assure the husband peace, privacy, and comfort in the home.[57] But for all that, the socialists before the war and the Social Democratic Parties after the war attempted to soften the contours of traditional masculinity, and although the new man in Adler's definition was not to be realized, he remained a distinct if a distant presence.

The Communists, with their emphasis on the class struggle not diluted by the Social Democrats' commitment to parliamentary democracy, championed an aggressive, powerful masculinity. It could have been different if the changes in morals that took place in the early years of the Soviet Union had continued, but as we shall see, that experiment was aborted. The Communist writer and filmmaker Béla Balázs, a former member of the Hungarian Soviet, living in exile in Germany, tells us in 1929 that manliness means having a passionate will, to do battle with a goal firmly in mind, and to take a stand without flinching.[58] The pseudo-military German and Communist Rote Frontkämpferbund (the association of red frontline fighters), founded in 1924, took as its symbol a raised fist held in a threatening gesture. Here the new socialist man of Adler had abdicated in favor of a decidedly masculine militancy that would finish off the bourgeoisie, a class that Communists believed was already declining.

The Roter Fröntkampferbund apparently felt none of the ambivalence toward war that plagued the Social Democratic Reichsbanner. This shock troop of the German Communist Party, while deploring the need to kill the enemy, stated that one must, nevertheless, learn to kill; blood must be spilled, including one's own, so that once the proletariat was victorious, there would be no need for further bloodshed. Hermann Remmle, one of the longest-serving members of the German Communist Party's Central Committee, summed up its attitude toward wars and warriors when he said that the difference between the world war that had just ended and the ongoing class war was that the latter was a revolutionary and not a counterrevolutionary war.[59] Yet, it was a war nonetheless, one in which a militant masculinity replaced the nonaggressive socialist man. Not only the German but also the French Communist man was supposed to project an image of an aggressive virility.[60]

The new Communist man, a product not so much of self-cultivation or education as of the class struggle, was, above all, a disciplined fighter, even though his humanism was mentioned occasionally.[61] However, the man of the future, living in a socialist society, would indeed be a "new man," and in the new Soviet Union, where victory had been achieved, Trotsky attempted to define him. He was immeasurably strong, wise, and subtle; his body would become more harmonious, his movements more rhythmic, his voice more musical.[62] The actual conditions in the one new socialist society that existed did at first hold the promise of a new departure. During the first ten years of the Bolshevik state it looked as if a new man, different from the accepted norm, might actually emerge as moral bonds were loosened and eternal moral truths were no longer said to exist: they must grow out of actual socialist practice.[63] And socialist practice, as the young revolutionaries charged with a new code concerning marriage and the family saw it in 1918, must, according to Marxist theory, reflect the withering away of the family and the state. They would leave behind a society based upon individual freedom.[64] Moral purity had been an important element of the masculine ideal, and now this seemed to lose some of its force as religious influence was eliminated, homosexuality decriminalized, de facto marriages recognized, abortion decriminalized, and total equality between the sexes guaranteed. For a brief time even a "Down with Shame" movement was allowed to exist.[65] Here there was to be no room for the chaste male stereotype. Moreover, it seemed for a moment as if a piece of the wall erected between insider and outsider, so important in the construction of modern masculinity might fall.

The new man who could have emerged—surrounded and inspired by avant-garde writers and poets—was, in any case, confined to a few urban centers. Moreover, the conventional standards of morality had already been questioned in Russia during the czarist regime before the war,[66] and the Bolshevik break with the past was not as radical as it might seem. The more relaxed social attitudes were threatened from the start by the conventionality of the Bolshevik leaders, who, as in the case of Lenin, voiced disapproval of a morally permissive society. Thus Bukharin, who in 1924 stated that the communist society would witness the disappearance of prostitution and the family,[67] a year later condemned as decadent groups with names like "Down with Shame." And an old Bolshevik wrote during this period concerning free love, regarded as a symbol of the search for a new socialist morality: "What can be put up against this theory? Parental authority? There is none. Moral feeling? But the old morality has died and the new has not yet come into being. The old form of the family has by and large been thoroughly destroyed, while the new does not yet exist."[68]

But even during this period of relaxed morals the so-called new socialist man had resisted fundamental change; he was still supposed to be hard in his dedication to the cause, simple in his habits, strong and silent.[69] Richard Stites has written that the ideal worker of the 1920s played an active, creative part in the productive process and behaved like a seasoned, conscious, well-trained warrior. The factory was his battlefield.[70] Masculinity devoted to a cause, disciplined and purposeful—even if it was in the service of productive labor rather than war—approximated the image of normative manhood, rather than presenting a true alternative to modern masculinity. It is this image that won out in the Soviet Union, for with Stalin's ascent to power, moral purity and chastity were reaffirmed as characteristics of the true worker. When the prudish Sidney and Beatrice Webb, in 1935, published their fulsome praise of the Soviet Union as an example to England, they could in good conscience single out its "healthy moral tone" as a sign of superiority. Any self-indulgence, they wrote, was contrary to communist ethics.[71]

On the one hand, the new communist man of Soviet propaganda was now said to be a restless fighter; on the other, he was said to have internalized the rules of daily life that had stayed constant over millennia, producing morally pure and beautiful men and women. Woman was now also put back in her place when in 1936 abortion was recriminalized, implicitly conceding the failure of revolutionary reforms.[72] The great experiment that attempted to create a new morality and with it a new man seemed to have failed.

Nevertheless, the Bolshevik man departed in several ways from the traditional ideal of manhood. The formal equality of women was recognized, they were comrades in the workplace rather than mere helpmates confined to the home. Yet with the fading of social experimentation in the Soviet Union, the scope of this equality was diminished by an emphasis upon the role of women as mothers, as well as upon the importance of the home and family. Lenin had always disapproved of free love, and it was perhaps a traditional view of woman's purity that had fueled the campaign against prostitution begun immediately after the revolution, when some prostitutes were sent to labor camps. Among most Western Communist Parties, and especially in the German party, women by and large retained their traditional image despite the leadership roles of a few women. We draw our examples from Germany once more, though they could probably be duplicated by other nations that contained strong Communist Parties. Women, typically enough, at first joined men as fighters in the Roter Frontkämpferbund, but soon their presence was thought to be inappropriate. Indeed, Hans Marchwitza, a popular "red" novelist, saw women as a distraction from the good fight that had to be waged; for Willi Bredel, a highly acclaimed Communist writer, party activists tended to become unreliable through their association with women.[73] Both men were highly orthodox and much-acclaimed Bolsheviks. This trend would continue throughout the existence of Bolshevism, despite all declarations to the contrary, as would Bolshevik iconography, in which woman was usually pictured as the equal of man.

This ambivalence about the role of women, which in the end preferred tradition over equality, was reflected in Karl Grünberg's *Brennende Ruhr* (The Ruhr on Fire, 1929), a novel much acclaimed by the Communist Party, both for its content and because Grünberg was, in fact, a factory worker who was self-taught. Here two women play major roles, the temptress Gisela, a "demonic female,"[74] who tries to corrupt the hero, the leader of a general strike, and Mâry, who joins in the fight, refuses to flee in defeat, and has the stuff to become a real *kampf-kamerade*, a true comrade in arms. A *femme fatale* such as Gisela was almost a stock character in so-called proletarian literature, while Mâry, though a fighter, nevertheless kept her womanliness intact: she is a nurse who tends the wounded, and as she converts a dying adversary to communism, the analogy to the Virgin Mary seems close at hand. Grünberg documents in exemplary fashion both the urge to give women greater equality with men in fighting the class war and, at the same time, the final victory of traditional femininity.

The keen-sighted, taut, and tightly muscled man who, as Frank Trommler tells us, came to the forefront of Communist iconography with the Russian Revolution,[75] brooked no rival. And, indeed, Grünberg's hero was described as such a broad-shouldered man. But here the worker departs from the image that informed the norm, this time in a rather more important manner. The aesthetics of masculinity were not emphasized, even when Soviet realism depicted men as tall and strong workers. They were fully dressed, their bodies fully covered in conformity with Lenin's and Stalin's devotion to respectability. Although for National Socialism, as we shall see, the nude male body in the tradition of Winckelmann's Greeks became a potent political symbol, Soviet ritual was restrained in the use that it made of body symbolism.[76] The abstract image of "the worker," whether man or woman, stood in the forefront of Bolshevik iconography. The European Communist Parties, as we mentioned, had never really imitated the greater permissiveness of the new Soviet Union, and they supported Stalin's return to a fighting spirit and strict respectability.

Yet for all the difference in emphasis between the Bolshevik man and bourgeois manliness, masculinity was used by both as the predominant symbol of strength, of work, and of the dynamic that must inform modern society. The ideal of energy and order, to which we have referred so often, was reflected in most official representations of masculinity, and it seems as if there was only a limited space for the expression of difference among such symbols in their representational function. Soviet realism and Nazi representations of masculinity, for example, also had many salient features in common: the inspired pose, the carriage of the head, the straight and honest look. Nor were the projections of willpower, solidity, and strength different, and even some of the favorite themes, such as camaraderie, were the same.[77] Thus it is not surprising that when the German Democratic Republic after the Second World War inherited some sculptures of Arno Breker, Hitler's favorite sculptor, it made use of them. Breker had sculpted nude youths in the tradition of ancient Greece, supplying the Nazis, as we shall see, with one of their most important symbols. Now the Soviets used his figures to decorate a sports arena,[78] which was appropriate, even if in their nudity and sensuousness they were not really in tune with socialist realism. The commonly accepted ideal of masculinity, which we have been discussing throughout, was present in all these representations of masculinity, whether Communist, bourgeois, or National Socialist, heightened, sharpened, and often given a more aggressive cast.

The chance to create a new man as an alternative to normative masculinity had been missed. The first socialist state had not produced the socialist man of Max Adler's dreams, instead, with some exceptions, it held fast to a disciplined masculinity that shared its principal attributes with the enemy in the class struggle. Proletarian literature meant to be read by the masses reflected a normative masculinity with astounding consistency, demonstrating once more the power of the masculine stereotype, documenting how little, in the end, an alternative image of masculinity counted.

"Der Rote Eine-Mark Roman" (the red one-mark novels) published during the Weimar Republic were a unique attempt by the German Communist Party to create political literature as mass entertainment, and to break the hold that cheap novels published by the large Berlin publishing houses had over the workers' imagination. Johannes R. Becher, much later to be the longtime minister of culture in the German Democratic Republic, called on those who had both brains and broad shoulders to support the venture.[79] Grünberg's book was one of this series. All of these cheap novels used an aggressive masculine vocabulary, admired sheer physical strength, domination, and victory. To be sure, this was not a military victory but the victory of the strikers as the slogan had it: "All wheels stand still if your strong arm commands it." Here, in these popular novels, women were, once again, not truly equal to men; instead, the broad-shouldered proletarians kept women at bay.[80] The enemies of the Communist Party, such as the Social Democrats, were said to be effeminate, and indeed the image of the enemy in these novels was usually the same as that of the traditional masculine countertype: weak, pale, old, womanly, in a word, "unmanly."[81]

Among not only Communists but most Social Democrats as well, the ideal of a new and different manhood never became firmly rooted in spite of repeated attempts by socialist intellectuals to change the direction of normative masculinity. Socialism advocated normal masculinity under another guise. Even the traditional warrior image was present. As far as the image of masculinity itself was concerned, the different kinds of war to be fought did not make a vast difference or present a true alternative to the soldierly figure as the culmination of traditional manliness. Here, warriors and socialists do belong in one and the same chapter.

The socialist ideal of a humane and pacifist masculinity seems to have failed in practice and even, to great extent, in theory. Yet in the end the warrior ideal did not triumph either. Both were too extreme, too opposed to the steady temper of life that most men and women desired. The warrior ideal left its imprint upon the Bolshevik and fascist parties, and Adler's socialist ideal was kept alive among some Social Democrats, and may even have contributed to soften the pre-Stalinist Soviet ideal. But it was the bourgeois stereotype of masculinity, which we have traced since its beginning, that continued to provide the bedrock of modern manliness and determined the view of masculinity of the vast majority of the population, regardless of their political loyalties.

7

THE NORMAL SOCIETY OF MEN

The masculine ideal held firm through war and revolution, all attempts at fundamental change had been destined to failure. Modern masculinity reflected the aspiration of a modern society that remained largely unchanged, not necessarily in its economic or even social composition—after all, the Bolshevik revolution changed both—but in its acceptance of respectability as a vital cement of society and the nation. Ever since the time of Winckelmann, true manliness had symbolized an essentially healthy society, and this society, in turn, did not merely posit manliness as an ideal to be reached but made it an integral part of its function. Before we discuss the climax of modern masculinity to be reached between the two world wars, we must pause to consider the principal means through which society itself transformed manliness from theory into practice. We have up to now stressed the masculine stereotype as an ideal, or as representative of society, but have paid relatively little attention to how it was institutionalized—how the very functioning of normative society became linked to the masculine ideal. Western society had always been run by men, but in modern times the stereotype of masculinity was institutionalized and firmly anchored within the modern state.

The masculine ideal had overcome the challenges of the fin de siècle, and yet such challenges increased after the First

World War as those marginalized by society attained a new self-confidence. The indispensable function that modern masculinity performed in established society, and that was even accepted by its enemies, like the communists, must be set off against the continued visibility of its challengers, at least until fascism came to dominate much of Europe. But even during the years of relative freedom, in the decade after the First World War, the strength of the masculine stereotype and its successful institutionalization was further documented by the strong desire of most outsiders, even if they accepted their own identity, to conform to the image of normative masculinity.

Education played a crucial part in the institutionalization of the stereotype, but so did a wide variety of social and political associations. The process through which the ideal of manliness penetrated into the population is important as well, it not only affected the workings of middle-class society but also socialized the working class. Here, once more, we must proceed by example, for giving a full account of the institutionalization and the penetration of this stereotype would mean writing the social and cultural history of the nations of Europe. We have already addressed some institutions, such as the military and the English public school, which played a vital role in projecting masculinity as necessary to the working of modern society. From the beginning of the nineteenth century onward, secondary education was apt to include education for manliness, indeed the proper masculine behavior and comportment was a vital part of the upbringing of middle-class boys in much of the West. As the middle classes slowly took over the reins of power, they had to build a nonaristocratic elite that could lead society and the state, and here education in manliness played its role. The new male stereotype, as we saw at the beginning of this book, had grown up in close alliance with middle-class sensibilities at the same time that it assumed a practical role in building a new bourgeois elite.

England was the most advanced industrial country in Europe, and it was here that education in manliness as the preparation for a new governing elite was furthest advanced during the nineteenth century. Aristocratic values were still present, such as the ideal of chivalry, but dominated by virtues that were an integral part of the male stereotype. Thus in a article called "Mens Sana in Corpore Sano" (A sound mind in a sound body)—echoing the importance of athletics and sport for the training in manliness—an English journal wrote in 1864, "[T]he sinews of a country like England cannot depend on its (old) aristocracy. A good wholesome cultivated mind and body, taught to endure, disciplined to obedience, self restraint and the sterner duties of chivalry, should be the distinguishing mark of our middle class youth."[1] The English public schools, newly reformed by the 1830s, provided such training. There the chapel and the playing field were often singled out as the two centers of school life: one to instill the proper morality, the other to train a fit masculine body and to provide experience of fair play. But the public school was not the only institution that gave such training; other organizations spread the message deeper into the population. Robert Stevenson Smythe Baden-Powell's Boy Scouts, founded in 1908, provide an example readily at hand. Here military experience played its part as Baden-Powell applied lessons he had learned in the Boer War to making men out of boys. Michael Rosenthal was quite correct when he entitled his book on the history of the Boy Scout movement *The Character Factory*. As such, its influence was great, and not confined to any one national elite as scouting and organizations modeled upon it became popular in many nations.

The military aspect of the organization, learning how to scout, was secondary to clean living, which entailed the proper posture and habits: "The boy who apes a man by smoking will never be much good, a strong and healthy boy has a [foot]ball at his feet."[2] Indeed, *Scouting for Boys* (1908), the handbook of the movement, typically enough, contrasts the proper type of boy with his countertype: the boy who smokes has a bad posture and a slovenly appearance, his hands deep in his trouser pockets; the boy who plays ball stands straight and strong. Baden-Powell told his Boy Scouts that "a clean young man in his prime of health and strength is the finest creature God has made in this world."[3] Small wonder that Baden-Powell thought the shape of a face provided a good guide to a man's character, addressing a tradition that has roots in Johann Caspar Lavater's physiognomy. The Boy Scout was closely related to the public school boy in appearance and moral outlook, for both received much the same training in manly virtue.

The Boy Scout was trained to follow orders in wartime, as part of a general education in obedience, duty, and endurance, which also prevailed in many public schools. However, chivalry was not forgotten; we saw earlier how it had become an integral part of the definition of an English gentleman. The section "Manliness" in *Rovering to Success* (1922), for example, starts with a paragraph, on chivalry before it exhorts the boy to "Be Master of Yourself." This meant that "kind heartedness" was considered as important as the sterner qualities of character, and the Scouts were, at times, seen as knights, united by strict loyalty as well as by patriotism.[4]

Concern with the social function of masculinity was a strong motivating force in setting up the Scouts. Baden-Powell discovered the amount of good there was in men as well as among boys, so it was said, through scouting. Men will sacrifice their time and pleasure, he wrote, and submit to discipline, until by "persistent pluck" they bring the task at hand to a successful conclusion.[5] Here the masculine ideal is clearly summarized, an ideal that served to form a middle-class elite, and that organizations such as the Boy Scouts with their large and diverse membership spread downward to most other segments of the population as well. The Boys Brigade, founded in 1883, affiliated with the Anglican Church, helped in the cause, and so did the message of work and prayer spread by books and teachings largely inspired by Evangelical piety. The Boys Brigade was aimed at organizing and disciplining the leisure time of working-class boys who had left both the Sunday and the state schools. Such boys were to become "brave, true, Christian men" while both "muscular Christianity" and the public school cult of sports were transmitted to them in this manner.[6] The individual Brigades, which were established throughout Great Britain, remained small, though they exemplified a widespread Evangelical drive. Organizations such as the Salvation Army and the YMCA also spread the "manliness of faith" into the population. The importance of such piety for the construction of masculinity in England was pointed out in an earlier chapter, and it was never truly to decline until after the Second World War.

"National Progress is the sum of individual industry, energy and uprightness, as national decay is of individual idleness, selfishness and vice"[7]—these words written by Samuel Smiles in his book tellingly called *Self-Help* (1859) held as true for the manly ideal of the twentieth century as they did in the nineteenth century when they were written. The book, which we mentioned before, was supposed to be a practical manual for achieving success through one's own efforts in all undertakings. The true gentleman was said to have a keen sense of honor, scrupulously avoiding mean actions,[8] and this in a book destined not for the elite but the general public. The book with its examples of statesmen, generals, doctors, and artists who had made an impact upon their society was a success all over the world.

Masculinity as basic to the functioning of society was not merely dependent, however, upon proper attitudes of mind, for a healthy mind must reside in a fit body. Toward the end of the nineteenth century many middle-class men became increasingly conscious of their own bodies, as we noted in chapter 5, and there was a surge of support for building and disciplining the body among British working-class men as well.[9] This it was hoped would help adjust the working class to normative manliness, and aid its members in becoming more productive. The Health and Strength League, a working-class and lower-middle-class organization whose slogan was "Sacred thy body even as thy soul," went from 13,000 members in 1911, five years after its founding, to 125,000 members by 1935, and in 1910 its *Annual* was circulated to some 90,000 young men.[10] The *Annual* itself estimated that in 1908 there were 100,000 physical culturists in England, many fewer, in its opinion, than on the Continent.[11] The *Annual* combined patriotism—raising the standard of the race (the English did badly in international athletic competitions)—with adoration of the male body, to make man, "so beautiful, so strong, so noble."[12] Working-class as well as middle-class youths were engaged in physical exercise in order to make manliness function correctly. Beauty here seems confounded with strength and the developing of one's muscles rather than with attaining a harmoniously proportioned body.

The penetration of the ideal of manliness into the working classes of other nations is still more difficult to chart. However, German workers toward the fin de siècle also began to be conscious of the potential beauty and strength of the male body, and, as we saw in chapter 6, through a wide variety of workers' sports organizations cultivated their health and strength. Male beauty as a sign of probity made finding employment easier, according to Siegfried Kracauer's book *Die Angestellten* (The Employees, 1930), published during the Great Depression. He defined such wage earners as neither proletariat nor middle class, documenting for our purposes, once again, the spread of the male ideal. Newspaper advertisements directed at men and not only at women employees asked, "How can I become beautiful?"; the newly acquired enthusiasm for sport and women's visits to beauty parlors was said to be caused, at least partly, by fear of losing one's job.[13] Looks had surely always mattered in gaining employment, especially when dealing with the public (and Kracauer's remarks we have cited were based largely upon the retail trade), and here the "true manliness" that has concerned us becomes crucial in gaining a living.

Physicians in Germany, always important in putting forward the stereotype of manliness, also played their part in the way in which the middle-class pattern of manliness was spread down the social scale. Here the workmen's insurance schemes, such as the one initiated by Bismarck in Germany, forced workers to consult officially designated physicians, where in all probability they received not only a medical examination but also advice about personal hygiene, including codes of personal conduct. "Moral disease" and physical disease were closely linked in both England and Germany,[14] just as they were joined in the "disease" of degeneration that had characterized the countertype at the fin de siècle.

German education in manliness, for all the differences in schooling, was in many aspects similar to that of English boys. This can be illustrated through the stories that young boys were supposed to read on their way to a productive manhood. They dealt with both fighting the good fight and adventurous living but at the same time were supposed to instill a communal spirit. Here masculinity within the dictates of middle-class society did not have to be aggressive or military. The books of Karl May, for example, many of which were set among the Indians of North America, were by far the most popular reading for German boys of all classes, from the end of the nineteenth century until well after the Second World War. They are singularly peaceful; the hero, a trapper called Old Shatterhand, is strong and manly, but he avoids a fight if at all possible. Old Shatterhand conquers the prairie not by fire and sword but with due regard for law and order. When he has defeated an evildoer, he does not kill him but brings him before a judge. May believed in the survival of the fittest and that the weak must be subordinated to the strong, but his Social Darwinism was embedded in bourgeois values and compassion that triumph in the end. Life among his heroes on the North American plains resembled the middle-class society he knew at home. Moreover, May's novels are marked by a Pietistic tradition that serves to soften the cruelty that at times informs his triumphant heroes.[15] The morality that suffuses his stories is not so different from that which at the same time informed those of G. A. Henty, the most popular writer of boys' stories in England. His heroes are both "Christian and manly": a young fellow who thinks more of others than of himself, who puts duty first, and is ready to devote himself to helping women and making children happy deserves to get on in the world.[16]

At the same time, the masculine activist ideal spread by English boys' weeklies and popular adventure stories, which were read by almost all classes of the population, could often be cruel. Foreigners were treated badly and the heroes "did not stop to wonder whether they really had a right to torture a dago bartender in Valparaiso or hang a Hebrew jewel thief because he had pawed an English girl."[17] Adventure stories often had a hard edge to them, and here the countertype entered once more. There are German boys' stories with a similar aggressiveness, but the most popular of these, like their English counterpart, were also tempered by a certain chivalry. However, in Germany the chivalric tradition as such plays little part; instead, heroes—such as those in the popular turn-of-the-century novels of Ludwig Ganghofer—are diamonds in the rough who possess a tender heart and protect the weak. May's heroes may look frightening, like bears, but they have compassion for even their worst enemies. The hard and domineering manly posture is maintained, but it contains a Christian, bourgeois core that tames its fearsomeness.

However, this taming must not be pressed too far; fair play was not an important ingredient in the makeup of the usual German hero. If Leslie Susser was undoubtedly correct when he wrote that fascism failed in Britain because its strong-arm tactics violated the rules of the game, no such rules existed in Germany.[18] The German social structures and political traditions differed from those of England, giving a sharper edge to the functioning of German masculinity. Above all, the linkage between patriotism and militarism was largely absent in England, but in Germany the military and the war veterans' associations played an important part in institutionalizing and spreading the ideal of masculinity into broad sections of the population.

The so-called Kriegervereine (Soldiers' Associations), for example, were founded after the German Wars of Liberation against Napoleon, and rapidly increased in size after the wars of German unification, until by the eve of the First World War they counted nearly three million members.[19] However, through their public appearances and festivals many more people came under their influence. The core of their membership was lower middle class and working class (craftsmen and rural laborers were strongly represented). Their ideology was nationalistic, in favor of the military, cultivating a manly and soldierly spirit. Members were called upon to be faithful to emperor and fatherland even unto death, and to demonstrate bravery, courage, decisiveness, strength, and toughness of will.[20]

Veterans after the First World War continued this tradition, adding racism to the mix of patriotism and manliness. Long before the paramilitary movements of the political Right became important in the Weimar Republic, the divergence between the ways in which the manly stereotype was transmitted in Germany and England was obvious, always remembering that there were similarities as well; after all, masculinity even in Germany did not have to be aggressive or military. Looking at education once more brings into sharp relief the different ways England and Germany trained their governing elites.

The German secondary school—the so-called gymnasium—was supposed to train an elite, but this type of education had little in common with the English public school. Boys in England learned to obey and command, first in serving the prefects—always boys in their last year at school—and then in turn becoming prefects themselves. Moreover, the pupils were disciplined by the prefects, without interference by teachers; they were taught early on lessons in self-discipline and responsibility, so different from the gymnasium, where students were at the mercy of the strict and rigid discipline of their elders.

There were too many teachers in German gymnasiums who, though ordinary men in daily life, "played God among their students."[21] That such schools left a host of bad memories is not astonishing, and the revolt of youth at the fin de siècle was above all directed against the school as symptomatic of an oppressive society. Here something of a military discipline and the language of the barracks invaded the classroom, and the title "Professor" given to teachers at the gymnasium only deepened the distance between them and their pupils. Typically enough, German schoolboys wrote bitter accounts of their school days disguised as novels or plays; here famous authors such as Hermann Hesse and Thomas Mann castigated the stifling atmosphere and the sadism of school life. In the gymnasium obedience and discipline counted—character training of sorts—but also, in the last resort, the camaraderie among students in the face of their oppressors. Even right-wing political movements that could be expected to support such an education eventually became dissatisfied. The Nazis, for example, were impressed by the English public school as they organized their own all-male national boarding schools designed to produce the future leaders of the nation. These Nationalpolitische Erziehungsanstalten were supposed to create "new men" to serve the new Reich, instilling in boys soldierly virtues such as self-control, love of order and action, and a willingness to sacrifice.[22] They quite consciously adopted some of the methods of the English public school to accomplish this end. That the young members of the Nazi elite were supposed to learn both to obey and command through exercising both functions within their squad[23] provides an especially telling example of an English educational principle adopted by these Nazi institutions. Moreover, like their English counterpart, they held each boy and not just the teachers responsible for the smooth functioning of the whole school. The English schoolmaster who thought that the Nazi boarding schools taught the same lesson as the English boarding schools, even though they used different methods, had gotten it upside down; some methods of the English school and even shared manly virtues were put into the service of a racist party and volk.[24] Perhaps Hitler's admiration for England played a part in this pro-English orientation, but so also did the experience of many Nazi leaders who had once regarded themselves as rebels against an establishment, characterized by the traditional gymnasium, from which they thought themselves excluded.

Student fraternities at the universities, with their duels, their drinking, their social rules and regulations, and all of their rituals, provided a more general education in manliness than the gymnasium. They provided a much rougher tone and environment than the colleges at Oxford or Cambridge that trained the English elite. Moreover, until 1918, all university students, although excused from conscription, had to do one year's military service. The one year's service became a sign of status, for those who had passed through it were automatically promoted to officerships in the reserves, and many teachers as well as other professionals proudly printed their military title on their visiting card. The attempt of the military to influence German students was quite different from what went on in England, where a military spirit had no place in the formation of the English elite.

A speech given at the University of Munich at the opening of the fall semester 1928, well after the Great War, was typical for a continued belief in discipline and obedience: Germany places a great responsibility upon your shoulders, the students were told; steel your will and heart in order to become men who are free, upstanding, and independent. The speech up to this point could have been given in England, but it goes on: "[F]reedom, true freedom, is inward, opposed to passion and egoism."[25] Such inward freedom tended to be indifferent to any demand for freedom of speech or action, and in this context opposition to passion and egotism meant self-discipline in the service of established society and the nation. Here the ideals that formed men (very few women were admitted to universities) pointed in a direction that was not really different from that which the gymnasium represented. The German bourgeois elite accepted all the proper values that they shared with their English counterparts, but gave them a military twist in which obedience and discipline threatened to take the place of individual responsibility. German educators had strayed far from the ideal of personal self-cultivation that had stood at the origin of the humanistic gymnasium in the previous century.

However, other male groups—choir societies, gymnastic clubs, associations for cultural, charitable, or purely social purposes—did not necessarily follow suit. These were voluntary associations that one could join and leave at will, and most of them were self-governing. Individualism was a precondition for their existence,[26] quite different from the system of education we have described. But, then, such *Männerbünde*, as they were called, as a rule, had no specific educational goal in mind, such as making men out of boys.[27] Germany was covered by a whole network of mostly middle-class or lower-middle-class male associations. England also possessed its system of male organizations, such as the London clubs where matters of state, literature, or the arts were discussed. An upper-class Englishman would spend his adolescence and most of his adult life in exclusive male company. But then, this held true for most Western societies that segregated or excluded women from the system of upper-class education and from playing any part in running society or politics, except that here, in England and Germany, *Männerbünde* were institutionalized.

Manliness as an integral part of settled bourgeois society raised questions about the dynamic of masculinity that had always been one of its chief attributes. The controversy in 1929 about the nature of so-called manly literature between the former German Expressionist writer Kurt Pinthus and the Communist critic Bélà Balàsz, whose definition of a firm and decisive manliness we quoted in chapter 6, illustrated this problem perfectly. Manliness for Pinthus meant a matter-of-fact attitude toward life, without any illusions, and at the same time the cultivating of a robust and blunt ("*derb und rauh*") disposition.[28] Pinthus contrasts such manly attitudes to what he calls the "weak and effeminate" cry of Expressionist youth and to those nationalists who brag about their strength.[29] His masculinity seems well attuned to bourgeois society, to manly behavior and attitudes, including moderation as well as sobriety, where any show of weakness or suspicion of effeminacy could unmake a man.

Balász, attacking this definition of masculinity, asked about the defiant commitment and uncompromising ethical stance of true manliness.[30] Balász posed his question from the Communist point of view, but it could have been asked by a nationalist as well. It seems as if Pinthus had not only omitted but negated the subordination to a higher cause that had been an integral part of the definition of modern manliness. However, passionate commitment, indeed any extreme, had no place in bourgeois society, except perhaps in times of national crisis. As a rule it seemed better and more practical to be without illusion, to take things as they came. The shedding of the spontaneous, of the passionate dedication to a cause, of the phoenix-like aspects of masculinity, was the price to be paid when manliness became part of daily life, of the normal working of society. Here there was no room for heroes.

The manly ideal was always a goal to aim at, but in the soberness of daily existence, of running a peacetime society as opposed to war, it could not so easily be put to the test. What remained was the stereotype of looks and virtue that people could discern, and that men who were lucky enough to have the right body symbolizing the proper morality could live up to. It was, after all, not too difficult with the proper education and physical exercise, to become a "clean-looking Englishman" or a good-looking German reflective of the national character. The predominance of the male stereotype, whose origin and evolution we have tried to analyze, asserted itself. Sometimes aspects of this stereotype that had been latent came to the surface, as in the First World War; at other times an alternative manliness was proposed, as we saw in chapter 6. But the stereotype as a standard of judgment, as an expression of modern, bourgeois society, even if low key, always retained its importance.

Such an ideal of manliness not only was thought necessary for running bourgeois society but also served to define it, side by side with family life, which was said to be at the heart of modern culture. Yet, as we have seen, masculinity tended to escape from the restraints imposed by the family. Schiller's poem, *The Cavalry Song*, standing at the beginning of modern masculinity, had exalted the freedom of the man who cast off the burden of daily life, and in 1924 Hans Blüher in praising the German Youth Movement asserted that masculine creativity could flourish only among male camaraderie and that the family destroyed man's spirit. He found some support but also critics, who accused him of advocating a *Bund* of monkeys and of poisoning the health of the *Volk*.[31] Such controversy could not erase the tension between masculinity and the demands of family life. This troubled relationship will come to a climax in the Third Reich, as we shall see, in the first modern state that saw itself in large measure as a *Männerbund*, and yet wanted to further and preserve the family.

Nevertheless, the truly masculine man integrated into daily life and, deprived of his sharper edges—as we have just described him—was, for the most part, held to be a good family man. Indeed, the "clean-cut Englishman" and his German cousin had to be surrounded by a family, if only to escape the imputation of homoeroticism or worse, an accusation that lay readily at hand in such a male-oriented society. Blüher in Germany was exceptional: as a rule family life and true masculinity were reconciled, a precondition for the proper ordering of settled society. This reconciliation depended upon the status of women. As long as women were subordinate to men, and the differences between the sexes clearly marked in every respect, man enjoyed a certain amount of freedom, even if it was paired with responsibility. But if women should aspire to greater independence, as the women's rights movement at the fin de siècle advocated, he was threatened in his so-called inborn superiority, and his individual freedom seemed unduly restricted as well. He was no longer the sole commander of the family, responsible only to himself.

Enough in the status of women had changed at the beginning of the twentieth century as a result of the movement for women's rights to cause anxiety among men. During the First World War many women had worked outside the home and earned money, though most of them were dismissed when the war was over. Moreover, a new type of woman seemed to have emerged, the so-called new woman, whom we have mentioned already as a subject of ridicule.[32] And yet men's superiority was not yet seriously at risk, and the tension between the family and the claims of true manhood were kept under control. Modern historiography has concentrated upon women's struggle for equality and neglected the deep cultural currents that even among women continued to support a traditional view of their status. Popular literature can give us an insight into generally accepted attitudes that more sophisticated writings cannot provide, even though such writings may have been agents of change and the much-beloved popular authors were as a rule deeply conservative. But, then, popular culture was still wedded to tradition, a fact that society could only ignore at its peril.

Agnes Günther's *Die Heilige und Ihr Narr* (The Saint and her Fool, 1913) was one of the German best-sellers of all time, a book that hundreds of thousands read between the wars, many more than even the most popular classics. The book was really a fairy tale whose central character, a young princess, creates another-world atmosphere, where people are delicate, their feelings pure, and from which all meanness is banished forever. She worships her beloved and future husband, a tall man who walks proudly and with firm manly strides. The princess is called affectionately *Seelchen* or "little soul," a name that refers not only to her gift of second sight but to her whole personality. Indeed, the affectionate nickname tells us everything about her submissiveness, her oversensitivity, and purity.

The attitude toward women Günther projects was matched, though in a lower key and without much of the purple prose and bombast by Hedwig Courths-Mahler, arguably one of the most popular German writers between the world wars. When the Nazis wanted to forbid her books because of her courageous stand against the regime (she refused to join the official writers union), they did not dare do so—a rare case of an author's defeating Nazi censorship because of her popularity.[33] Her novels are love stories in which the women practice kindness from the bottom of their hearts, are gracious, and stay in the background. Courths-Mahler preached the necessity of firm family ties as a bulwark against lack of character, unsteadiness, and self-indulgence. She paints a happy and healthy bourgeois world, with men and women in their accustomed place.

Germany was not alone; England and most other European nations possessed such highly popular romances. Sometimes they have different settings and a different thrust, but the result is much the same. Thus in the so-called English desert romances, popular between the two world wars, the sheik, a virile, sensuous male, masters females by physical force.[34] Yet these women do not object but remain faithful to their masters even after having been forced to bend to their will. Here violence and a certain cruelty is added to romance, unthinkable in Courths-Mahler's love stories. But it was precisely the activism of the hero that gave such novels their widest circulation, for they were ready-made for the new medium of the film, and the middle and late 1920s saw the rise of the male film star as a sex symbol. Rudolph Valentino exemplified full-blooded romance, a hero who was said to stimulate the sexual imagination of women.[35] Though Valentino was a predatory male, his dancer's body and languid posture signaled not a truly masculine but a more androgynous beauty that combined masculine brutality with an almost feminine tenderness. Valentino and his many imitators were attacked by other men as unmanly "lounge lizards."[36] Such androgynous masculinity, however, points to the future, to a time after another world war when, as we will see in the last chapter of this book, such confusion of gender was more easily accepted. As yet men were men, as the saying goes, and it was said that it was better to be ruled by masculine women than effeminate males,[37] but then there was no danger of this happening as long as most of the heroes of these early films represented true masculinity.

The literature we have discussed in these past pages was usually written by and for women, who must also have provided the bulk of the readership. Thus many women themselves had internalized their traditional role, just as women applauded the virile and possessive actions of Valentino or Ramon Navarro, which, to be sure, were less violent and cruel than those of the literary sheiks.[38] Social custom supported this image of women as opposed to that of men. The French writer Rachilde tells us, with perhaps some exaggeration, how in the time of her youth, in the early 1870s, girls were not allowed to drink wine or eat red meat (apparently privileges reserved for men), that they had to sit up straight and wait to speak until spoken to. Traditional customs had relaxed somewhat since that time. Indeed, Denis de Gourmont, a considerable figure in fin de siècle Paris, wrote admiringly that Rachilde's books showed that even a woman can write virile prose;[39] nevertheless, the thrust was still the same. Such stereotypes of women were part of the pattern of bourgeois life in which, despite his ties to the family structure, man retained a certain freedom of action. However, masculine freedom was circumscribed by middle-class morality and patterns of behavior that unlike the sheik but like Günther or Courths-Mahler tamed a potentially turbulent manhood into a respectability that was needed for the proper functioning of society.

II

Modern masculinity had been successfully institutionalized over a long period of time, nevertheless the countertype also continued to be a visible presence, as it had been ever since the end of the past century, continuing its challenge at an increased rate after the First World War. But, once more, normative society and with it "true manhood" managed to co-opt the new and to draw its sting. This time it was aided not just by the strength of society itself but also by the consensus supporting true masculinity, which, as we saw earlier, prevailed even among its opponents from the left and right.

The women's rights movement, ever since the end of the nineteenth century, had challenged the position of men in bourgeois society, though many women even on the radical fringe of the movement emphasized their femininity and saw themselves as destined for motherhood. From the 1890s onward, however, in England, and a little later in Germany and France, a different type of woman seemed to pose an equal and perhaps even more immediate threat. This so-called new woman seemed sexless, homeless, and unmaternal, providing an endless source of amusement for the English popular press. But it was after the First World War that the "new woman" came into her own, and through her high visibility and appearance—as much as by her demand for equality—challenged all men. With her short hair, mannish clothes, and the cigarette dangling from her lips, she seemed to efface gender. The flapper—as the British "new woman" was called—by trying to look like a boy, was said to destroy the character of her sex and—one might add—that of the male sex as well. France had its own flapper, *La Garçonne* (The Single Girl), so called after the title of a novel by Victor Margueritte published in 1922. *La Garçonne* increasingly took on the appearance of a man, cutting her hair short and wearing tailored clothes.[40] However emancipated she turned out to be, eventually it was the heroic deed of a man who saved her from certain death. All the despair and loneliness that Margueritte's "new woman" deprived of clear gender division is made to feel could not stop the advance of the new female style she represented. Was the advent of a third sex at hand—when human beings would be neither men nor women, obliterating traditional gender and giving women the same role in running society as that held by "true men"?

The "new woman" presented the identical problem for French and

English as for German men. She seemed to have no sexual feelings that man could awaken and play upon. The *Berlin Illustrated*, with its huge circulation, at the beginning of the century saw in her the woman of the future: nothing, so we read, could slow or hinder her march to victory; today she can be a member of parliament, a lawyer, or a judge who passes sentence without mercy (shades of the *femme fatale*). This was a woman who knows neither how to flirt nor how to love, and as revenge for her past slavery has given proof that man can be dispensed with.[41] After the war, the "new woman" drew universal attention from the German political Left as well as the Right. Not all those inclined to socialism saw in the *Bubikopf* a sign of progress, as we mentioned in chapter 6; thus Otto Dix painted a rather cruel picture of the journalist Sylvia von Harden, sitting in a Berlin cafe, smoking a cigarette. He emphasized her aggressive chin, the attempt to disguise all that might be considered feminine in her appearance, the use of her hand to cover the part of her short dress that concealed the womb (see Figure 1.2).

The embarrassed defenders of Dix have argued that the painting was in reality an attack upon intellectuals because the Berlin cafe in which she sat and smoked was their preferred meeting place. Sylvia von Harden herself remembered that Dix addressed her on the street one day, saying, "I must paint you! I simply must! You are representative of an entire epoch." Dix described the painting as concerned not with the outward beauty of a woman but with her psychological condition.[42] That condition was not promising. Whatever importance one might assign to the psychology involved, here the stereotype of the "new woman" was created not by a right-wing painter accustomed to upholding tradition but by a left-wing artist with anarchist leanings. The "new woman" was a harbinger of things to come, not in immediate terms but in the 1960s, when the traditional image of masculinity was eroded and a more radical feminist movement seemed set for success. Even then, however, the traditional gender image, though badly dented, was still partly in place; witness the continuing popularity of the literary romances in the tradition of Courths-Mahler in Germany and in the England of Barbara Cartwright as well. The "new woman" after the First World War did portend the future rather than characterize the present, but the men at the time saw the "new woman" as a serious challenge to their dominance.

Although ever since the fin de siècle one of the most urgent challenges to true manhood had come from emancipated women, the existence of unmanly—so-called womanly men—doubled the threat to the proper functioning of manhood. The specter of "unmanly men" had accompanied modern masculinity from its birth, such as, for example, the effeminate dandy early in the nineteenth century, and then that of the decadent. The latter refused to vanish: Oscar Wilde may have been sent to prison in England, but he had many successors, not only in England but throughout the Continent. The "new woman's" brother—the effete artist, a frequenter of cafes, with his languid pose and a cigarette dangling from his mouth, was considered a twentieth-century decadent. (Here, as with the "new woman," the cigarette became one of the symbols of depravity as opposed to manly pipes and cigars.)

But now it was some of the unmanly men themselves, the descendants of the Baron de Montesquiou, who in one of their first openly homosexual publications attempted to present themselves as truly masculine, and this for both ideal and functional reasons. The notion, put forward by some of their own defenders, that homosexuals possessed a female soul in a male body or that they were somehow a third sex was widely repudiated.

The first and longest-lived homosexual periodical in Germany, *Der Eigene* (1898–1933), for example, promoted a militant masculinity. Its owner and editor, Adolf Brand, lamented the unmanly times in which he lived and which were marked by a lack of reverence for strong men and monarchs. The illustrations that accompanied the texts were the same pictures of youthful masculinity that could be found in normative publications, except that here some of the men were in the nude or affectionate with one another, poses not allowed in the mainstream media. But the bodies and comportment of the men were in complete conformity with the normative masculine ideal. Typically enough, many contributors considered woman's emancipation the most objectionable consequence of a more democratic age.[43]

Indeed, an examination of the love stories taken at random from German gay journals published between 1929 and 1979 document an unchanging male stereotype. They are filled with "beautiful young men," blond, tall, and slender, with sharply chiseled faces, fulfilling Winckelmann's ideal. Normative masculinity was affirmed rather than challenged.[44] The worship of classical beauty and the frequent references to Greece as legitimizing homosexuality led to a strong reaffirmation of the male stereotype not only in Germany but in England and France as well. Effeminate men, so André Raffalovich, himself a homosexual, tells us in his *Uranisme et Unisexualité* (Homosexuality and Unisex, 1896)—to cite another and different example—are sick liars and criminals, unable to control their passions.[45] It was unfortunately not unusual for homosexuals to turn the accusations leveled against them back upon other homosexuals who did not fit the ideal of a beautiful and virile masculinity.

Havelock Ellis, the English sexologist, thought that what homosexuals wanted was beauty, strength, and youth,[46] and although this may have been true, most heterosexuals worshipped at the same shrines. The majority of homosexuals, so it seems, clung with great tenacity to this masculine stereotype. They continued perhaps in its purest form the heritage of Winckelmann himself into the modern age. The pictures of men such as those in *Der Eigene*, with their hairless bodies and Greek profiles, attest to that fact. Small wonder that such men were attracted to the normative manly stereotype that, as we have seen throughout this book, was built upon Winckelmann's heritage. Most homosexuals, then, actually shared a masculine stereotype with society at large, even if for them it was charged with sexual meaning projecting a human beauty that must never be compromised. To be sure, homosexuals, like any minority at the time, wanted to gain admission to society and help it to function, and thus were under intense pressure to prove that they were real men. That a continuity exists here as well was demonstrated when many of the twenty-four homosexuals interviewed by the U.S. Army in a case study during the Vietnam War in the mid-1960s said that they hoped that the army would be a curative experience for them through its discipline and emphasis upon virile behavior.[47]

Clearly, such men had internalized not only the normative masculine stereotype but their own ugly stereotype as well. Entering into society and its functions was considered a species of cure for homosexuals. Such feelings of inferiority and a corresponding desire for normalcy were shared by virtually all minorities; they were preeminent not only among homosexuals but, as we shall see, among Jews as well. This need for acceptance by normative society was no doubt tragic as far as the dignity and self-confidence of members of the minorities were concerned, and because in any case they were rarely completely accepted however much they might support society's ideals. *Der Eigene* provides a prime example of this futility: the Nazis, worshippers of masculinity, shut down the journal as soon as they had attained power.

However, as indicated earlier, by no means all homosexuals gave strong support to the masculine ideal. The first writer to defend homosexuality, Karl Heinrich Ulrichs, had written in mid–nineteenth century that "we are women in spirit."[48] And Magnus Hirschfeld, one of the most famous sexologists practicing in the first decades of the twentieth century, founder of the first gay defense association, himself a homosexual, believed that gays were, in fact, a third sex. He classified men and women according to their male or female characteristics, and although he held that all men and women contained some feature of both sexes, he still considered masculinity and femininity clearly distinct categories. Homosexuals possessed more female characteristics than a true male ought to possess and hence constituted an intermediate sex placed somewhere between male and female.[49] Moreover, the men described in chapter 5, such as the Baron de Montesquiou or Jean Lorrain, far from wanting to be normal men, flaunted their effeminacy, and Oscar Wilde repudiated the Greeks as providing legitimacy to homosexuality and instead was proud of his difference.

Here those homosexuals, perhaps the majority, who believed in the normative masculine stereotype have been addressed in order to demonstrate the power of co-optation of modern manliness: the majority of a group traditionally regarded as the foil of masculinity in reality rallied to its support in the name of a pure manhood. Jews had, if anything, still more reason than homosexuals to co-opt the masculine ideal. As a minority rather recently emancipated from ghetto life, they could adopt such an ideal both as a sign of assimilation and a repudiation of the past. The ghetto life of poverty and religious oppression (as most Western Jews saw it) was kept constantly before their eyes in the villages and towns of Poland at Germany's eastern border, as well as within the European cities themselves, where East European Jewish immigrants lived in their own crowded quarters. These "ghetto Jews," as they were often called, seemed to keep their distinct dress and speech (Yiddish), as well as their religious orthodoxy—a way of life that singled them out as different in body and mind from normative society. A "new Jew" would have to be created to counter this stunted image, which had haunted Jews throughout their assimilation. It had been part of their past in a way that the image of the effeminate man had haunted the past of homosexuals.

To be sure, one of the most important factors that drove homosexuals to seek integration into society was present among Jews as well, namely, the internalization of one's own stereotype as it had been created by society and the urgent wish to escape from its shadow. The desire to play a positive role in the evolution of modern society was also present. Jews were heavily concentrated in the cities, as well as in the commercial professions, and this factor had a decided influence upon the fashioning of a new Jew. Jews, in order to become true men, must become reacquainted with nature. Even in the 1920s some young Jews were told to marry German peasant women in order to freshen up the tired old blood. Here Jews took over a prejudice from society at large, and reacted once more to their own stereotype of pale, ugly, puny, and inbred men, crowded together in cities. Just like homosexuals, they were branded as degenerate by their enemies, and degeneration, as we saw earlier, was the foil of masculinity. Just so, a Jewish publication blamed the supposed lack of interest in gymnastic exercises among young Jews upon nightly sessions in coffeehouses from which pale figures were seen slinking home at dawn.[50]

The new Jew was supposed to "expose as lies the fairy tale of the bent and crooked Jew, as our youth grows to maturity in good health and with straight bodies."[51] Max Nordau's contrast between "coffeehouse Jews" and "muscle Jews" tells the whole story. Nordau was to be influential beyond his own time at the end of the nineteenth century, and he defined the new Jews as he defined normal men in contrast to so-called degenerates, as we saw earlier: they are "men who rise early and are not weary before sunset, who have clear heads, solid stomachs and hard muscles."[52] Such Jews had attained the proper masculinity, and in contrast to the "ghetto Jew," they now had the posture, body size, and capability to engage in productive work and to play their part in the advancement of society (Figure 7.1). Many Jewish organizations, from the end of the century onward, wanted to create a new Jew—foremost among them Nordau's Zionists—but mainstream organizations joined in as well as Jewish sports and gymnastic clubs sprang up throughout central Europe.

Once the Nazis cast their shadow over the land, even the left-liberal and pacifist author Arnold Zweig, a self-conscious Jew, wrote admiringly about the new type of Jew, well-formed and taking joy in his body and trained muscles, who according to the Anglo-Saxon example treated sport with the same consideration as intellectual accomplishment. Zweig described what he saw as the new German of 1931, but in his eyes this German was supposed to set an example for the new Jew.[53] The new Jew, then, represented the ideal of masculinity writ large, and

7.1 The new Jew at work, a postcard issued by the kibbutz movement in the 1930s.

like the homosexuals, he strengthened that stereotype in the modern age. Here manliness could also be based on high ideals such as the nation, though most Jews were not nationalists but liberals. Self-control, willpower, and "quiet strength" were as much part of the masculine ideal of these groups as of society as a whole, and for both Jews and homosexuals, appearing and acting manly was considered an entrance ticket into society.

The masculine ideal had overcome the period of its greatest challenge at the end of the nineteenth century, had been strengthened by the war, and retained its dominance in the interwar years. Long before and after the Great War it had become firmly rooted and had made its way as a symbol and as supposedly essential to the proper working of society. The outsiders themselves had internalized this ideal. The willingness to sacrifice for an ideal was always latently present, but in daily life and in its social function, masculinity reflected a moral stance—the practice of manly virtues—rather than single-minded national or political commitment. And yet, after the Great War, masculinity as a national and political symbol reached its climax. The ideal of masculinity was close to the heart of fascism, which, together with communism, was about to become the most fateful political movement of the interwar years. Manliness as a public symbol reached new heights, even as manliness as a social imperative continued to co-opt its challengers.

8

THE NEW FASCIST MAN

I

The history of modern masculinity now reaches a climax. Never before or since the appearance of fascism was masculinity elevated to such heights: the hopes placed upon it, the importance of manliness as a national symbol and as a living example played a vital role in all fascist regimes. Manliness was a principle that transcended daily life. To be sure, fascism merely expanded and embellished aspects of masculinity that had always been present, and that we have discussed in the previous chapters. The fascist ideal of manliness was in immediate terms built upon the Great War, for the movement considered itself the true inheritor of the war experience, but it also included other images of masculinity, such as those put forward, for example, by the German Youth Movement or by the Italian Futurists. Wherever the manly ideal rose above ordinary life, it was co-opted by the fascist movements. Fascism used manliness both as an ideal and in a practical manner in order to strengthen its political structure, but devotion to a higher cause was at the center of its concept of masculinity.

A speech by an Italian Fascist party functionary given to the Ballila—the fascist youth organization—around 1930 expresses this priority perfectly: *mens sana in corpore sano* is not enough, (though in daily life manliness stressed just this fact), nor are school and sport. What is needed is a spark that inflames the enthusiasm and the will to serve the fatherland.[1] Service and sacrifice in a higher cause had been part of the definition of the manly ideal almost from the beginning, but now such a demand was couched in the rhetoric of the First World War. That war made the greatest contribution to the formation and goals of the fascist man: the new Italian fascist man, Emilio Gentile has written, is a warrior-crusader in the service of a faith.[2] That faith was the civic religion of nationalism, but even before the war, extreme nationalists had wanted to create a new man in order to fulfill their dreams for a new Italy. Mussolini was in close touch with such movements in the formative period of fascism, and they, as well as the war, would help shape the image of fascist man.

Italian nationalists from the turn of the century onward proclaimed a revolutionary nationalism that would depart from tradition. Like the literary and artistic avant-garde of the fin de siècle of which they were a part, such men wanted to accept modernity, and above all the new speed of time made possible by technology that had impressed so many of their contemporaries. Nationalism was not supposed to fulfill its traditional function of making time stand still but, instead, was meant to revolutionize Italy. This was supposed to be a spiritual revolution leading to the creation of new elites.

The Futurists from the beginning of this century onward were both an artistic avant-garde and a political movement, influential within Italian nationalism as well as upon the formation of a fascist man. They were not nationalists of the old school, for they opposed ideas of immutability and joyfully embraced modernity. Futurists believed in the creation of a new man who was not tied to the weight of past history but could take off into uncharted spaces proclaiming Italy's glory through his personal drive and energy. Nevertheless, this new man must be disciplined, at one in spirit with like-minded men through a way of perceiving the world, of acting and behaving, based upon the sober acceptance of the new speed of time and a love of combat and confrontation. Futurism took concepts like manliness, energy, and violence, and sought to tear them loose from the historical traditions in which conventional nationalist movements had anchored them. And once again, in apparent contradiction to its dislike of tradition, the new man was ready to fight and to sacrifice his life for the fatherland. Filippo Marinetti, the leader of the Futurists, summed up the qualities that such a new man should possess: he was a disciple of the engine, the enemy of books, and a believer in personal experience as well as Italy's power and glory.[3] These notions are obviously contradictory, for although he is supposedly an autonomous person, the futurist is also disciplined and limited in freedom of action by his service to Italy. The Futurists, it must be remembered, were not systematic thinkers but artists who believed in spontaneity.

Other Italian nationalists at the start of the twentieth century also toyed with the idea of a new man. Giovanni Papini one of their most important publicists, pointed to the importance of this ideal when he called a collection of his essays, written at the beginning of the new century, simply *Maschilità* (1915), that is to say, manliness. Here Nietzsche is praised as a model for the true man, as is Otto Weininger's *Sex and Character*, discussed in earlier chapters, because of its sharp separation between men and women, the one—as Papini paraphrased him—forceful, energetic, hard, and proud; the other weak, flabby, bland, and tearful.[4] Men must free themselves from bourgeois icons like the family, schools, and the love of women, for loving them means to become their servant.[5] *Maschilità*, so Papini proposes, is a "male discourse written for men," by which he means that it is written in a Nietzschean style, exhorting its readers to break with established traditions in order to discover the true Italy: they must fling themselves at life in a sober, unromantic manner. They must have the courage to become more brutal, more bestial, more barbaric.[6] Papini and Enrico Corradini, another influential nationalist, writing in their journals, thought that war and a spiritual revolution would complete the process of Italian unification. The generation that followed the Risorgimento had been unequal to its task.[7] This was a very Nietzschean nationalism, always in movement, aggressive and hard: "honey and stone" was another way in which Papini compared women and men.[8]

This Italian "new man" was a Nietzschean nationalist, a combination the German philosopher would have repudiated. The Nietzschean nationalist as a new man was not totally unknown in Germany,[9] but German nationalism itself, though it used Nietzsche, drew his sting—there was to be no influential Papini to invoke the true Nietzsche on behalf of a nontraditional, antihistorical nationalism. The new man described in Papini's book influenced the new man of Italian fascism, but, then, Mussolini himself came from a restless, revolutionary tradition, and during the war he was full of praise for Papini and his journal

Lacerba. These Italian nationalists (and Papini's ideas were shared by others), in turn, were closely aligned with the Futurists. This was a constellation that had a lasting influence upon Italian fascism and its concept of masculinity, in contrast to National Socialism whose nationalism lacked this particular dynamic.

Intense nationalism, faith in Italy's greatness and destiny, was permeated with a revolutionary fervor that would create new men ready to transform Italy. Such nationalists believed in regenerative violence, which, as Renzo de Felice has argued, suited Mussolini's temperament.[10] Their influence on fascism was largely inspirational, though they joined Mussolini in agitating for Italy's intervention in the First World War, believing, as he did at the time, that the war would precipitate a revolution. The new man of fascism shared the dynamic of the nationalists as well as their patriotic fervor, nevertheless he was also tightly disciplined and self-controlled—closer to the ideal of the Futurists—characteristics mostly absent from the rhetoric in which Papini and his fellow nationalists cast their men of the future.

The First World War and its consequences were more important than either Futurists or extreme nationalists in forming the concept of the new fascist man. Fascism itself as a political movement was a product of that war, and the movement as a whole—whether Italian fascism or German National Socialism—thought of itself as the inheritor of the war experience. It was precisely the actual experience of war that, in fascist eyes, predestined veterans to lead the new men of the future. Those who had faced death were said to have been the true heroes who knew the meaning of sacrifice, even though they had lived life to the full. Soldiers who have passed the test of war challenged death precisely because of their vitality and love of life.[11] The glorification of the First World War played a major role in fascist ideology: to have experienced the war led to true manhood, opposed to the bourgeoisie who knew neither how to live nor how to die. Yet, this idealized veteran was no individualist, he was at one with his squad and his people.

Wartime camaraderie was for all of fascism the paradigm of society and the state. This camaraderie, as we mentioned in a previous chapter, was, of course, a camaraderie of males, and such male bonding was considered the foundation upon which the state rested. The German ideal of the *Männerbund* (Figure 8.1) was often invoked by the Nazis, but Italian fascists also conceived of the state in this manner, despite Mussolini's brief flirtation with women's rights in the 1920s.[12] But

8.1 "The Party lifted on high by athletic men," a postcard of the *Männerstaat*, issued in honor of the NSDAP Reichsparteitag in Nürnberg, September 6–13, 1937.

although camaraderie was thought to embrace the whole nation, in reality attention was focused upon the Fascist Party and its formations. Here camaraderie was supposed to be voluntary, not enforced, as in the trenches: to join such elites required willpower, legitimizing once more the importance of the human will to the construction of the new man. The former combatant imbued with the proper spirit, who had truly experienced the war as it should have been faced, became a member of the Italian fascist squadrista, the fascist shock troops, representing the prototype of the new man.[13]

The ability to face death without flinching had also been the key characteristic of Ernst Jünger's new race of men formed by the war, and it became a defining moment for the fascist or National Socialist man after the conflict. The cult of the war dead, of the fascist or Nazi martyrs, was the centerpiece of the fascist and Nazi political liturgy. Such a preoccupation with death and sacrifice was a product of the war itself and of the apocalyptical call for destruction and renewal: the destruction of the old world and the renewal of the nation.

Mussolini's new man, then, was to be inspired by the war experience, and indeed he lived in a state of permanent war. The constant wearing of uniforms, the marches, the emphasis on physical exercise, on virility, were part of the battle against the enemy. This enemy was not, until the Ethiopian war of 1935 and the racial laws of 1938, a minority like the Jews or a foreign nation but, rather, the menace of degeneration that would sap the strength of the nation from within. The emphasis on camaraderie, discipline, and fitness was accompanied by a high moral tone. For example, Achille Starace, secretary-general of the Fascist Party from 1931 to 1938, mounted purity crusades and called for greater austerity. Here also the new fascist man was exemplary, battling degeneration and embodying through his comportment the manly purity that had accompanied modern masculinity from the start. Lando Ferretti, a committed fascist involved with the fascist youth movement, and in official sport organizations, even called for the closing of dance halls, "which have nothing in common with hellenic beauty."[14]

Fascist preoccupation with the human body needs special emphasis. The rise of modern masculinity had always centered on the cultivation of the human body, a hallmark of the modern as over against earlier ideals of masculinity, and this concern also reached its climax in fascism. The new man's body represented his mind as well. The nude male body reflecting the classical ideal of beauty became, as we shall see, an important National Socialist symbol, but Italian fascism also made use of it, if to a lesser degree. Thus a nude youth with a beautiful Greek body was at times said to symbolize the fascist era. More important, the Forum Mussolini in Rome, the main sports stadium, completed between 1932 and 1937, was surrounded by sculptures of nude athletes, men and women, each one contributed by one of Italy's provinces. These were classical figures, once more, documenting the remarkable continuity of such inspiration, in this case encompassing both men and women. Women, after all, had to be strong and vigorous as well in order to become better wives and mothers.[15] This changed little in their dependent position. Athletics, for example, was supposed to be a means to enhance female grace, and in 1931 Mussolini's press office ordered publications to eliminate all sketches of "excessively thin and masculinized female figures."[16] Men's bodies in all their well-sculptured nudity became fascist symbols; women, with some exceptions such as the one just mentioned, kept their bodies at least partly clothed.

Still, a German observer watching Italian youth marching in serried ranks into the Forum Mussolini gave them too National Socialist a reading when he asserted that it was their very dearest wish to model themselves in spirit and looks after the statues of Greek athletes surrounding the stadium.[17] Italian fascist writers on sport and gymnastics, unlike those of Germany, did not constantly stress the formation of male beauty. Yet Mussolini himself bemoaned the fact that Italians walked as if they were crippled; they must learn to walk straight.[18] Nowhere, however, does he show the unbridled enthusiasm for manly beauty that Hitler demonstrated when he wrote in *Mein Kampf* that the Greek ideal of beauty is immortal because it combined the most glorious bodily beauty with a sparkling spirit and a noble soul.[19] We shall return at some length to the use the Nazis made of the so-called beautiful male body.

The difference between Germany and Italy in the emphasis they placed upon looks and bodily structure was a matter of degree and not of absolutes. Once the racial laws were passed in 1938, the attempt to invent Italian Aryans on the German model fell rather flat. The overriding importance of physical exercise in Italy, then, was not so much centered on the symbolic importance of the beautiful body as, above all, on its use to instill discipline and a sense of order, and proper comportment was considered essential. That physical exercise furthered comradeship was considered vital as well; here a real camaraderie was said to exist (as it had in the war), one that knew neither class nor caste. The fact that sport encouraged camaraderie was also praised in Germany. There one Nazi educator wrote that sport reenforced a manly joy in life that derived from true comradeship. This was no small matter, remembering that the ideal of male comradeship, as far as fascism and National Socialism were concerned, provided the foundation of the state.[20]

But there was another way in which fascism made use of the human body: in Italy rather than in Germany, body language, not merely looks and comportment, was important, building upon an expressiveness that was common in southern but not in northern Protestant Europe. Mussolini used body language as a means of communication in a theatrical manner quite foreign to Adolf Hitler, who would have thought it unbecoming, if not effeminate. To be sure, the stiff and disciplined bodies at marches or mass meetings spoke their own language, but here it was the Duce's extremely malleable body that spoke to the masses (such as, for example, his jutting chin, which was supposed to demonstrate his willpower).

Physical exercise played a crucial part in forming the fascist man; fascism accepted the by then traditional notion that a fit body was the sign of a manly spirit. Physical exercise was not regarded as just a preparation for wars to come; it was supposed to build character, and indeed all the justifications for sport that we have discussed held the male body hostage for the qualities the new fascist man should possess. But, in the last resort, acquiring physical strength, discipline, and agility, and sculpting the body, were considered useless without strength of will. The will, so the editor of the official Italian fascist sports journal tells us, is the spark that ignites the fervent desire for service and sacrifice.[21] The will took on the same role that it had always played in the history of masculinity, and fascist masculinity repeated, if in extreme form, normative ideals.

Here too the needs and hopes of contemporary society as it perceived itself were reflected in the very construction of the male stereotype symbolizing both a dynamic and restfulness. The extreme of fascist manliness mattered, of course, for it brought into sharp relief the warrior elements of masculinity, even while it attempted to direct and channel manly aggression and energy. Discipline was all-important, and the need for self-restraint was frequently invoked in fascist publications and speeches, and with good reason, for the constant and unremitting stress on action and on permanent war might easily get out of hand.

The emphasis on action was supposed to distinguish the new man from the bourgeois, associated in the fascist mind with passivity, cynicism, and decadence. In contrast, the fascist man, according to the official history of Italian fascism, written by Giocchino Volpe in 1936, unites culture, knowledge, and action. However, education must treat knowledge as a dynamic force directed toward the realization of fascist ideals.[22] Such notions could be found among National Socialists as well; indeed, they were common among all fascists. But in Italy, the fascist man was not so firmly anchored in the past or in a clearly defined ideology and therefore gave much greater play to the dynamic that the new man must exemplify.

Mussolini himself, like Papini, was much taken by Nietzsche. Hitler also sought to enlist Nietzsche in his cause, but his Nietzsche was expurgated, adjusted to traditional, historically centered nationalist and racist ideas. Mussolini's Nietzsche had not come under racist influence, and for him Nietzsche's highly unsystematic thought meant seizing ideals different from those in which an older generation had believed. A new order of "free spirits" steeled in war would arise, so he wrote, who could grasp Nietzsche's ideals, they would know the winds and the glaciers of the high mountains, and have looked into the abyss as well. They would give men back their hope.[23] Mussolini wrote this Nietzschean vision at the turn of the century. As we have seen, however, the ever-present ideal of sacrifice and salvation also played a role in forming a new order of men. Given this spirit and these goals, it is not astonishing that willingness to act became one of the principal attributes of the fascist new man driven by a quasi Nietzschean vision of Italy's future but at the same time disciplined and obedient, however much the latter might contradict the original impulse.

At the beginning of the 1930s, for example, some young Italians took this challenge to action seriously and turned it against a fascist regime apparently grown fat in power. Young fascist intellectuals—students for the most part—began to criticize the fascism of their day on behalf of what they considered to be the original revolutionary impetus. This criticism had no great effect, except that it might have contributed to the start of the Ethiopian war (1935) as an outlet for frustrated activism.[24] But it demonstrated an élan, a continuing drive present in Italian and other fascisms in southern Europe, but much more strictly controlled in National Socialism.

The so-called new man of National Socialism was deeply rooted in the past, and although the Italians' ties to ancient Rome were often invoked—after all, fascism's trademark, the *Littorio*, had been the Roman insignia of public office—Mussolini considered him only a point of departure, a springboard toward the future. The new man of Italian fascism, moreover, was a constant presence; the new German as an individual was rarely mentioned. Thus when Achille Starace handed over his position as the secretary of the Fascist Party to his successor in 1939, he said that the creation of a new man was the constant object of the party's attention, a task to which the party must devote itself with all its might.[25] The same tension that had plagued the Futurists existed in fascism: between the revitalized, active, individual and the duties of the "citizen soldier." This soldier must have faith and be disciplined, possess willpower and courage.[26] But, then, as Renzo de Felice has shown, Mussolini's ideas themselves were contradictory: the image of a new man was created by a state that was both authoritarian and populist, activist and yet contemplative, dynamic and realistic, nationalist and Western.[27] In the article on fascism in the 1933 edition of the *Encyclopedia Italiana*, Gioacchino Volpe writes that there are two Mussolinis: one who does not love the masses and sympathizes with the individual; and the other, who knows that discipline is necessary as a means of integrating the individual into the nation and, because he himself is disciplined, wants it for others as well. Moreover, discipline is vital for effective action, and for the day—soon to come—when the battle against the decay of Italy will give way to Italy's reconstruction.[28] These contradictions are reconciled in the name of a vague totality.

The Nazis, however, had no such ambivalence; they were apt to think only about people in the mass; any individualism was foreign to their cast of mind, This is, perhaps, a rather subtle but nevertheless real distinction, for it leads to a crucial difference between the Italian fascist and the Nazi ideal of masculinity. Italian fascism put much of its trust in the new fascist man who would lead Italy into utopia. But the future was never detailed; it was safe in the hands of the new fascist man, who could be trusted to make the right use of it. Here the difference from National Socialism is startling, for the Nazis left nothing to chance, and the true German was meant to execute a set plan for the racial state, which was always supposed to grow organically out of the nation's past.

The picture of Hitler creating a new man (Fig. 8.2) was therefore strictly speaking inaccurate. And yet in general the figure created by the "sculptor of Germany," as portrayed in that country's leading satirical journal, was true. This new man Hitler created could well be anchored in the past. The important message was that, with the Nazi access to power, a new man was being born, a "new German," as over against the present and presumably decadent manhood.

For all the difference between the new German and Italian man, however, both movements shared a tension to which we have referred

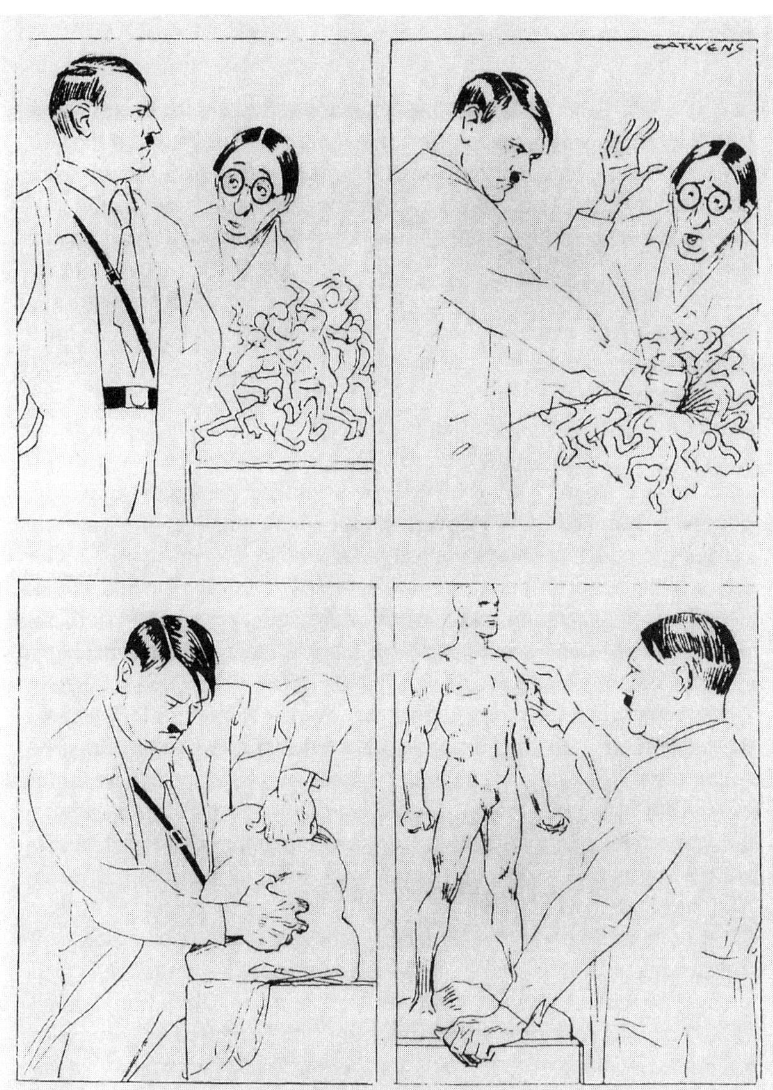

8.2 *Germany's Sculptor*; Hitler creating the new German, from the satirical newspaper *Kladderadatsch* 86, no. 49 (1933).

briefly already: between a triumphant masculinity and the ideal of family life. The tension between manliness and the family was only to be expected in movements that were organized along paramilitary lines, and that took up much of every man's time. Thus boys were members of the Balilla or the Hitler Youth before entering other, adult party organizations, sometimes the tightly knit shock troops of the respective movements. Yet both movements also praised family life as a foundation of the state. Italian popular literature, approved by the regime, extolled "the poetry of the hearth" and the tranquility of family life, seemingly contradicting the activism and virility of the ideal fascist.[29] Yet, at the same time, *Critica Fascista*, an important organ of the party, wrote that exercising the male body demolished, and will continue to demolish "the limited aspirations, the feebleness and the mediocre inspiration bourgeois family life can offer the individual, in order to make him capable of understanding the needs of the state."[30] But it was in Germany rather than Italy that the rivalry between family life and the all-male party organizations was openly addressed, for Italy, after all, had no tradition of the *Männerbund* with its claim to be the originator and sole custodian of the state.

In the struggle for power during the Weimar Republic, for example, the Nazi storm troopers, the S.A., faced the dilemma of deciding between family life and the rough lifestyle of street fighters. Thus, in one officially sanctioned book of reminiscences about the clashes between the S.A. and the Communists at that time, a member of a squad, resting after doing battle, exclaims: "The family does not concern us, we are National Socialists and our only loyalty belongs to the party," whereupon he is rebuked by his leader for whom the family, restored to its rightful place by National Socialism, is the most important cell of the state. There is no rebuke, however, when in the Nazi film *Kolberg* (1945) an officer during the German Wars of Liberation renounces the love of an idealistic girl, not only for the sake of the fatherland, but also because he prefers the masculine world of fighting to a settled family life.[31] This book of reminiscences of life in the S.A. was published when the party was in power and had to demonstrate its respectability, but the very fact that such an exchange was part of a reconstruction of the early days of National Socialism, shows that this problem existed and that the family had to be defended even then. Fascism represented the fullest expression of modern masculinity, as we stated at the beginning of this chapter, and it brought to the surface the always-present tension between family life and the *Männerbund*. This tension could be resolved, as it had been resolved earlier, by subordinating women and children to the dominance of the male: women and children had their predetermined place in family life, and the man as activist was filled with a dynamic that, in the service of a higher cause, could not easily be confined to the home. The picture on the cover of the S.S. calendar for the year 1936 makes this clear: here the father stands at the top of the picture dominating the family, and below him, in descending order, stand the wife and child.

Fascism, as we have mentioned, saw itself as the inheritor of the Great War. The heroes of that war were co-opted as fascist heroes, and if Italians were told that "our heroes are the fallen of the war,"[32] then Nazi Germany built many of its rites and ceremonies upon memories of the heroism shown in that conflict. Fascism regarded the heroic as expressing true manliness, defining masculinity not so much through virtues that could be expressed in ordinary life but by its climax as a fighting force, ready for sacrifice. Manliness was once more co-opted at the moment when it transcended ordinary, routine existence. The hero had always been masculine, and woman in modern times was heroic only as victim or martyr, usually defending her purity.[33] Sir Walter Scott's Rebecca was heroic in this manner, not only facing her enemies but also defending her innocence, as we saw earlier, or, a century later, Agnes Günther's "Seelchen" in all her suffering. The term *heroic* was a staple of the fascist vocabulary and it had a different meaning for men than for women, for the one it was active and for the other passive, in tune with the generally perceived difference between the sexes.

Italian fascism and National Socialism, then, shared certain heroic and activist concepts in their definition of masculinity and also the tensions that were bound to exist between such manliness and bourgeois respectability. They differed on the degree of individualism allowed to the new man they wanted to create and, above all, on his relationship to the past and the future. National Socialism was a racist regime, unlike Italian fascism during its first sixteen years, and this fact determined in large measure the differences between the fascist and National Socialist man. Racism could not tolerate an indeterminate future, it had its own utopia of blood and soil, its nostalgia for the national and racial past. Moreover, racism's foremost symbol was the human form itself, the "ideal Aryan," described and illustrated in great detail according to past models that had never changed. Racism demanded precision, and Italian fascism and those fascisms that took their inspiration from Italy, until the racial laws of 1938, were not concerned with sketching out every detail to the same extent as National Socialism.

The many pictures of Mussolini projecting the cult of the Duce were an exception here, and it seemed as if he himself, in his own person, symbolized all the virtues of true masculinity. Mussolini was pictured taking physical exercise, engaged in productive work like harvesting or driving an engine—indeed, he was meant to exemplify for his people strength and decisiveness, as well as productivity. Mussolini was pictured as the model of a youthful and virile man. Indeed, the word *virility* appears often in fascist writings, seemingly used as proof of the writer's fascist credentials.[34] Mussolini's public image as a new man was carefully preserved: no news of the Duce's birthdays or illnesses could be printed, nor the fact that he had become a grandfather.[35] The Duce, as the symbol of the regime, illustrates the triumph of the fascist masculine ideal. This was reaffirmed when lights that could be seen from the large square below, the Piazza Venezia, were left burning in Mussolini's empty office until late at night. This was meant to signal not only attention to duty but youthful vigor and stamina as well.[36]

The Hitler cult rarely showed Hitler in action and then only on exceptional occasions, mostly at public ceremonies. He was the symbol of the movement but at the same time removed from it, more like a religious symbol rather than as someone engaged in the same activities as ordinary men. This did not exclude a certain personalization when it came to illustrating Hitler's bravery in war or on a stormy flight in his airplane, but by and large these were not in the foreground when it came to the worship of the Führer. Mussolini was only occasionally, and Hitler never, pictured as a family man. Mussolini was, of course, married, but although his children were often photographed, at times with their father, his wife was almost nonexistent in public life. Mussolini's exemplary masculinity was in the foreground, not his role as family man, and Hitler himself had no proper family. The leader had to be perceived as totally masculine, given the virtues and the world of action he was supposed to symbolize.

II

The appearance of the ideal male was usually derived from Greek models, as we have seen throughout this book, and in this regard German fascism was no exception. Thus students on Nazi work-study fellowships were told that through training and education they were on the way to becoming Greek ideal types.[37] National Socialism's preoccupation with manly beauty and with every detail of male appearance and comportment was due to the fact, as we have mentioned, that it was and considered itself first and foremost a nationalist and racist movement. The origin of racism in anthropology and aesthetic speculation about human beauty made it highly conscious of the appearance and structure of the body as symbolic of a man's inner worth. For example, one of the most widely read books on racism—which expressed Nazi views—after a general introduction to racism starts with eleven chapters detailing the appearance of the Nordic race and other racial strains native to Germany. The Nordic race, for example, is tall and lean, with broad shoulders and small hips; ideal measurements are provided. It would take up too much space to list all the bodily features of Nordic man, besides his pink-red skin and light hair color that becomes darker with age.[38] Only when the bodily structure of the race has been thoroughly examined, do we hear about the qualities of the Nordic soul. Typically enough, books illustrating and describing the appearance of the Italians were scarce up to the introduction of the racial laws in 1938; afterward the number of such books increased substantially, trying rather feebly to imitate the German example.

Apart from some minor details, this racist manly ideal was familiar; its structure was that of the normative male stereotype, not far removed from the "clean-cut Englishman." Racism always co-opted familiar ideas of beauty and ugliness, of how men and women should look, and locked them into place. Racism's attraction was its certainty, decisiveness, and abhorrence of ambiguity. It claimed immutability, and its content rested upon an established consensus of beauty and ugliness, health and sickness. Here in its stereotype of manliness, it merely heightened the so-called masculine features, helping to drive masculinity to its extremes.

Physical exercise had always been important in the construction of masculinity, and from the beginning it was not undertaken for its own sake but for the purpose of sculpting the ideal male body and for character training. Fascist preoccupation with the human body as representative of the proper spirit meant an emphasis on physical exercise, as we have seen, but in National Socialism, this absorption was expressed in absolute and far-reaching terms. The German man, an official National Socialist publication tells us, sees in sport not just the steeling of his body but the fulfillment of his worldview. Man must prove that his words will be followed by deeds: "his body is a gift of God, it belongs to his Volk, which he has to protect and defend; through steeling his will he serves his people."[39] This hymn to the male body is followed by a list of the usual manly virtues that a man so steeled is said to possess: loyalty, honesty, comradeship, obedience, discipline, and courage. The sequence is important here: from physical exercise and body sculpting, it proceeds like the book on racism, to manly virtues and ethical commands.

Sacrifice in a higher cause had already inspired ideals of true manliness during the German Wars of Liberation, yet at no time was it ever quite explicitly stated that a man's body belongs not to himself but to his people. The Nazis took a belief that had been operative in wartime—the necessity of sacrifice—and transformed it into an absolute principle. Here the male body itself played an important part, countering what the Nazis saw as the moral swamp of the Weimar Republic, and, once the Third Reich was established, symbolized Germany's renewal and strength. The male body had never before been elevated so self-consciously into a central political symbol; Italian fascism did not use the male body in this way for all its belief in physical exercise and in mass gymnastic display. The Nazis made frequent use of the idealized nude male body on public buildings. Thus, for example, two naked male figures by Arno Breker were the first sight that greeted visitors to Hitler's new Reich's Chancellery (Figure 8.3).

The nude male body as a Nazi symbol was, of course, of Greek inspiration. The ideal Aryan was often compared to the ancient Greek ideal type, which was said to exemplify a healthy mind in a healthy body. Racism enters here as well. According to its theorists, the Aryan race had stopped by Greece on its trek from India to the north of Europe, and in the process had taken with them all that was best in Greek civilization.[40] The so-called rediscovery of the human body in fin de siècle Germany also played its part, not through nudism, which the Nazis rejected, but by drawing attention to the human form as both natural and beautiful. The German Youth Movement had almost made a cult of the steeled and sculptured male body,[41] and Walter Flex's highly popular book *Der Wanderer zwischen beiden Welten* (The Wanderer Between Two Worlds, 1917), had at one point presented its hero, a former member of that movement, in the nude in all his supposedly

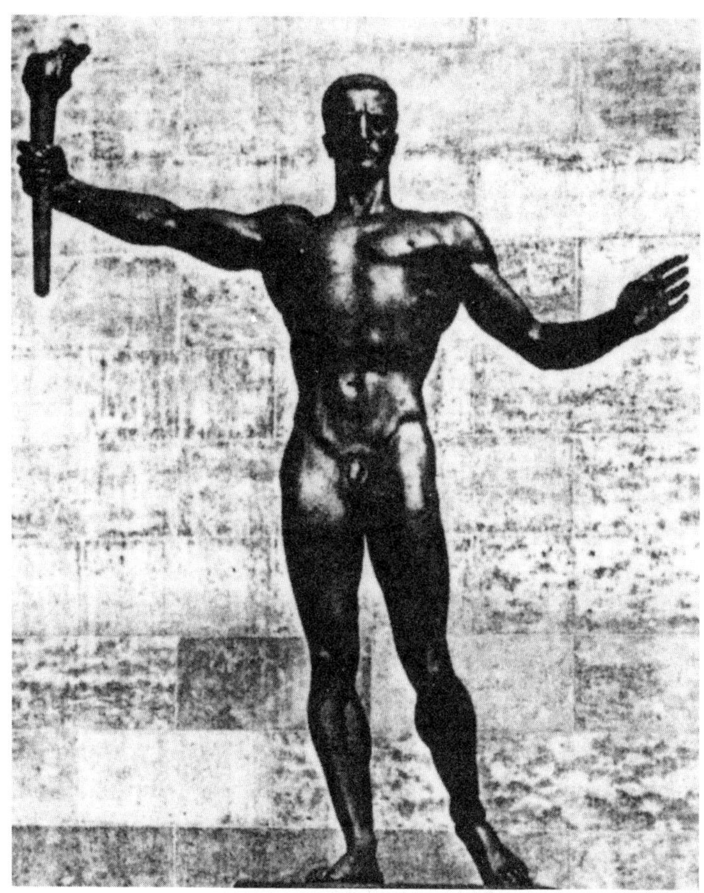

8.3 *The Party* by Arno Breker; created for Hitler's new Reichchancellery (1936).

youthful beauty. Nude soldiers on war monuments were quite common, not just in Germany but Italy as well.[42]

The use of the idealized male body as a national symbol was shrewdly chosen, for it already reflected society with its need for both a dynamic and order. Moreover, as we mentioned at the beginning of this book, the very ideal of beauty served many men and women as an addition to, and often as a virtual substitute for, established religion.

]And with its echoes of classical beauty, the sculpted male body was considered nothing if not beautiful. The full beauty of the male body could be truly appreciated only in the nude, according to Greek examples, and in its representational functions it continued to project much the same image as Winckelmann's Greek youths.

Using the male body in this fashion, however, presented a special problem for National Socialism, for how could such nudity be reconciled with the respectability so important to the movement's political success? This tension is parallel to that between the *Männerbund* and the family, which we discussed earlier. Moreover, could such an emphasis upon the beauty of the male body, like that upon male bonding, not turn back upon itself and lead to a homoeroticism that might transform sturdy men into unmanly men, the ideal type into its countertype? Asking these questions is important not only because the Nazi themselves asked them but also because they can deepen our understanding of some of the problems associated with masculinity as a political force. Winckelmann himself had already attempted to make his Greek sculptures acceptable to middle-class sensibilities by raising his naked youths to an abstract plane, transforming them into a stylistic principle. The transparent whiteness of these figures, their tranquility—a key to Winckelmann's attempt at minimizing their erotic impact—had supposedly stripped them of all sexual connotations. Classical beauty, as Winckelmann and his successors saw it, transformed the naked youths of Greek sculpture into universally valid and immutable symbols. The Nazis took up this argument and extended it in their all-important distinction between the private and the representational.

The Nazis discouraged public displays of nudity in non–symbolic representation. At the annual Exhibition of German Art held in Munich, for example, paintings of individual so-called typically German men and women were, with a very few exceptions, fully clothed. The public nudity of private persons, according to the Nazis, would deaden shame.[43] Where such nudity seemed inevitable, it was often circumscribed according to the example Winckelmann had set. For example, the problem arose in physical exercise, as well as in body building, greatly encouraged by the Nazis. In his much-used and semiofficial *Gymnastik der Deutschen, Körpers Schönheit und Schulung* (German Gymnastics, Physical Beauty and Training, 1938), for instance, Hans Surèn advocated nearly complete nudity in the pursuit of sport and while jogging through the countryside. However, the male body had to be prepared carefully before it could be offered for public scrutiny. The skin must be hairless, smooth, and bronzed. The body would thus be almost transparent; with as few individual features as possible, it would lose any sexual appeal. Such a bronzed body became an abstract symbol of Aryan beauty, not unlike the athletes in Leni Riefenstahl's film of the 1936 Olympics.[44]

Statues of athletes were generally presented in the nude, their bodies sculpted "according to the nordic race, following the example of antiquity . . . combining the ideal of beauty with a life force that transcends the individual, symbolizing . . . a powerful Volk," as a Nazi art critic tells us.[45] Such a male figure could be worshipped but neither desired nor loved. To be sure, the figures of athletes surrounding the Forum Mussolini were nude as well, but their form was less strict than that of Nazi athletes, nor did they bear the ideological weight that Germany heaped upon the shoulders of such men.

Arno Breker, the semiofficial sculptor of the Third Reich, long after that Reich had come to an end still praised the revolutionary youth of his day who had torn the veil from the body hidden in shame, and thus permitted us to see our origins in paradise. Greece deified the human and humanized the divine.[46] Nearly forty years after the end of the Third Reich Breker asserted that he had never wanted to glorify Nazi rule, only to praise the beauty of the human body. But the beauty he praised was a powerful expression of Nazi ideology, creating a portrait —as he put it—that was not threatened by the hectic speech and nervousness of the times.[47]

The nude body was not merely symbolic of true beauty but also pointed backward as the paradigm of a healthy world before the onset of modernity. Nazi male symbols were often equipped with a sword or pictured in a natural setting. Breker worked from live models, and his favorite model was not surprisingly an athlete and decathlon champion whose well-honed body was reproduced in most of Breker's sculptures. The model, Gustav Stührk, provided a living example of the new man, and the realism involved in such sculptures pointed to an Aryan stereotype that was not merely an abstract ideal of masculinity but one that seemed to exist: as one of Breker's admirers said (echoing Herder), only sculpture can transmit a true likeness of man.[48] Racism, as we mentioned, had already gained strength from working with human stereotypes, and now it was apparently vindicated.

Breker's sculptures and reliefs of nude males played a prominent part in the self-representation of the Third Reich. His figures were said to symbolize heroic will and readiness to sacrifice. For Adolf Hitler, two of Breker's statues—nude figures representing the party and the army—were among the most beautiful of all German artistic creations (see Figure 8.3).[49] These particular statues give the appearance of quiet strength. Arms outstretched and legs apart, they are on the alert, but in contrast to some of the reliefs that Breker created, they are not in violent, almost threatening, motion. Many of his sculptures and reliefs were destined for the monumental buildings planned for the rebuilding of Berlin after the Second World War had been won, further proof that the nude male body became an important symbol of the strength and beauty of the new Reich.

The realism of such figures enhanced their symbolic value; they were easily understood, especially because more often then not their posture suggested that they were engaged in the tasks of assuring protection or were geared for battle. As we have mentioned, Germans were accustomed to seeing classical sculpture and to hearing praise of the beauty of their human form. In addition, the ceremonial function of such sculptures as symbols of the new Reich further reduced any individualism that might have remained, and therefore any erotic temptation they may have presented. Here, the conflict between such nudity and respectability was latent rather than overt, though it pointed to the tension between a movement that placed its fate in the hands of men regarded as warriors for the cause, to be admired in all their masculine beauty, and the settled bourgeois society whose support was crucial for its success.

Such male beauty was not confined to Germany. The opening of the exhibition of Breker's sculptures in Paris on May 14, 1942, was an important event during the German occupation of France, and was accompanied by a barrage of publicity.[50] Some eight thousand French visitors mingled with Germans in uniform. Vichy France's education minister, Abel Bonnard, admired the sculptures, and so did the playwright Jean Cocteau (who likened his friend and lover Jean Marais to a typical Breker sculpture).[51] Indeed, Breker became the fashion among many Paris intellectuals. Two of his nude males even guarded the approach to a Soviet barracks in Germany after the Second World War until the collapse of the Soviet Union.[52]

Although the nude male body could be abstracted, yet another, more pressing conflict between Nazi symbolism and respectability lurked in the background. Racism always attempted to make the abstract concrete, and that was one of its great strengths. Rather than inert and abstract symbols like national flags, national monuments, or even sculptures, racism liked to use living human symbols as its means of self-representation. Publications and posters during the Third Reich were filled with photographs of typical Aryans as countertype to so-called typical Jews. This contrast, we have mentioned in an earlier chapter, had already been used in order to impress occupied Paris a year before the Breker exhibition. The exhibit *Les Juifs et la France* (The Jews and France, 1941) had contained a statue called "the perfect athlete," in contrast to the pictures of morally inferior Jews that surrounded it.[53] Racism tolerated no ambiguities, and therefore these stereotypes were fixed and could not be altered, though racial theorists, faced with the fact that few Germans looked the way Aryans were supposed to look, asserted that it was the preponderance of Aryan appearance that mattered rather than total conformity to the ideal. Nevertheless, so-called Aryan looks with blond hair and blue eyes often sufficed to gain an entrance ticket to the elite schools and cadres of the party.

The S.S.—the Black Corps—as the most prominent Nazi elite was most likely to present a presumptive challenge to normative masculinity. Here was an organization of carefully selected so-called pure Aryans faithful to the proposition, as their leader Heinrich Himmler expressed it, that the Third Reich was a state based upon the comradeship of men: "for centuries, yea millennia, the Germans have been ruled as a *Männerstaat*."[54] But such male bonding raised the fear of homoeroticism and even homosexuality. Himmler emphasized the difference between the male bonding encouraged within the S.S. and erotically charged friendships. Strict punishment was to be meted out to S.S. men who touched each other even when fully clothed, and S.S. men convicted of homosexuality were to be executed. No executions actually took place; suspected homosexuals were expelled or retired from the S.S. instead. Himmler nevertheless looked back to times when the ancient Germans supposedly drowned homosexuals in swamps, nature thus taking back its own mistake.[55]

National Socialism made every effort to appear as the guardian of respectability. Nudism, together with pornography, was banned shortly after the Nazis came to power, as indeed was all printed material that through pictures of nudes, title, or contents could produce an erotic effect. The German Purity Leagues greeted the advent of the Third Reich enthusiastically. Small wonder that a movement that made every effort at middle-class respectability was conscious of the dangers presented by its masculine symbols and by the male bonding that dominated its fighting and elite formations.

The strict separation of gender that the party advocated must have added to the fear that male camaraderie might serve to create unmanly men. Manly adornments, so a National Socialist book of portraits of "German men" tells us, do not exist merely for decorative purposes but belong to its wearer as does his own face: these are decorations, chains of office, or other honors that bind him to his nation[56]—this in contrast to the baubles women are supposed to wear. Not that the Nazis ignored woman's constitution. The Nordic woman, we are told, is feminine, full-bosomed, with broad hips and small shoulders (the exact opposite of the bodies of men).[57] There was no Italian fascist or Nazi attempt to create a "new woman" parallel to the new man, except perhaps in 1944, when the Italian Social Republic, the rump fascist state granted to Mussolini by the Germans after Italy's defeat, formed a woman's auxiliary of the armed forces, and even gave women the vote.[58] Even before this time, however, women were encouraged to engage in athletics appropriate to their sex—a point to which we will return. Woman could not so easily be reinvented; after all, as wife and mother she fulfilled functions that had to be kept intact. National Socialism was preoccupied with demographic concerns. The German population must be increased in order to make the race more powerful, obtain a large army, and fill the new spaces about to be conquered. Moreover, women in several countries had in the preceding century and a half served as symbols of national continuity, whether as Germania, Marianne, or Brittania; any nationalist movement, for this reason alone, might find it difficult to place a new and different woman next to one who fulfilled her historic mission as the procreator and the mother of her people.

Yet in the Third Reich, from time to time, nude women made an appearance, quite different from the sedate and chaste stereotype. When ordinary women were shown in the nude, in German film, for example, they were apt to be foreigners, Russian tavern dancers or various Africans or Polish tramps.[59] Glimpses of naked German women were rare, as for example, the short glimpse of a semi-nude girl escaping the clutches of Jud Süss, in the film of that name. However, the nude beauty of a true German woman could be exhibited if it was symbolic and not that of a particular person. Especially in sculpture such nudity was a matter of chaste, supposedly unerotic edification: the sculptures of nude women athletes were no rarity, and their bodies were prepared like those of men, smooth, almost transparent, and the female form was often hinted at rather than executed in the lush manner becoming an Aryan woman. Moreover, especially in racial texts, nude women illustrating the proper bodily structure were usually set in the past, not in the present. Yet, in private, once again, greater latitude was allowed, for how else can we interpret Hitler's patronage of the painter Adolf Ziegler, whose female nudes left nothing to the imagination, and which even hung in the Führer's own Munich apartment?

Women were encouraged to do physical exercise in order to enhance their female grace and beauty. Here once more, women could be pictured in the nude, but against the background of nature, suffused by the sun. Nature was supposed to take the sting out of such nudity, emphasizing woman's natural grace. Such beauty was supposedly inherent in Aryan women, together with their skill in managing the family and bearing children. The nude woman as symbol of Aryan feminine beauty, in any case, presented no immediate threat to respectability, for unlike the male, she performed no important public function either for the party or for the Third Reich. She continued to symbolize through her purity and chastity the normative ideal of femininity.

The countertype was present in all of fascism as the familiar enemy who had to be vanquished. Except that here the danger that he represented was magnified because fascism and National Socialism reenforced all the sharper edges of masculinity. The idea of struggle was basic. After all, these regimes came to power, however legally, by first creating conditions of civil war and then, once in power, continuing the battle against real or imagined domestic and foreign enemies. Italian fascism and the movements that followed its model had some difficulty designating the enemy once communism and socialism had been vanquished, and the attack continued mainly as rhetoric against all of those still holding oppositional beliefs rather than against a clearly defined and distinct group of people. This changed to some extent with the Ethiopian war in 1935–1936, when blacks were often singled out for ridicule, and the mixing of races was strictly forbidden in order to preserve the so-called dignity of the white Italian race. Indeed, the declaration of the Fascist Grand Council, which in October 1938 sanctioned the exclusion of Jews from Italian life, starts by stating that the empire with its black population had made acquisition of racial consciousness a priority.[60] The black enemy, however, was far away and rather easily conquered; he could hardly be transformed into a frightening menace.

The Jews, by contrast, were a clearly defined community inside the nation and they could serve to pinpoint enemies otherwise not so easy to detect. Once again, racism simplified recognition of the enemy. Thus the Nazis as well as Italian fascists, after their own racial laws of 1938, equated Jew and communist, and the Nazis themselves also identified the Jews with the Weimar Republic *(Judenrepublic)*. The racial enemy was the cause of all of Germany's tribulation, the obstacle to utopia.

The Jew could not be completely divorced from the Aryan, for Aryan and Jew were tied to each other by the struggle that the Aryan had to wage in order to justify his own existence. To be sure, if Hitler had won the war, Europe would be without Jews, but another enemy and countertype would undoubtedly have taken their place. As we can read in one Nazi book on racial research, all Nordic people would have to unite in order to counter the yellow peril.[61] The Nazis once again sharpened and made more absolute modern society's apparent need for an enemy.

Jews, blacks, and Gypsies were all singled out as the sworn enemies of the health and well-being of the Aryan race. Following the passage of the Nuremberg racial laws, which defined who was or who was not an Aryan, semiofficial commentaries on these laws classified Gypsies along with Jews and blacks as people with "alien blood."[62] But even here there was a clear-cut hierarchy that made the Jews the root of all evil. However, others who did not necessarily belong to a so-called inferior race also helped to undermine Aryan society; they were established as countertypes as well: homosexuals, vagrants, habitual criminals, beggars, the handicapped, and the feebleminded—all those who were unable to do so-called productive work or who had no established place of residence. These the Nazis called "asocials," and defined them broadly as people who could not be integrated into the community of the *Volk*, and who lacked the generally accepted norms that guaranteed so-called productive work within a settled community, be it the family or the state.[63]

The racial policy office together with the secret police began in 1934 to compile a catalogue of asocials. Some of the asocials could be redeemed; after all, they were Aryans. Others such as the Gypsies, blacks, or Jews had inherited their condition and must be exterminated. The so-called asocials were precisely those who were always supposed to stand in the way of the smoother functioning of modern bourgeois

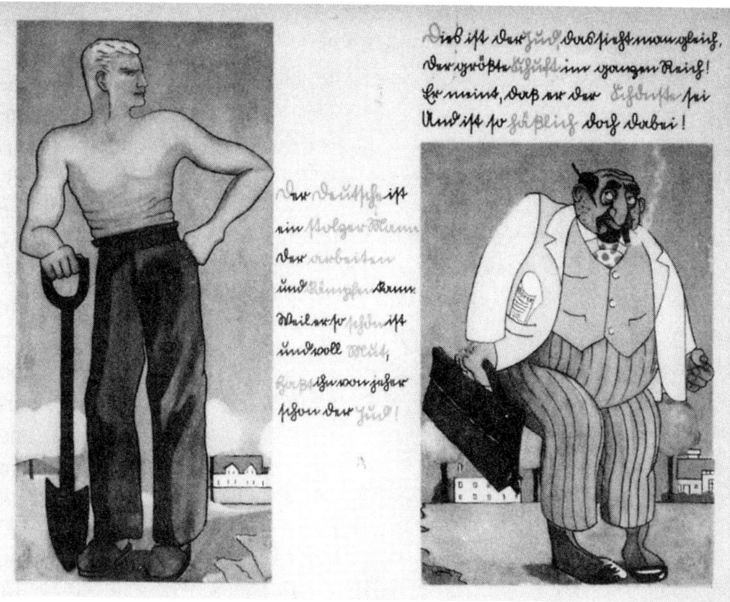

8.4 Illustration from Eva Bauer, *Ein Bilderbuch für Gross und Klein* (A picture book for children and adults [Nürnberg: Stürmer Verlag, 1936]. The text reads: "The German is a proud man who knows how to work and to fight. Because he is so beautiful and courageous, the Jew hates him. That this is a Jew one can see at a glance, the greatest scoundrel in the German Reich. He thinks he is a beauty, when in reality he is so ugly!" Author Bauer was an eighteen-year-old who wanted to transmit "weighty knowledge to German youth in simple verses and joyous colors." (Fred Hahn, *Lieber Stürmer! Leserbriefe an das NS-Kampfblatt, 1924–1945* [Stuttgart: Seewald Verlag, 1978], 158–59.)

society, they were the sworn enemies of utopia.[64] We have dealt with these countertypes in an earlier chapter, and the Nazis through their rigid system of classification and subsequent extermination, brought such outsiderdom to its logical conclusion. The word *logical* is important here, for in reality most people could not have envisioned that such a mass murder could take place in twentieth-century Europe, and refused to take Hitler seriously when he prophesied that the Jews would vanish from Europe.[65] That all the countertypes, including the Jews, were made to look alike, the exact opposite of manly in looks and behavior, we have mentioned earlier. Here, again, the Nazis left nothing to the imagination (Figure 8.4). National Socialism took over racism's clear-cut distinctions between enemy and friend.[66]

The new fascist or National Socialist man, then, was not so new after all. Most of his basic traits were shared with normative masculinity, but he extended them, giving them an aggressive and uncompromising cast as an essential tool in the struggle for dominance. There is, surely, a world of difference between the clean-cut Englishman, the all-American boy, and the ideal member of the SS. Yet all shared essentially the same masculine stereotype with its virtues, strength, and aesthetic appeal, whether it was restrained, nonviolent, and even compassionate, or uncompromising, ready to do battle by all means at hand. Fascism, and especially National Socialism, demonstrated the awesome possibilities inherent in modern masculinity when it was stripped down to its warlike functions.

These possibilities did not have to become reality; they were only latent in the construction of modern masculinity. After all, as we have seen, manliness could emphasize fair play or chivalry, and even Italian fascism did not go in for mass murder. It was racism that pushed National Socialism over the edge, it was the race war that led to the extermination of those whom Hitler had always seen as the principal enemies of the German people. Fascism heightened the warrior qualities of masculinity; racism brutalized them and transformed theory and rhetoric into reality.

9

TOWARD A NEW MASCULINITY?

The Second World War did not bring about any immediate change in the normative masculine stereotype. Even if the new fascist man had been an ideal to aim at, and had attracted attention in all of Europe, he did not truly survive into the postwar world. Nevertheless, a certain nostalgia for such a heightened manly ideal could be found on the fringes of postwar society, where the Nazi SS stirred the imagination, informing, for example, some German memoirs and postwar popular fiction: sober, sovereign figures of manhood.[1] But there was no longer much talk about fashioning a "new man" who would guide the nation into a brighter future. Instead, in western Europe, a consensus emerged that the torn fabric of society must be mended as soon as possible, and as part of this new traditionalism, prosaic, normative masculinity was at first reaffirmed.

The masculine stereotype whose construction has provided the theme of this book confronts us once more from all sides, in advertisements, film, and literature: clean-cut and fit. This traditional ideal of manhood will not vanish, even if eventually it were to be challenged more successfully than ever before. As late as 1989 one of the most popular West German magazines noted that advertisements constantly featured men who were lithe, athletic, and tall, with chiseled faces.[2] To be sure, the war did not pass entirely unnoticed as far as the male stereotype was concerned. It did not, however, change but once again in immediate terms strengthened some aspects of normative masculinity. In this it was not so different from the First World War, except that after 1945 the political dimension that had been so fateful was missing. A tougher manliness was in fashion after the war ended, reflected by movie stars like Humphrey Bogart or John Wayne, popular not only in the United States but in western Europe as well. Indeed, a certain cruelty came to the fore, not in the stereotype itself but, for example, in widely distributed comic books filled with violent action, often directed by men against women.[3] Perhaps a continuity did exist between the violence of the war, popular literature, and the ever more violent Western society in the making. However, conditions did vary from nation to nation, and this kind of male cruelty seemed more pronounced in the United States than in Europe. However, the prevailing tendency after the war—whether in Europe or the United States—was to rebuild a peaceful, traditional, and normative society that would erase the memories of the conflict.

The part of Europe under Soviet control by and large continued the same image of man that the Bolsheviks had advocated in the past, and that, as we saw earlier, under Stalin had approximated the Western stereotype. Here every deviation from respectability was considered a social crime and punished accordingly. Sexual or social deviance was said to be the hallmark of Western degeneracy, at least until the final years of the Soviet period, when attitudes toward sexuality seemed to change. Prostitution became more visible, homosexual organizations were established, and explicit sex scenes were shown in the cinema.[4] Nevertheless, in Soviet Europe during most of its existence time had stood still. Both West and East, in spite of the Cold War, shared the same ideal of respectability and gender difference, though at least theoretically women were for a time given greater rights in Soviet Europe. Ironically, the nations of Soviet Europe that boasted of their revolutionary origins became, until the last years before the fall of the Soviet empire, the most traditional and conservative postwar powers; in the West, in spite of restorative tendencies, slow change was under way that would in the end erode the normative masculine stereotype as well as challenge the traditional divisions between genders.

Those who wanted a change in manners and morals pushed ahead, while the traditional manly ideal continued to prove its strength. In

Europe the movement for women's rights made the most spectacular advances in the postwar world. If, for example, in 1965 the majority of men and women in the German Federal Republic thought that woman's place was in the home, by 1983 a bare majority of men and the vast majority of women rejected such traditional attitudes. Not just in Germany but throughout western Europe the once-ridiculed "new woman" seemed set to triumph.[5] Women entered public spaces previously closed to them, and even within the family a greater balance of rights between men and women was being established. Perhaps in a wider perspective the movement for woman's equality was part of the liberation movements that seemed to forge ahead in the 1960s and 1970s: the civil rights movement that emancipated blacks in the United States and the movements abroad that liquidated the colonialism of the past centuries. At any rate, the women's movement, which had frightened men at the fin de siècle, was now set to achieve most of its aims.

This time the reaction among men was much less violent; indeed, as figures from the German Federal Republic show, there was much acceptance even among men of the new status and independence of women. To be sure, insecurity and fear remained as some men faced the new woman, and by the 1990s a so-called men's literature had come into being that tried to reassure men through attempting to locate a virile masculine essence that solely men could claim as their own.[6] The masculine stereotype was under greater pressure now than it had been at the turn of the century, and the much milder reaction demonstrates that it was already being eroded and not just by the challenge of a revitalized women's movement but by men themselves. This was a change through erosion, not confrontation, and it seems of equal if not of greater symbolic importance for the fate of the masculine stereotype at the end of the twentieth century than the increased presence of liberated women. The change came not from the outside but from inside the manly ideal itself and advocated what had been regarded as a distinctly unmanly lifestyle.

Once again, just as at the end of the nineteenth century, it was youth who after the Second World War were in the vanguard of a change in manners and morals, but this time a youth culture emerged that was not avant-garde but encompassed all classes of the population and that informed many of the popular media as well. This was a threat of a different order from the threat of the earlier youth revolt. Within Europe, England for a while set the tone, and it was, for example, the so-called Teddy Boys and after them the Beatles who influenced the new youth culture, as well as the rock 'n' roll craze of the 1950s and early 1960s.[7] The nervous stimulation they projected set the tone for the future, though the much larger market, resources, and pool of talent from across the Atlantic was in short order to exercise a dominant influence over the lifestyles of Europe.

It has been possible up to this point in the book to confine our analysis to western and central Europe, but the post–Second World War era must widen our perspective because it is in this period that the United States came to set the example for the music that European youths loved, the clothes they wore, and the fashions they followed. All these knew no national boundaries. And it was this youth culture that pressed for a change in postwar manners and morals. Media such as film, also dominated by the United States, introduced new dimensions into the quest for change, popularizing competing images that in the varieties of manliness they projected had not existed before the war. Popular culture had played very little part in either fashioning or challenging normative masculinity; it had acted as a conservative force, and the challenges to masculinity had come from the educated and the intellectuals. But now, for example, mediated by the United States, popular music with its rhythms became an effective engine for change in the sober and controlled paradigm of masculinity.

The "Beat Generation" of the 1950s in the United States was a harbinger of change that by the 1960s at the latest was destined to influence all of European youth. The beats were said to be "completely untyrannized by normative American stereotypes,"[8] did not seem to care about their manhood, and experimented sexually with men or with women—though the use of drugs was for a time apparently more important to them than sex. The beats were much taken with jazz, which seemed to correspond to the frantic rhythm of their own lives. Popular music fulfilled this function for all the various youth cultures after the war: it provided, on both sides of the Atlantic, the rhythm and frantic movement for a youth that wanted to escape from the confines of modern life and its respectability while affirming their own individual identity.

Popular music encouraged joy in bodily expression, which in turn stimulated the rediscovery of the human body, long imprisoned by respectability. This rediscovery had also been a feature of the revolt of youth at the fin de siècle when nature in all its harmony and immutability had mediated between man and his body and, as in the German Youth Movement, had drawn the sting of uncontrolled passion. But now, popular music, whatever its composition, whether rock 'n' roll or the so-called new sound, encouraged wild, passionate, and disharmonious movements of the body and stimulated each youth "to do his own thing." The search for a personal identity was an important motivation whether for the "Beat Generation" and Britain's "Angry Young Men" of the 1950s, or, much later, for "hippies" and "punks": youth demanded to be itself without much regard for tradition.

It cannot be our task to write the history of the post–World War II youth culture, but we must note that it encompassed most youths, including those in the student movement of the 1960s, who possessed not just a personal but a social and political agenda. Moreover, in contrast to prewar days, youth was now being discovered as a mass market that further served to democratize youth culture. The relationship of this youth culture to modern masculinity seems obvious: joy in bodily movement and expression, in rhythm and the undisciplined release of feeling was diametrically opposed to the manly qualities we have mentioned so often. If persons such as Walter Pater, Krafft-Ebing, or Charcot had visited a modern discothèque, they would have confined its visitors to the Salpetrière to be treated as neurasthenics or in our context as (unfortunately) hysterical men.

The joy in bodily movement was accompanied by a more natural look, which by the 1970s seemed to have become firmly established. Some young women rejected all fashion or adornment to present themselves without artifice; men in rebellion against the semimilitary haircut of the day began to wear their hair long and even to sport short pigtails. Gender distinctions were at issue here: clothes and appearance tended to blur such distinctions, and yet they were not meant to question a basic heterosexuality. However, this gender-bending, as it was called, made men seem unmanly, often giving them an androgynous appearance.

The androgyne, as either a man with female sex organs or a woman with male genitals, was, by the end of the nineteenth century, regarded as a monster menacing men and women alike. Homosexuals and lesbians, as we saw earlier, had praised the androgyne as a gender-bending ideal that could help end their marginalization by society. But now, some forty years after the Second World War, the so-called androgynous look became itself a matter of fashion and a statement directed against normative masculinity and femininity, pushing opposition to tradition to a new extreme. Popular English and American entertainers of the 1980s and 1990s such as David Bowie, Boy George, and Michael Jackson spread this look far beyond their nations. As public figures they questioned perceived notions of masculinity in a manner that would have been impossible earlier, and in 1984 one male singer, Dee Snider, was even voted best-dressed woman of the year.[9]

Advertising, too, took up this theme in mainstream newspapers and magazines, seeking to sell new fashions (Figure 9.1). The models they used were not transsexuals—they had undergone no sex change—but

9.1 Versace advertisement, 1994. By permission.

men who seemed to have discarded most vestiges of the manly stereotype, and that to a large measure of public acclaim, though their particular androgyny must be seen in concert with the fashion in dance and music they represented: filled with violent rhythm and ear-splitting sound. There can be no doubt that this phenomenon represents an erosion of the manly stereotype when even the beats, in all their rebellion, had kept a certain manliness intact. Even a popular icon of the 1950s and early 1960s, film actor James Dean, a fragile, seemingly "unmanly" loner who was not afraid to cry in public, stressed his masculinity. When his father in the film *Rebel Without a Cause* (1955) was pictured as a feminized man who wore fur coats, Dean exclaimed, "I don't ever want to be like him."[10] The importance of this androgynous image must not be exaggerated. It was a sign of the times rather than an identity that was widely shared; a statement of fashion in clothes and appearance rather than the adoption of what some in earlier times had called the Third Sex.

The so-called skinheads who emerged in England around 1968 illustrate the complexity of this youth culture. They shared that culture's unorthodox lifestyle, as well as the centrality of popular music as a means of self-identification. However, they also projected a "formalized and hard masculinity."[11] Skinheads walked with a swagger and were, on the whole, neatly dressed, perhaps reflecting their working-class origins, different also in this respect from the contemporary youth culture. Skinheads had no proper political agenda, but they were tough and militant, and carried a chip on their shoulder. In contrast to the majority involved in the youth culture, they were not peaceful but loved confrontation and violently attacked imagined enemies; they called for blacks, Jews, and Asians to get off their backs.[12] Here was a group that imitated man as the warrior, while accepting in comportment but not in behavior the link between masculinity and respectability. Androgyny, long hair, and gender-bending were abhorrent to them as opposed to true manliness. Here, then, is a group that in spite of having one foot in the youth culture, worshipped a heightened masculinity.

Androgyny, as a statement of principle, was, in any case, of greatest importance for some in the women's rights movement. Radical feminists in recent times, for example, regarded the androgynous human being as one who is free to choose a number of different sexual and therefore social roles, to move back and forth between masculine and feminine genders.[13] Here the androgynous vision provided radical feminists with a utopian ideal for social change through which women could escape the place that normative society still assigned them and make full use of their talents and capabilities. At the same time, the androgyne was being freed of its monstrous reputation even for men, and as a part of the youth culture it presented a challenge to modern masculinity. For all this, women wearing so-called masculine clothes such as trousers and shirts were widely accepted, but men in women's clothing were and are still regarded with abhorrence. Masculinity is safeguarded even here, as deep-rooted tradition triumphs over innovation. After all, clothes had always been one of the chief signs of gender.

Ever since the Second World War, youth culture, however diverse, had celebrated outsiderdom. Many European or American youths cherished their role as countertypes, and asserted their superiority over society's norms. The countertype had always been present but marginalized by society. Here, as we saw earlier, the last fin de siècle seemed to have brought about a change as unmanly men and unwomanly women became ever more visible. They had always presented a fundamental challenge to normative masculinity and now they did so in even greater measure. During the interwar period, the German Weimar Republic saw a great number of openly gay and lesbian men and women active in cultural life, and for right-wing political parties the lively gay nightlife of Berlin symbolized the degeneracy of the republican system.

Nazi Germany, and indeed fascist Europe, had persecuted homosexuals and had ended a few years of relative tolerance. However, in Germany, for example, the law that since 1870 outlawed homosexual acts was not to be repealed until 1969, more than twenty years after the end of National Socialism. The stereotype of the outsider was not at first affected by the defeat of fascism and National Socialism, no more than, in immediate terms, the normative masculine stereotype was changed by the new world order. The Gypsies, for example, were once again marginalized and received no compensation for their persecution (250,000 were murdered in death camps), and the existence of homosexuality continued to reinforce the self-confidence of so-called normal men and thus to strengthen the masculine stereotype in which they found refuge.

It was not until well after the end of the Second World War, however, that homosexuals seemed to move from the margins of society to challenge the normative stereotype in a much more effective manner than ever before. The deliberate confusion of gender by the heterosexual members of the youth culture helped to provide a better atmosphere for this challenge, and the American struggle for civil rights by blacks and by women reinvigorated a homosexual rights movement that, although it had existed ever since the beginning of this century, had been neither broadly based nor very effective. The visibility of unmanly men and unwomanly women was now established, but the challenge to true masculinity went much further than a mere presence that would have been provocation enough to have enraged past generations. It still took several decades after the war for many legal discriminations to end, as we mentioned, and nearly one more decade after that until, at least in a few nations, homosexual rights were officially recognized.

During the 1970s and 1980s a gay subculture established itself that affected the dominant normative culture and interacted with and reinforced the youth culture that we have discussed. It also helped to transmit that youth culture to society at large. Here gays distinguished themselves as designers and creators of fashion, colorful and for the most part unorthodox. Moreover, by the 1980s a canon of gay literature was in the making, much of it so-called "coming-out" stories—making one's gayness public—which was readily available throughout Europe. This was no longer a love that dared not speak its name; newspapers covered almost all aspects of gay life and, above all, advertisements used obviously gay figures to market men's fashions. The homosexual was still stereotyped, but now sometimes in a more positive manner, not exactly manly but still beautiful. Although the exact influence of this gay subculture is impossible to measure, it contributed to a general atmosphere: it was a visible sign and symptom for a general shift in sexual attitudes and behavior brought about by the youth culture and the triumph of the "new woman"—no longer to be ridiculed but taken as a role model instead.

These cultural changes at the new fin de siècle constituted an unprecedented menace to the masculine stereotype, and seemed to threaten its erosion over a period of time. The challenge to the manly stereotype which we have discussed included what to many seemed a decline of morals: a discarding of clearly defined traditional virtues that manliness and society as a whole had required, substituting values defined vaguely as a personal choice.[14] Nevertheless, even if the former countertype could no longer so easily assume its traditional role, and if the new youth culture remained pervasive, the old masculine stereotype that long ago had saturated society still seemed to hold firm. Even some of the youth culture for all its so-called unmanliness, nevertheless showed a certain nostalgia for so-called real men. James Dean was no exception in rejecting effeminate men; after all, the very masculine Marlon Brando had, in the 1950s, been an idol of youth, and later, even androgynous singers strenuously denied any association with homosexuality. Indeed, for all their newly found self-confidence, many gays themselves wanted to accent their own masculinity.

The normative ideal of manly beauty had captured the imagination of homosexuals and not only that of society at large; this was not just an ideal to be aimed at in order to shed their own unfavorable stereotype. The continuity of the normative ideal among homosexuals through a time of change can be illustrated by examples already used in Chapter 7, taken from German gay love stories written between 1924 and 1979, in which "beautiful young men" are invariably lithe, muscled, and blond, with faces hewn in stone (a description reminiscent of Ernst Jünger's fighters)—and except for the coloring, the descriptions and pictures of these youths would have fitted Winckelmann's Greek statues.[15] The bodies of such youths were hairless and smooth, in the same way that the normative masculine ideal had always represented itself. Here, there was no difference between normative masculinity and its foes. This kind of continuity of the manly stereotype among those who were rejected as countertypes was not confined to homosexuals; Jews as a European minority had also internalized the masculine ideal, as Max Nordau's advocacy of "muscular Judaism" demonstrates.

Nordau had written his famous polemic against degeneration in 1892, reaffirming the linkage between so-called normal society and belief in the masculine stereotype. This was a powerful association, which we have illustrated throughout this book, and one that once again confronted the possible erosion of masculinity. For Nordau, so typical of his time, the restlessness of modernity signaled "the end of an established order," and the manly stereotype that had always countered the nervousness of the modern age constituted the cure for degeneration: men, as he had it, with solid stomachs, hard muscles, and power of will.[16] Western European nations after the First World War attempted to maintain or even to tighten ordinances meant to protect long-established morality; in our time conservative governments such as that in England in 1988 attempted to stem the tide of change in manners and morals by forbidding the so-called promotion of homosexuality in state schools.

The Purity Leagues had tried to counter what they saw as the threat of degeneracy at the end of the last century, but now both a more conservative Catholic church and Protestant fundamentalists took their place, allied with many conservatives. In their struggle against vice, however, even the Purity Leagues had maintained a ubiquitous relationship to the Christian churches that had given them additional weight.[17] The polemic against any modification in manners and morals had not changed much for over a century. Needless to say, the commitment to traditional society by old and more recent purity movements put the maintenance of gender division and of the masculine stereotype high on their agenda.

The analogy between this and the previous fin de siècle is, however, of limited usefulness in comparing how traditional society was infiltrated by the new because much of today's youth was caught up in its own and radically different culture. However, the traditional fabric of society proved strong once again. For one thing, the political establishment in western Europe was not affected by the youth culture that was the driving force for change. Even while gays and lesbians were more visible and assertive than ever before and the woman's rights movement was undoubtedly winning its battles, a general change in the accepted morals and manners, basic to any change in the stereotype, was as yet—by the 1990s—very much in doubt. Here another factor may well be decisive, one we have mentioned before: the great capacity of normative society for co-optation. Indeed, it had integrated the earlier revolt of the young through making use of patriotism or encouraging them as an unpolitical but interesting avant-garde. At the same time the ambiguous masculinity of the present youth culture may be more difficult to integrate into a fixed masculine stereotype. Perhaps, just as the war had heightened certain features of normative manliness, so the contemporary challenge to the masculine image may in the end soften its sharper edges and give the stereotype a greater flexibility.

Images of masculinity, men asserting what they believe to be their manhood, are still pervasive in our culture. And as late as 1993 one writer could describe men's anxiety about their manhood as "the masculine curse"; after all, concrete signposts on the road to masculinity were missing, a simple test of manhood that had to be passed no longer seemed to exist.[18] A certain standard had been set in the past, and certain tests had made it easier to ascertain if one were a true man: the duel, courage in war, and more generally, the possession of willpower as well as the manly virtues of "quiet strength" and of an acceptable moral posture. Proper looks and comportment had provided proof of true manhood: the correspondence between the appearance of the body and the quality of the soul furnishes the essence of any stereotype. Now the contours of the male stereotype were getting blurred, even if the ideal itself might still be present. The new wave of bodybuilding toward the end of the twentieth century was no longer motivated, for the most part, by a wish to pass the test of manhood through acquiring a properly structured body, which had played such a prominent role in the gymnastics movement well over a century earlier.

The idea of manliness with which we have been concerned was an ideal proclaimed in public, though privately many different interpretations of masculinity existed—and yet, the normative stereotype of manliness undoubtedly played its part in most individual lives. It had penetrated too deeply into society and reflected too many of its needs and hopes. Normative manhood had become central to society's manners and morals, to the respectable pattern of behavior that informed all aspects of life from attitudes toward the human body and sexuality, clothes, appearance, and the conduct of personal relations.

Bourgeois patterns of respectability had grown up at the same time as the construction of modern masculinity; both were an integral part of middle-class culture. The discussion of what a man should be constantly referred to that culture, whether, for example, it be to the bourgeois cult of beauty as background to the male stereotype or to middle-class sensibilities that co-opted the old ideal of male honor. Although the masculine ideal was vital to the maintenance of respectability, however, the male stereotype had been equally important in the making of nations. Modern masculinity and modern national consciousness had grown up at the identical time, and while the image of the warrior was needed, the nation itself looked beyond war to an ideal type, a living symbol, that like other national symbols might breathe life into an abstract concept. Words and pictures told of "the German" or "the Englishman," and they nearly always connoted a definite type who would represent the national character. The man who was said to fulfill this role, with some national variations, approximated the masculine stereotype. We have seen that even socialists and Bolsheviks could not resist its appeal as they, too, sought to become respectable.

The fate of modern masculinity was and is bound up with that society of which it is a part, and especially with society's attitude toward respectability. Respectability, however, provides society with essential cohesion, and it is difficult to envision its downfall or even radical change. Nationalism is still alive and well—though many pronounced it dead after the Second World War—and with it the cult of national symbols, even if the search for a national stereotype may have been temporarily discredited because of its association with National Socialist racial policy. The question, then, is not whether the manly stereotype will vanish but about its erosion. Throughout the past century we have already seen many changes, such as the heightening of normative manliness by war or fascism, but also the softening of its contours by socialism or bourgeois sensibilities.

If manliness has reflected the hopes and wishes of modern society, what then would happen if these changed drastically, if there was no further need to reconcile order and progress, and if the dynamic thought vital to the functioning of society was no longer perceived as threatening the longing for harmony? Such a change would deprive the masculine stereotype of much of its traditional function. But this change does not seem likely in the near future. It is possible, however, that different symbols could replace that of manliness and its function, given the relative indifference to a manly appearance and what this was meant to express. Moreover, more people are becoming suspicious of human stereotypes than ever before: the word today often has a negative connotation, which forced us to explain at the very beginning of this book that positive stereotypes also existed, and that we would be dealing with one of the most powerful of such mental images.

The recent youth culture continues to thrive side by side with normative masculinity, but there are as yet few signs that it will triumph over the needs of traditional society. However, the battle is still joined, and the unanswerable question is not whether true manliness will be overturned but just how far it can bend. Here the women's movement is of prime importance, for it raises the question of whether the masculine stereotype can survive a downfall of patriarchy. Given the greater equality that prevails among men and women today, however, especially in the family, the manly ideal has still managed to hold its own. That ideal was never merely dependent upon power relationships but fed upon the whole network of manners and morals and the social ideals we have mentioned so often. The importance of modern masculinity as part of the cement of modern society makes the manly ideal difficult to defeat. History cannot so easily be undone.

Whatever the outlook at present, it seems important to understand

and to come to grips with a historical phenomenon that was and is both abstract—an ideal—and concrete, like "a placard hung up to be read," as manliness was defined so long ago.[19] Moreover, this was and is a placard whose contents changed relatively little over the span of time. Even today, when it seems more at risk than ever before, it still informs the outlook upon the world and the self-understanding of perhaps the majority of people in Western society.

Although the future of modern masculinity is a matter for speculation, its past importance is without doubt because it touched nearly every aspect of society. Concentrating upon the male stereotype has meant discussing the history of manliness through its public image. This cannot claim to be a complete history of masculinity, nor can it explore all that the image touched or the actions it stimulated, for that would mean writing a history of modern society. But it can give us an insight into the social and political significance of one of the most important and lasting symbols of modern life.

All those who want to change society, as well as those who want to escape their marginalization, have to take the stereotype of modern masculinity into account. Without addressing it, for example, any history of the women's or the gay emancipation movements must be incomplete. Taking the measure of men makes a hoped-for contribution to our understanding of the society in which we live and in this manner may provide some signposts of possible change.

NOTES

CHAPTER 1

1. Anne-Charlotte Trepp, "The Emotional Side of Men in Late Eighteenth-Century Germany (Theory and Example)," *Central European History* 27 (1994): 127–52.

2. Lynn Hunt, *Politics, Culture and Class in the French Revolution* (Berkeley, 1984), 92.

3. Friedrich Ehrenberg, *Der Charakter und die Bestimmung des Mannes* (Hildburghausen and New York, 1834), 14. Ehrenberg was a preacher in Berlin's (Protestant) cathedral.

4. "Character Reading," *Phrenological Magazine* 3 (1882): 18.

5. Michael Rohrwasser, *Saubere Mädel Starke Genossen* (Berlin, 1975), 93.

6. Ehrenberg, *Der Character*, 14, 15.

7. Ibid., 21, 52.

8. Quoted in Hans Weil, *Die Entstehung des Deutschen Bildungsprinzips* (Bonn, 1930), 47.

9. George L. Mosse, *Nationalism and Sexuality* (New York, 1985), chap. 5.

10. Ute Frevert, *Women in German History* (New York, 1989), 178.

11. Stefan Zweig, *The World of Yesterday* (Lincoln, Nebr., 1964), 90.

12. Frevert, *Women in German History*, 173.

13. Quoted in Ronald Hyam, *Britain's Imperial Century, 1815–1914* (London, 1976), 134.

14. Mosse, *Nationalism and Sexuality*, 84.

15. Martin Green, *The Adventurous Male: Chapters in the History of the White Male Mind* (University Park, Pa., 1953), 8.

16. Lewis D. Wurgaft, *The Imperial Imagination* (Middletown, Conn., 1983), 10.

17. Ibid., 11.

CHAPTER 2

1. Norman F. Cantor, *Inventing the Middle Ages* (New York, 1991), 381; Léon Gautier, *Chivalry* (London, 1891), 485.

2. Ute Frevert, *Ehrenmänner: Das Duel in der bürgerlichen Gesellschaft* (Munich, 1991), 22.

3. Norman Vance, *The Sinews of the Spirit: The Ideal of Christian Manliness in Victorian Literature and Religious Thought* (Cambridge, 1985), 9.

4. Frevert, *Ehrenmänner*, 32.

5. Robert A. Nye,"Fencing, the Duel and Republican Manhood in the Third Republic," *Journal of Contemporary History* 25 (May–June 1990): 369.

6. Maurice J. Quinlan, *Victorian Prelude: A History of English Manners, 1700–1830* (London, 1965), 69.

7. A. Mangan and James Walvyn, eds., *Manliness and Morality: Middle-Class Masculinity in Britain and America, 1800–1940* (New York, 1987), 98.

8. Pierre Birnbaum, *Anti-Semitism in France* (Oxford, 1992), 165.

9. See Robert A. Nye, *Masculinity and Male Codes of Honor in Modern France* (New York, 1993), 46.

10. Frevert, *Ehrenmänner*, 133ff.

11. Kevin McAleer, *Dueling: The Cult of Honor in Fin de Siècle Germany* (Princeton, 1994), 35.

12. Nye, "Fencing, the Duel and Republican Manhood in the Third Republic," 371.

13. Frevert, *Ehrenmänner*, 197.

14. Nye, *Masculinity and Male Codes of Honor in Modern France*, 32.

15. McAleer, *Dueling*, 59.

16. Ibid., 43, 183–84.

17. Ibid., 141.

18. Ibid., 41.

19. i.e. Frevert, *Ehrenmänner*, 196.

20. Brenda Keiser, *Deadly Dishonor: The Duel and the Honor Code in the Works of Arthur Schnitzler* (New York, 1990), 13.

21. Quoted in Nye, "Fencing, the Duel and Republican Manhood in the Third Republic," 370.

22. Nye, *Masculinity and Male Codes of Honor in Modern France*, 162.

23. Theodor Fontane, *Effi Briest* (Harmondsworth, 1987), 221.

24. Alan Corkhill, "Abwandlung des Duellrituals in der Deutschsprachigen Literatur des 19. und frühen 20. Jahrhunderts," *Neophilologus* 72 (1988): 244.

25. Willy Ritter Liebermann von Wahlendorf, *Erinnerungen eines deutschen Juden, 1896–1936*, ed. Ernst Reinhard Piper (Munich, 1988), 64.

26. Ernst Moritz Arndt, "Die Leipziger Schlacht" (1913), *Sämtliche Werke* (Leipzig, n.d.), 4: 83.

27. Pierre Bayle, *Historical and Critical Dictionary*, trans. Richard H. Popkin (Indianapolis: Library of Liberal Arts, 1965), 236.

28. Ibid., 236.

29. Quoted in George L. Mosse, *Toward the Final Solution* (New York, 1978), 19.

30. Johann Kaspar Lavater, *Ausgewählte Schriften*, ed. Johann Kaspar Orelli (Zürich, 1859), 1: 21.

31. Henry Caraway Hatfield, *Winckelmann and His German Critics* (New York, 1943), 111.

32. See Heinrich Funck, ed., *Goethe und Lavater. Briefe und Tagebücher* (Weimar, 1901), 46.

33. Lavater, *Ausgewählte Schriften*, 73.

34. Ibid., 88.

35. See Sander L. Gilman, *Disease and Representation* (Ithaca, N.Y., 1988), passim.

36. M. Tissot, *L'Onanisme. Dissertation sur les maladies produite par le masturbation* . . . (Lausanne, 1716), 220.

37. Jean-Jacques Rousseau, *Émile, Julie and Other Writings*, ed. R. L. Archer (Barron's Educational Series, Woodbury, N.Y., 1964), 122.

38. Lynn Hunt, *Politics, Culture and Class in the French Revolution* (Berkeley and Los Angeles, 1986), 90–92.

39. John Caspar Lavater, *Essays in Physiognomy* (London 1804), 3: 205, 206, 210–11.

40. Wilhelm von Humboldt, *Schriften zur Anthropologie und Geschichte* (Stuttgart, 1960), 296.

41. See Isabel V. Hull, *Sexuality, State and Civil Society in Germany, 1700–1815* (Ithaca, N.Y., 1995), forthcoming.

42. Jean-Jacques Rousseau, *Émile*, 218.

43. Von Humboldt, *Schriften*, 298.

44. Bernhard Ruprecht, "Plastisches Ideal und Symbol im Bilderstreit der Goethezeit," *Probleme der Kunstwissenschaft* (Berlin, 1963), 1: 204.

45. Johann Joachim Winckelmann, "Gedanken über die Nachahmung der Griechischen Werke in der Malerei und Bildhauer Kunst," *Ausgewählte Schriften* (Insel Bücherei, No. 130) (Leipzig, n.d.), 22.

46. Goethe an Herder (1771), in *Genius der Jugend*, ed. Gerhard F. Hering (Stuttgart and Hamburg, 1931), 47.

47. Winckelmann, *Gedanken über die Nachahmung*, 39.

48. Simon Richter, *Laocoön's Body and the Aesthetics of Pain* (Detroit, 1992), 44.

49. Alex Potts, *Flesh and the Ideal: Winckelmann and the Origins of Art History* (New Haven, 1994), 138.

50. Winckelmann, *Gedanken über die Nachahmung*, 38.

51. Hatfield, *Winckelmann and His German Critics*, 42.

52. Tadeusz Namowicz, *Die Aufklärische Utopie. Rezeption der Griechenauffassung J. J. Winckelmann's um 1800 in Deutschland und Polen* (Warsaw, 1978), 71.

53. Ibid., 71.

54. Adolf Hitler, *Mein Kampf* (Munich, 1934), 453.

55. This is one of the theses of Alex Potts, *Flesh and the Ideal*, passim.

56. Ibid., 4.

57. Max Baeumer, "Winckelmann's formulierung der klassischen Schönheit," *Monatshefte*, 65, no. 1 (Spring 1973): 61–74.

58. Peter Gay, *The Enlightenment: An Interpretation* (New York, 1969), 2: 297.

59. *Winckelmann's werke*, ed. Heinrich Meyer and Johann Schulze (Dresden, 1811), 4:37.

60. Potts, however, stresses the eroticism in Winckelmann's view of these sculptures, and the conflict between their nude form and his own suppressed sexuality; *Flesh and the Ideal*, esp. chap. 4.

61. *The Literary Works of Sir Joshua Reynolds*, ed. Henry William Beechy (London, 1870), 1:343.

62. Martin Jay, *Downcast Eyes: The Denigration of Vision in Twentieth Century French Thought* (Berkeley and Los Angeles, 1993), 22.

63. Thomas Nipperdey, *Deutsche Geschichte, 1800–1866; Bürgerwelt und starker Staat* (Munich, 1983), 540.

64. Otto Jahn, *Winckelmann. Eine Rede gehalten am 9. Dezember 1843, in der Akademischen Aula in Greifswald* (Greifswald, 1844), 3, 28.

65. See Winckelmann, *Gedanken über die Nachahmung*, 38. The phrase is "Edle einfalt und stille grösse."

66. Ibid., 21.

67. See Walter Pater, *Winckelmann* (London, 1911), 18.

68. Potts, *Flesh and the Ideal*, 131.

69. Quoted in Paul Derks, *Die Schande der heiligen Päderastie, Homosexualität und Öffentlichkeit in der deutschen Literatur, 1750–1850* (Berlin, 1990), 193.

70. Hatfield, *Winckelmann and His German Critics*, 145.

71. Namowicz, *Die Aufklärische Utopie*, 140.

72. Derks, *Die Schande der heiligen Päderastie*, 204, 207.

73. Friedrich Schiller, *Über die ästhetische Erziehung des Menschen* (Stuttgart, 1981), 32, 33.

74. Derks, *Die Schande der heiligen Päderastie*, 200.

75. Eduard Pommier, *Winckelmann und die Betrachtung der Antike im Frankreich der Aufklärung und der Revolution* (Tübingen, 1992), 6, 7.

76. Eduard Pommier, *Winckelmann und die Betrachtung der Antike*, 22ff.

77. Max L. Bäumer, "Winckelmanns Auffasung republikanischer Freiheit und sein Einfluss auf die Kunst der Französichen Revolution," *Beiträge zur internationalen Wirkung Winckelmanns* 4/5 (Stendal, 1986), 23–25.

78. Thomas W. Gaethgens, "Jacques-Louis David: Léonidas bei den Thermopylen," *Ideal und Wirklichkeit in der Bildenden Kunst im Späten 18. Jahrhundert*, ed. Herbert Beck et al. (Berlin, 1984), 230.

79. Elmar Stolpe, *Klassizismus und Krieg: Über den Historienmaler Jacques-Louis David* (Frankfurt a. Main, 1985), 149.

80. Pater, *Winckelmann*, 46.

81. Robert Knox, *The Races of Man* (London, 1862), 400.

82. Sir Charles Bell, *The Anatomy and Philosophy of Expression, as Connected with the Fine Arts* (London, 1844; first published, 1806), 21 and passim.

83. Walter Pater, "The Age of Athletics," in *Greek Studies*, ed. Charles L. Shadwell (London, 1885), 302.

84. Pater, *Winckelmann*, 40.

85. Pater, "Age of Athletics," 303.

86. George L. Mosse, *Toward the Final Solution: A History of European Racism* (New York, 1978), 68.

87. Julius Langbehn, *Rembrandt als Erzieher* (Leipzig, 1900), 64.

88. See page 141.

CHAPTER 3

1. Johann Joachim Winckelmann, "Gedanken über die Nachahmung der Griechischen Werke in der Malerei und Bildhauerkunst," *Ausgewählte Schriften*, Insel Bücherei 130 (Leipzig, n.d.), 24.

2. Jacques Ulman, *De la Gymnastique aux Sports moderne* (Paris, 1965), 133.

3. Ibid., 212.

4. Gerd Steins, "Wo das Turnen erfunden wurde," *Berliner Forum* 6 (1986): 17.

5. H. De Genst, *Histoiree de L'Éducation Physique* (Brussels, 1949), 2: 46.

6. J. C. F. Guts Muths, *Gymnastik für die Jugend . . .* (Schnepfenthal, 1804), 24, 28.

7. Ibid., x.

8. Ibid., 3, 5.

9. Ibid., 6: "Wer schätzt wohl nicht den überall so vorlaut sprechenden Empfehlungsbrief der schönheit?"

10. Ibid., 271.

11. Ibid., 129.

12. Ibid., 9.

13. Ibid., 12, 133.

14. Friedrich Ludwig Jahn and Ernst Eiselen, *Deutsche Turnkunst* (Berlin, 1816), xiii, xiv.

15. Gerd Steins, "Wo das Turnen erfunden wurde," 22.

16. J. C. F. Guts Muths, *Spiele zur Übung und Erholung des Körpers und Geistes* (Hof, 1893), 314, 315.

17. Letter to the Gymnasts of Frankfurt (1843), *Die Briefe Friedrich Ludwig Jahns*, ed. Wolfgang Meyer (Leipzig, 1913), 489.

18. See ibid., 495.

19. Jahn and Eiselen, *Deutsche Turnkunst*, cited in Carl Euler, *Friedrich Ludwig Jahn* (Stuttgart, 1881), 164.

20. Ibid.

21. Jahn and Eiselen, *Deutsche Turnkunst*, 233.

22. Ibid., vii.

23. *Die Briefe Friedrich Ludwig Jahns*, 57.

24. Ulman, *De la Gymnastique aux Sports moderne*, 287.

25. Franz Passow, *Turnziel. Turnfreunden und Turnfeinden* (Breslau, 1818), 180.

26. *Die Briefe Friedrich Ludwig Jahns*, 57.

27. Ronald Hubscher, Jean Durry, and Bernard Jeu, *L'Histoire en Movements: Le sport dans la société française (XIXe–XXe siècle)* (Paris, 1992), 19.

28. Patrizia Ferrara, *L'Italia in Palestra* (Rome, 1992), 29.

29. Gaetano Bonetta, *Corpo e nazione* (Milan, 1990), 61.

30. Ibid., 63.

31. Ibid., 117.

32. Walter Pater, "The Age of Athletics," *Greek Studies*, ed. Charles L. Shadwell (London, 1885), 296, 297.

33. Jonathan Gathorne-Hardy, *The Old School Tie* (New York, 1977), 147.

34. Ibid., 147.

35. Ibid., 145.

36. Konrad Koch, *Die Erziehung zum Mut durch Turnen, Spiel und Sport* (Berlin, 1900), 6.

37. See Ludwig Gurlitt, *Erziehung zur Mannhaftigkeit* (Berlin, 1906), passim.

38. *The George Eliot Letters*, vol. 4, *1874–1877*, ed. Gordon S. Haight (New Haven, 1955), 312.

39. Gurlitt, *Erziehung zur Mannhaftigkeit*, 233.

40. Gerhard Kaiser, *Pietismus und Patriotismus im Literarischen Deutschland* (Wiesbaden, 1961), 23.

41. Philip Greven, *The Protestant Temperament* (New York, 1977), 126.

42. Leonore Davidoff and Catherine Hall, *Family Fortunes: Men and Women of the English Middle Class, 1780–1859* (Chicago, 1987), 113.

43. Charles Kingsley, *Westward Ho!* (London, 1899), 16, 160.

44. Quoted in David Newsome, *Godliness and Good Learning* (London, 1961), 213.

45. Ibid., 197.

46. Carl Friedrich Pockels, *Über Gesellschaft und Geselligkeit und Umgang* (Hannover, 1813), 67, 75.

47. Honoré Riouffe, *Mémoires d'un détenu pour servir a L'Histoire de la Tyrannie de Robespierre* (Paris, 1795), 16.

48. Alex Potts, "Beautiful Bodies and Dying Heroes: Images of Ideal Manhood in the French Revolution," *History Workshop*, Autumn 1990, 11.

49. Elmar Stolpe, *Klasizismus und Krieg, Über den Historien-Maler Jacques-Louis David* (Frankfurt a. Main, 1985), 84.

50. Thomas Carlyle, "Heroes and Hero Worship," *The Complete Works of Thomas Carlyle* (New York, n.d.), 2: 406.

51. Ibid., 333–34.

52. John Buchan, *Men and Deeds* (London, 1935), 98.

53. Ibid., 273.

54. Peter Beer, *Die Macht der Religion*, in P. Moritz, ed., *Aus der Zeit*, vol. 3, *Aufrufe, Dichtungen, Reden* (Berlin, 1935).

55. Cited in Pascal Hintermeyer, *Politique de la Mort* (Paris, 1981), 72.

56. Wilhelm von Humboldt, "Die Amazonen," *Wilhelm von Humboldts Werke*, ed. Albert Lietzmann (Berlin, 1912), 216.

57. Wilhelm von Humboldt, *Schriften zur Anthropologie und Geschichte* (Stuttgart, 1960), 307.

58. Von Humboldt, "Die Amazonen," 216.

59. Carl Friedrich Pockels, *Versuch einer Charakteristik des Weiblichen Geschlechts* (Hannover, 1797), 1: 16.

60. Mona Ozouf, *La fête revolutionaire* (Paris, 1976), 120.

61. Johann Gottlieb Fichte, *Grundlage des Naturrechts nach Prinzipien der Wissenschaftslehre*, ed. Fritz Medicus (Leipzig, 1908), 309.

62. Ibid., 212, 317.

63. Carl Friedrich Pockels, *Versuch einer Charakteristik des Weiblichen Geschlechts* (Hanover, 1797), 35.

64. C. Wilmanns, *Die "Goldene Internationale" und die Notwendigkeit einer socialen Reformpartei* (Berlin, 1876), 195.

CHAPTER 4

1. Galit Hasam-Rokem and Alan Dundes, eds., *The Wandering Jew* (Bloomington, Ind., 1986), 238.

2. George L. Mosse, *Toward the Final Solution* (New York, 1978), 22.

3. See Friedrich Schiller, *Über die ästhetische Erziehung des Menschen* (Stuttgart, 1965), 60.

4. Ibid., 61.

5. See page 27.

6. Ibid., 193.

7. Klaus Doerner, *Madmen and the Bourgeoisie* (Oxford, 1981).

8. Erwin H. Ackerknecht, *Kurze Geschichte der Psychiatrie* (Stuttgart, 1957), 34.

9. Martin S. Staum, *Cabanis: Enlightenment and Medical Philosophy in the French Revolution* (Princeton, 1980), 162, 163.

10. Ibid., 163.

11. Christian Gotthelf Salzmann, *Carl von Carlsberg oder über das Menschliche Elend* (Carlsruhe, 1787), 5:94.

12. *Männerbibliothek, oder Handbuch aller Kentnisse welche der Mann in jedem Alter . . . zu wissen nötig hat* (Berlin, 1838), 1:356.

13. Ibid., 354.

14. See George L. Mosse, *Nationalism and Sexuality* (New York, 1985), 29.

15. Ute Frevert, *Krankheit als politisches Problem, 1770–1880* (Göttingen, 1984), 31.

16. See Michael Geyer, "The Stigma of Violence, Nationalism, and War in Twentieth Century Germany," *German Studies Review*, Winter 1992, 94.

17. Ute Frevert, *Das Duell in der bürgerlichen Gesellschaft* (Munich, 1991), 158.

18. See Elisabeth Frenzel, *Judengestalten auf der deutschen Bühne* (Munich, 1940), 170.

19. See Sander Gilman, *The Jew's Body* (London, 1991), passim.

20. Johann Winckelmann, *Geschichte der kunst des Altertums*, in *Sämtliche Werke*, ed. Joseph Eiselein (Donaueschingen, 1825), 3: 131, 132.

21. Mosse, *Toward the Final Solution*, 29.

22. Robert Badinter, *Libre et Égaux, L'Émancipation des Juifs (1789–1791)* (Paris, 1989), 82.

23. Adolf Hitler, *Mein Kampf* (Munich, 1934), 704–5.

24. Michael H. Kater, *Different Drummers: Jazz in the Culture of Nazi Germany* (New York, 1992), 11; Sander L. Gilman, *Freud, Race and Gender* (Princeton, 1993), 19–21.

25. Michèle C. Cone, *Artists under Vichy* (Princeton, 1992), 155.

26. Randolph Trumbach, "Sodomitical Subcultures, Sodomital Rules and the Gender Revolution of the Eighteenth Century: Recent Historiography," in *Unauthorized Sexual Behavior during the Enlightenment*, ed. Robert P. Macubbin, *Eighteenth Century Life* 9, no. 3 (May 1985): 118; Arthur N. Gilbert, "Buggery and the British Navy, 1700–1861," *Journal of Social History* 10, no. 1 (Fall 1976): 72–98.

27. Paul Derks, *Die Schande der heiligen Päderastie, Homosexualität und Öffentlichkeit in der deutschen Literatur, 1750–1850* (Berlin, 1990), 11.

28. *Winckelmann von Goethe* (Zürich, 1943), 91, 92.

29. Ibid., 209.

30. Derks, *Die Schande der heiligen Päderastie*, 255.

31. Ibid., 346.

32. Frenzel, *Judengestalten auf der deutschen Bühne*, 82.

33. *Getroffene Bilder aus dem Leben vornehmer Knabenschänder und andere Scenen aus unserer Zeit und herlichkeit* (Merseburg, 1833), passim. I owe this reference to James D.Steackley.

34. Ibid., 48.

35. Sander L. Gilman, *Freud, Race and Gender* (Princeton, 1993), 162–65.

36. Otto Weininger, *Geschlecht und Charakter* (Wien and Leipzig, 1920), 408, 409.

37. Ferdinand Probst, *Der Fall Otto Weininger, Grenzfragen des Nerven- und Seelenlebens*, ed. L. Loewenfeld and H. Kurella, Heft 31 (Wiesbaden, 1904), 24, 25.

38. Jacques Le Rider, *Der Fall Otto Weininger* (Munich, 1985), 144.

39. Eduard Drumont, *La France Juive* (reprint; Paris: La Librairie Francaise, 1986), 2: 466.

40. Joachim S. Hohmann, *Geschichte der Zigeunerverfolgung in Deutschland* (Frankfurt, 1981), 48.

41. Karola Fings and Franz Sparing, "tunlichst als erziehungsunfähig hinzustellen. Zigeunerkinder und jugendliche: aus der Fürsorge in die vernichtung," *Dauchauer Hefte* 9, Heft 9 (November 1993): 164. I thank Sybil Milton for this reference.

42. See Sander L. Gilman, *Seeing the Insane* (New York, 1982), passim.

43. Havelock Ellis, *The Criminal* (London and New York, 1913), 74.

44. Matt K. Matsuda, "Doctor, Judge, Vagabond: Identity Identification and Other Memories of the State," *History and Memory* 6, no. 1 (spring/summer 1994): 78.

45. Camille Spiess, *Ainsi Parlait L'Homme* (Paris, 1924), 87, passim.

46. Günter Grau, ed. *Homosexualität in der NS Zeit* (Frankfurt a. Main, 1993), 309.

47. Madame de Staël, *De L'Allemagne* (Paris, 1845), 499.

48. Ibid., 501.

49. Isabel V. Hull, *Sexuality, State and Civil Society in Germany* (Ithaca, N.Y. 1995), chapter 9.

50. Mario Praz, *The Romantic Agony* (New York, 1956), 204.

51. Friedrich Schlegel, *Lucinde* (Stuttgart, 1859), 84.

52. Johann Gottlieb Fichte, *Grundlagen des Naturrechts nach Principien der Wissenschaftslehré sämtliche Werke*, ed. I. H. Fichte (Berlin, 1845), 3: 313, 319.

53. *Winckelmann von Goethe*, 131.

54. Wilhelm von Humboldt, *Schriften zur Anthropologie und Geschichte* (Stuttgart, 1960), 307.

55. Schlegel, *Lucinde*, 103.

56. Carl Friedrich Pockels, *Versuch einer charakteristik des weiblichen Geschlechts* (Hannover, 1797), 1: 17.

57. Mosse, *Nationalism and Sexuality*, 100.

CHAPTER 5

1. The chief proponent of this warmed-over theory was the Marburg psychologist Erich R. Jaensch; see his *Apologische Forschungsmethode* (Leipzig, 1927), passim. It was only logical that Jaensch became a racist (with minor reservations), and a National Socialist; see his *Die Lage und Aufgaben der Psychologie, Ihre Sendung in der Deutschen Bewegung und an der Kulturwende* (Leipzig, 1933), passim.

2. Charles Morazé, *The Triumph of the Middle Classes* (London, 1966), xiii, xiv,

3. This is the point made by Michel Foucault, *The History of Sexuality*, vol. 1, *An Introduction* (New York, 1980), esp. 1–13; however the transgression of old taboos led at first not to greater freedom but to greater repression as identifying so-called sexual deviants became easier and more precise.

4. Albert Boime, *Thomas Couture and the Eclectic Vision* (New Haven and London, 1980), 131.

5. Quoted in Daniel Pick, *Faces of Degeneration* (Cambridge, 1989), 54.

6. Arnold Zweig, *Aufzeichnungen über eine Familie Klopfer und das Kind* (Munich, 1911), passim.

7. Oswald Bumke, *Die Grenzen der geistigen Gesundheit* (Munich, 1929), 5.

8. Janet E. Hogarth, "Literary Degenerates," *Fortnightly Review* (April 1895): 586.

9. Max Nordau, *Degeneration* (New York, 1968), 41.

10. Mark S. Micale, "Charcot and the Idea of Hysteria in the Male: Gender, Medical Science, and Medical Diagnostics in Late Nineteenth Century France," *Medical History* 34, no. 4 (October 1990): 387.

11. Oswald Bumke, *Gedanken über die Seele*, 4. Auflage (Berlin and Heidelberg, 1948, first published 1941), 29.

12. Advertisements quoted in Ulrich Linse, "Über den Prozess der Syphilisation, Körper und Sexualität um 1900 in ärtzlicher Sicht," in *Vermessene Sexualität*, ed. Alexander Schuller and Nikolaus Heim (Berlin and Heidelberg, 1987), 167.

13. Edward Shorter, *From Paralysis to Fatigue: A History of Psychosomatic*

Illness in the Modern Era (New York, 1991), 117, 118; Janet Oppenheimer, *Shattered Nerves* (New York, 1991), 143.

14. Andreas Steiner, *Das Nervöse Zeitalter: Der Begriff der Nervosität bei Laien und Ärtzten in Deutschland und Österreich um 1900* (Zürich, 1964), 20.

15. Shorter, *From Paralysis to Fatigue*, 212.

16. Micale, "Charcot and the Idea of Hysteria in the Male," 380.

17. Ibid., 380.

18. J.-M.Charcot, *Leçons sur les Maladies du Système Nerveux faites a la Salpetière* (Paris, 1872–1878), 8. Lesson, 116.

19. Micale, "Charcot and the Idea of Hysteria in the Male," 406.

20. Ibid., 407.

21. Ruth Harris, *Murder and Madness* (Oxford, 1989), 325.

22. *The Standard Edition of the Complete Psychological Works of Sigmund Freud*, vol. 1, *1886–1895* (London, 1966), 24, 25.

23. Richard von Krafft-Ebing, *Lehrbuch der Gerichtlichen Psychopathologie*, vol. 3, Umgearbeitete Auflage (Stuttgart, 1892), 72.

24. Günter Mann, "Dekandenz-Degeneration-Untergangsangst im Licht der Biologie des 19. Jahrhunderts," *Medizinhistorisches Journal* 20 (1985): 9.

25. Oswald Bumke, *Kultur und Entartung* (Berlin, 1922), 81.

26. Richard von Krafft-Ebing, *Psychopathia Sexualis* (Munich, 1984), 60.

27. Ibid., 157.

28. Quoted in *Der Unterdrückte Sexus*, ed. Joachim S. Hohmann (Lollar/Lahn, 1977), 25.

29. Richard Ellmann, *Oscar Wilde* (New York, 1988), 300.

30. Robert Hitchens, *The Green Carnation* (London, 1949), 15.

31. Quoted in Neil Bartlett, *Who Was That Man? A Present to Mr. Oscar Wilde* (London, 1988), 50.

32. See Jerrold Seigel, *Bohemian Paris* (New York, 1986), 223–24, though nothing is said about the homosexual aspect of the journal.

33. Jean Lorrain, *Correspondence* (Paris, 1929), 250.

34. Philippe Jullian, *Jean Lorrain ou le Satyricon 1900* (Paris, 1974), 60.

35. Philippe Jullian, *Robert de Montesquiou* (Paris, 1987), 288.

36. Linda Dowling, *Hellenism and Homosexuality in Victorian Oxford* (Ithaca, N.Y., 1994), 3.

37. Ibid., 998.

38. Nataly Barney, *Traits et Portraits, suivi de l'amour défendu* (Paris, 1963), 177.

39. George Wickes, *The Amazon of Letters: The Life and Loves of Nataly Barney* (London, 1977), 40.

40. Magnus Hirschfeld, *Berlin's Drittes Geschlecht* (Berlin and Leipzig,

1904), 37, 55, 43; P. Näcke, "Ein Besuch bei den Homosexuellen in Berlin. Mit Bemerkungen über die Homosexualität," *Archiv für Kriminalanthropologie und Kriminalistik* 15 (1904): 246ff.

41. Oscar Méténier, *Les Berlinois chez eux, Virtus et Vices Allemand* (Paris, 1904), 89, 126.

42. Henri de Weindel and F. P. Fischer, *L'Homosexualité en Allemagne* (Paris, 1908), 7.

43. Hubert Kennedy, *Ulrichs: The Life and Works of Karl Heinrich Ulrichs* (Boston, 1988), 116.

44. James D. Steakley, *The Homosexual Emancipation Movement in Germany* (New York, 1975), 24.

45. Hichens, *The Green Carnation*, 92.

46. Manfred Herzen, *Magnus Hirschfeld* (Frankfurt a. Main, 1992), 19, 20, and passim. Hirschfeld became the focus of accusations by the German Right that Jews and homosexuals worked hand in hand.

47. Ibid., 67.

48. Oscar Wilde, "Portrait of Mr. W. H.," in *Sexual Heretics: Male Homosexuality in English Literature from 1850–1900*, ed. Herbert Read (London, 1970), 392.

49. A. J. L. Busst, "The Image of the Androgyne in the Nineteenth Century," *Romantic Mythologies* (London, 1967), 38–39.

50. L. S. A. M. von Römer, "Über die androginische Idee des Lebens," *Jahrbuch für Sexuelle Zwischenstufen*, vol. 5 (Leipzig, 1903), pt. 2, 921.

51. Gert Mattenklott, *Bilderdienst: Ästhetische Opposition bei Beardsley und George* (Munich, 1970), 103.

52. Magnus Hirschfeld, *Sexualwissenschaftlicher Bilderatlas zur Geschlechterkunde* (Berlin, 1930), 490, 491.

53. Mario Praz, *The Romantic Agony* (New York, 1956), 332.

54. Nataly Barney, *Nouvelle Pensée de l'Amazone* (Paris, 1934), 197.

55. Charles Kains-Jackson, "The New Chivalry," in *Sexual Heretics: Male Homosexuality in English Literature from 1850–1900*, ed. Herbert Read (London, 1970), 316.

56. William Ernest Henley, "Rhymes and Rhythms" (1889–1893?), in *William Ernest Henley*, ed. Jerome Hamilton Buckley (Princeton, 1945), 148.

57. Colette, *The Pure and the Impure* (New York, 1966), 76.

58. Wolfdietrich Rasch, *Die literarische Decadence um 1900* (Munich, 1986), 6.

59. Frank Wedekind, "Spring's Awakening," in *The Modern Theater*, ed. Eric Bentley (New York, 1960), 6: 158.

60. George L. Mosse, *The Crisis of German Ideology* (New York, 1964), 104.

61. Ibid., 105.

62. Kurt Hans, "Jugend von heute," *Der Anfang* 1, Heft 3 (July 1913): 111.

63. Hans-George Stümke, *Homosexuelle in Deutschland* (Munich, 1989), 144.

64. Lesley Hall, *Hidden Anxieties: Male Sexuality, 1900–1950* (Cambridge, 1991), 21; Klaus Müller, *Aber in meinem Herzen sprach eine Stimme so Laut. Homosexuelle Autobiographien und medizinische Pathographien im neunzehnten Jahrhundert* (Berlin, 1991), 174ff.

65. Quoted in *Volkswart: Organ der Männervereine zur bekämpfung der öffentlichen Unsittlichkeit*, November 1915, 145.

66. Ibid., 147.

67. *Streitfragen, Wissenschaftliches Fachorgan der deutschen Sittlichkeits Vereine*, ed. P. Philips, 1. Heft (Berlin, 1892), 1.

68. A. Römer, "Das Sittengesetz vor dem Richerstuhl einer ärtzlichen Autorität," ibid., 5ff. A forthcoming work by John F. Fout will analyze these associations in greater detail.

69. Krafft-Ebing, *Psychopathia Sexualis*, 228.

70. Friedrich Nietzsche, "The Anti-Christ," in *The Nietzsche Reader*, selected by R. J. Hollingdale (Harmondsworth, 1977), 231.

71. Steven E. Aschheim, *The Nietzsche Legacy in Germany* (Berkeley, 1992), 150.

72. Erich Grassl, *Die Willensschwäche* (Leipzig, 1937), 216.

73. F. W. Foerster, "Sexualethik und Sexual pädagogie," *Volkswart* 1 (1908): 14.

74. Gaetano Bonetta, *Corpo e nazione. L'educazione ginnastica, igienica e sessuale nell'Italia liberale* (Milan, 1990), 130, 131; see also Anson Rabinbach, *The Human Motor, Energy, Fatigue and the Origins of Modernity* (New York, 1990), esp. 133–36.

75. Cited in Konrad Koch, *Erziehung zum Mutte durch Turnen, Spiel und Sport* (Berlin, 1900), 7.

76. G. Weitbrecht, *Die Sittlichkeit des Mannes Ehre* (Stuttgart, 1889), 7.

77. Krafft-Ebing, *Psychopathia Sexualis*, 317.

78. Shearer West, *Fin De Siècle* (Woodstock, N.Y., 1993), 81.

79. Richard Evans, *The Feminists* (New York, 1979), 107.

80. Alberto Cavaglion, *Otto Weininger in Italia* (Rome, 1982), 114.

81. Jean Pierrot, *The Decadent Imagination* (Chicago, 1981), 142, 143.

82. Elaine Showalter, *Sexual Anarchy* (London, 1991), 149.

83. Ibid., 149.

84. Patrick Kay Bidelman, *Pariah's Stand Up! The Founding of the Liberal Feminist Movement in France, 1858–1889* (Westport, Conn., 1982), 195.

85. Anneliese Maugue, *L'Identité Masculine en Crise au Tournante du Siècle* (Marseilles, 1987), 37, 103.

86. Ibid., 123.

87. See Lesley A. Hall, *Hidden Anxieties: Male Sexuality, 1900–1950* (Cambridge, 1991), esp. 114–69.

88. *Hirt's Deutsches Lesebuch*, ed. Johannes Eilemann et al. (Breslau, 1940), 243.

CHAPTER 6

1. Mario Isnenghi, *Giornali di Trincea* (Turin, 1977), 110.

2. Adrian Caesar, *Taking It like a Man: Suffering, Sexuality and the War Poets* (Manchester, 1993), 155.

3. See Modris Eksteins, *Rites of Spring: The Great War and the Birth of the Modern Age* (Boston, 1989), 281.

4. John Tosch, "What Should Historians Do with Masculinity? Reflections on Nineteenth-Century Britain," *History Workshop*, issue 38 (1994), 183.

5. See page 76.

6. Ernst Jünger, *The Storm of Steel* (New York, 1975), 235.

7. Robert Brasillach, *Notre Avant Guerre* (Paris, 1942), 282.

8. See page 52.

9. Caesar, *Taking It like a Man*, 67.

10. Ibid., 83, 84, and passim.

11. Ibid., 229.

12. Richard Aldington, *Death of a Hero* (1929), in *The Lost Voices of World War I*, ed. Tim Cross (London, 1988), 381.

13. *Lieutenant Sender: Blätter der Erinnerungen für seine Freunde*, ed. M. Spanier (Hamburg, 1915), 23.

14. George L. Mosse, *Fallen Soldiers* (New York, 1990), 74ff.

15. Jünger, *Storm of Steel*, 254.

16. Paul Weindling, *Health, Race and German Politics between National Unification and Nazism, 1870–1945* (Cambridge, 1989), 283.

17. Heinz-Peter Schmiedebach, "Sozialdarwinismus, Biologismus, Pazifismus—Ärztestimmen zum Ersten Weltkrieg," in *Medizin und Krieg*, ed. Johanna Bleker und Heinz-Peter Schmiedebach (Frankfurt a. Main 1987), 102, 117.

18. Henri de Montherlant, *Les Olympiques* (Paris, 1914); see 73, 74.

19. Robert Soucy, *Fascist Intellectual: Drieu La Rochelle* (Berkeley, 1979), 265.

20. Martin Green, *The Adventurous Male: Chapters in the History of the White Male Mind* (University Park, Pa., 1993), 56.

21. The writer was Hans Zöberlein in Michael Golbach, *Die Wiederkehr des Weltkrieges in der Literatur* (Kronberg i/T., 1978), 227.

22. A. J. Langguth, *Saki: A Life of Hector Hugh Munro* (New York, 1981), chap. 15.

23. Karl Hugo Sclutius, "Pazifistische Kriegspropaganda," *Die Weltbühne* 23. (erstes halbjahr 1929), 517.

24. Siegfried Kracauer, *Ginster. Von ihm selbst geschrieben* (Berlin, 1928), 23, 139.

25. Adolf Hitler, *Mein Kampf* (Munich, 1934), 181.

26. Ernst Jünger, *Der Kampf als inneres Erlebnis* (Berlin, 1922), 32.

27. Fritz V. Ostini, *Fritz Erler* (Bielefeld and Leipzig, 1921), 132; Mosse, *Fallen Soldiers*, 134.

28. Werner Picht, *Der soldatische Mensch* (Berlin, 1940), 16, 29.

29. See George L. Mosse, "The Knights of the Sky," in *War: A Cruel Necessity? The Bases of Institutional Violence*, ed. R. A. Hinde and Helen E. Watson (London, 1995), 132–42.

30. Peter Supf, *Das Buch der deutschen Fluggeschichte* (Stuttgart, 1958), 336, 338.

31. Johannes Werner, *Boelcke: Der Mensch, der Führer der deutschen Jagdfliegerei* (Leipzig, 1932), 10, 209; Werner V. Langsdorff, *Flieger am Feind* (Gütersloh, 1934), 40–41.

32. Hermann Grote, *Habe ich Veranlagungen zum Fliegen?* (Bochum-Langendeer, 1936), 2.

33. Emilio Gentile, *Il Culto del Littorio* (Rome, 1993), 127.

34. Christopher Hussey, *Tait McKenzie, a Sculptor of Youth* (London, 1929), 35–36.

35. Ibid., 67.

36. Ernst Toller, *I Was a German* (New York, 1934), 87, 99.

37. Alfred Pfabigan, *Max Adler: Eine politische Biographie* (Frankfurt a. Main, 1982), 210.

38. Max Adler, *Neue Menschen, Gedanken über sozialistische Erziehung* (Vienna and Munich, 1923), 69 and passim.

39. Josef Weidenholzer, *Auf dem Weg zum Neuen Menschen: Bildungs und Kulturarbeit der Österreicheschen Sozialdemokratie in der Ersten Republik* (Vienna, 1981), 263.

40. Alfred Pfoser, *Literatur und Austromarxismus* (Vienna, 1986), 42, 43.

41. This problem has been discussed at greater length in George L. Mosse, "La sinistra europea e l'esperienza della Guerra," in *Revoluzione e Reazione in Europa, 1917–1924*, ed. G. Spini (Florence, 1978), 151–67.

42. Ibid., 156.

43. Ilona Duczynska, *Workers in Arms: The Austrian Schutzbund and the Civil War of 1934* (New York and London, 1978), 100, 145.

44. Ibid., 145.

45. Anson Rabinbach, *The Crisis of Austrian Socialism: From Red Vienna to Civil War, 1927–1934* (Chicago, 1983), 210.

46. Duczynska, *Workers in Arms*, 126.

47. Pfoser, *Literatur und Austromarxismus*, 32.

48. Gerhard Hauk, "Armeekorps auf dem Weg zur Sonne—Einige Be-

merkungen zur kulturellen Selbstdarstellung der Arbeiterbewegung," in *Fahnen, Fäuste, Körper*, ed. Dietmar Petzina (Essen, 1988), 79.

49. Volker Schmidtchen, "Arbeitersport-Erziehung zum sozialistischen Menschen," *Flugblatt an die Arbeiterjugend!* (1906) (Archive of the Internationaal Instituut voor Sociale Geschiedenis, Amsterdam).

50. W. L. Guttsman, *Workers' Culture in Weimar Germany* (New York, Oxford, and Munich, 1990), 152.

51. Hauk, "Armeekorps auf dem Weg zur Sonne—Einige Bemerkungen zur kulturellen Selbstdarstellung der Arbeiterbewegung," 82.

52. *Arbeiter-Jugend* 17 (1925): 196.

53. Anson Rabinbach, *The Crisis of Austrian Socialism:* 71.

54. *Unser 3. Kreisfest!* (Flugblatt, Dresden, 1928?).

55. See Helmut Gruber, *Red Vienna: Experiment in Working Class Culture, 1919–1934* (New York, 1991), 156.

56. J. Robert Wegs, "Working Class Respectability: The Viennese Experience," *Journal of Social History* 15, no. 4 (summer 1982): 624; Joanna Bourke, *Working Class Culture in Britain, 1890–1960* (London, 1994), 630.

57. Gruber, *Red Vienna*, 178.

58. Béla Balázs, "Männlich oder Kriegsblind" (1929), in *Kritik in der Zeit, Fortschrittliche deutsche Literturkritik, 1918–1933* (Leipzig, 1985), 235.

59. Mosse, "La sinistra Europea e l'esperienza della Guerra," 162.

60. Francois Delpla, "Les communisted français et la sexualité (1932–1938)," *Mouvement Sociale*, no. 91, April/June 1975), 129.

61. Alfred Klein, *Im Auftrag ihrer Klasse: Weg und Leistung der deutschen Arbeiterschriftsteller, 1918–1933* (Berlin and Weimar, 1972), 208ff.

62. Leon Trotsky, *Literatur und Revolution* (New York, 1957), 254.

63. Ella Winter, *Red Virtue: Human Relationships in the New Russia* (London, 1933), 27.

64. Wendy Z. Goldman, *Women, the State and Revolution: Soviet Family Policy and Social Life, 1917–1936* (Cambridge, 1993), 1–2.

65. Richard Stites, *Revolutionary Dreams: Utopian Visions and Experimental Life in the Soviet Union* (New York, 1989), 133.

66. Laura Engelstein, *The Keys to Happiness: Sex and the Search for Modernity in Fin-de-Siècle Russia* (Ithaca, N.Y., 1992), 396, 397.

67. Nikkolai Bukharin, *Historical Materialism: A System of Sociology* (New York, 1965; first published 1925), 156.

68. Elizabeth A. Wood, "Prostitution Unbound," in *Sexuality and the Body in Russian Culture*, ed. Jane T. Costlow, Stephanie Sandler, and Judith Vowles (Stanford, 1993), 128.

69. Winter, *Red Virtue*, 115ff.

70. Stites, *Revolutionary Dreams*, 153.

71. Sidney and Beatrice Webb, *Communism, a New Civilization* (London, 1935), 74.

72. Jerome M. Gillison, *The Soviet Image of Utopia* (Baltimore and London, 1975), 168; Atina Grossmann, *Reforming Sex: The German Movement for Birth Control and Abortion Reform* (New York, 1995), 183.

73. Michael Rohrwasser, *Saubere Mädel/Starke Genossen* (Frankfurt a. Main, 1975), 68, 69; James M. Diehl, *Paramilitary Politics in Weimar Germany* (Bloomington, Ind., 1977), 186.

74. Karl Grünberg, *Brennende Ruhr* (Berlin, 1952), 254.

75. Frank Trommler, *Sozialistische Literatur in Deutschland* (Stuttgart, 1976), 489.

76. Christel Lane, *The Rites of Rulers: Ritual in Industrial Society. The Soviet Case* (Cambridge, 1981), 249.

77. See Igor Golomstock, *Totalitarian Art* (London, 1990), 214.

78. Peter Reichel, *Der schöne Schein des Dritten Reiches* (Munich, 1991), 369.

79. Franz Schonauer, "Der Rote Eine-Mark Roman," *Kürbiskern: Literatur und Kritik* 3 (1966): 13.

80. Rohrwasser, *Saubere Mädel/Starke Genossen*, 97.

81. Ibid., 100.

CHAPTER 7

1. Bruce Haley, *The Healthy Body and Victorian Culture* (Cambridge, Mass., 1978), 206.

2. Michael Rosenthal, *The Character Factory: Baden-Powell and the Origins of the Boy Scout Movement* (London, 1986), 181.

3. Robert Stevenson Smythe Baden-Powell, *Rovering for Success: A Book of Life-Sport for Young Men* (London, 1930), 139.

4. Ibid., 108–9,175.

5. Quoted in E. E. Reynolds, *Boy Scouts* (London, 1944), 140.

6. John Springhall, "Building Character in the British Boy: The Attempt to Extend Christian Manliness to Working Class Adolescents, 1880–1914," in *Manliness and Morality: Middle Class Masculinity in England and America, 1800–1940*, ed. J. A. Mangan and James Walvin (New York, 1987), 55.

7. Samuel Smiles, *Self-Help* (London, 1953), 14.

8. Ibid., 333.

9. Joanna Bourke, *Working Class Culture in Britain, 1890–1960* (London, 1994), 42.

10. Ibid., 42.

11. *Health and Strength Annual* (London, 1908), 4.

12. Bourke, *Working Class Culture in Britain*, 44.

13. Siegfried Kracauer, *Die Angestellten* (Allenbach and Bonn, 1959), 18.

14. Haley, *The Healthy Body and Victorian Culture*, 186, 187.

15. See George L. Mosse, "What Germans Really Read," *Masses and Man* (New York, 1980), 62–65.

16. A. G. Henty, "Black Pirates," *Beeton's Boys Own Magazine* (London), n.s., 3 (1889): 185.

17. Richard Usburne, *Clubland Heroes: A Nostalgic Study of Some Recurrent Characters in the Romantic Fiction of Dornford Yates, John Buchan and Sapper* (London, 1953), 6.

18. Leslie Susser, "Fascist and Anti-Fascist Attitudes in Britain between the Wars" (Ph.D. thesis, Oxford University, 1988), 89, 93–95.

19. Thomas Rohkramer, *Der Militarismus der kleinen Leute. Die Kriegervereine im Deutschen Kaiserreich, 1871–1914* (Munich, 1990), 271.

20. Ibid., 35, 59 n. 169, 216.

21. Friedrich Torberg, *Der Schüler Gerber* (Wien, 1954), 20.

22. *Stuttgarter N.S. Kurier* (22.4.1941), Wiener Library Clipping Collection.

23. *Mühlhauser Tageblatt* (3.5.1941), Wiener Library, Clipping Collection.

24. "Etonboy und Hitlerjunge," *Der gute Kamerad. Illustriertes Jahrbuch für Jungen* (Stuttgart, 1940), 54: 189; *The Spectator* (July 30, 1937), 196. For a good comparison of the two systems and their consequences: W. R. Hicks, *The School in English and German Fiction* (London, 1932).

25. Oswald Bumke, *Die gegenwärtigen Strömungen in der Psychiatrie, Fünf Vorträge* (Berlin, 1928), 24.

26. Thomas Nipperdey, "Verein als soziale Struktur in Deutschland im späten 18. und frühen 19. Jahrhundert," *Gesellschaft, Kultur, Theorie* (Göttingen, 1976), 180.

27. For *Männerbünde*, see Karen V. Welk, ed., *Männerbünde, Zur Rolle des Mannes im Kulturvergleich*, 2 vols. (Cologne: Rautenstrauch-Joest-Museum für Völkerkunde, 1990), passim.

28. "Männliche Literatur," reprinted in *Kritik in der Zeit* (Leipzig, 1985), 249.

29. Belá Balázs, "Männlich oder Kriegsblind?" Ibid., 254, 255.

30. Ibid., 255.

31. Jürgen Reulecke, "Das Jahr 1902 und die Ursprünge der Männer-Bund Ideologie in Deutschland," in Welk, *Männerbünde*, 1:7.

32. See p. 147.

33. Gabriele Strecker, *Frauenträume, Frauentränen, über den unterhaltenden deutschen Frauenroman* (Weilheim/Oberbayern, 1969), 114.

34. See Billie Melman, *Women and the Popular Imagination in the Twenties: Flappers and Nymphs* (London, 1988), chap. 6.

35. Steven Cohan and Ina Rae Hark, eds., *Screening the Male: Exploiting Masculinities in Hollywood Cinema* (London and New York, 1993), 25.

36. Ibid., 28–36.
37. Ibid., 91.
38. Melman, *Women and the Popular Imagination in the Twenties*, passim.
39. Rachilde, *Quand j'etais jeune* (Paris, 1947) passim; M. Auriant, *Souvenirs sur Madame Rachilde* (Paris, 1989), 91.
40. Mary Louise Roberts, *Civilization without Sexes. Reconstructing Gender in Postwar France, 1817–1927* (Chicago, 1994), 53.
41. *Berliner Illustrierte* 20 (1911): 143.
42. Sergiusz Michalski, *Neue Sachlichkeit* (Cologne, 1994), 53.
43. Harry Oosterhuis and Hubert Kennedy, *Homosexuality and Male Bonding in pre-Nazi Germany* (original transcripts from *Der Eigene*) (New York, 1991), 186 and passim.
44. See Joachim S. Hohmann, *Männerfreundschaften: Die schönsten homosexuellen Liebesgeschichten der vergangenen siebzig Jahr* (Frankfurt a. Main, 1979).
45. André Raffalovich, *Uranisme et Unisexualité* (Lyons and Paris, 1896), 354.
46. Vincent Brome, *Havelock Ellis, Philosopher of Sex* (London, 1979), 198.
47. Randy Shilts, *Conduct Unbecoming: Gays and Lesbians in the U.S. Military* (New York, 1993),32.
48. Hubert Kennedy, *Ulrichs: The Life and Works of Karl Heinrich Ulrichs, Pioneer of the Modern Gay Movement* (Boston, 1988), 50.
49. Manfred Herzer, *Magnus Hirschfeld* (Frankfurt, 1992), 60.
50. Erich Burin, "Das Kaffeehaus Judentum," *Jüdische Turnerzeitung* 9, no. 5/6 (May–June 1910), 75.
51. Ulrich Dunker, *Der Reichsbund Jüdischer Frontsoldaten, 1918–1938* (Düsseldorf, 1977), 99.
52. Max Nerdau, *Degeneration* (New York, 1968), 541.
53. Arnold Zweig, *Bilanz der deutschen Judenheit 1933* (Amsterdam, 1934), 189.

CHAPTER 8

1. Lando Feretti, *Essempi e Idee per L'Italiano Nuovo* (Rome, 1930), 178, 179.
2. Emilio Gentile, *Il Culto del Littorio* (Rome and Bari, 1993), 119.
3. George L. Mosse, *Confronting the Nation: Jewish and Western Nationalism* (Hanover, N.H., 1993), chap. 6.
4. Giovanni Papini, *Machilità* (Florence, 1915), 95.
5. Walter L. Adamson, *Avant-Garde Florence: From Modernism to Fascism* (Cambridge, Mass., 1993), 178.
6. Papini, *Machilità*, 41.

7. John A. Thayer, *Italy and the Great War* (Madison, Wis., 1964), 69.

8. Papini, *Machilità*, 7, 93.

9. Steven E. Aschheim, *The Nietzsche Legacy in Germany, 1890–1900* (Berkeley, 1992), 225.

10. See Renzo De Felice, *Mussolini il Rivoluzionario* (Turin, 1965), 271.

11. Roberta Suzzi Valli, "Squadrismo e Mito dello Squadrismo Nella Cultura Fascista" (Tesi di Laurea, Università degli Studi di Roma, "La Sapienza," 1991), 34, 39.

12. See picture of Mussolini attending the international congress of the women's suffrage movement (Rome, 1923), in Rezo de Felice and Luigi Goglia, *Mussolini, Il Mito* (Rome and Bari, 1983), picture 129.

13. Sandro Setta, *Renato Ricci* (Bologna, 1986), 114.

14. Ferretti, *Essempi e Idee per L'Italiano Nuovo*, 181.

15. Renato Bianda, Guiseppe Leone, Gianni Rossi, and Adolfo Urso, *Atleti in Camicia Neri* (Rome, 1983), 257.

16. Victoria De Grazia, *How Fascism Ruled Women* (Berkeley, 1992), 212, 220.

17. Louise Diehl, "Disciplin der Persönlichkeit im neuen Italien," *Neues Volk* (Rassenpolitisches Amt der NSDAP), Februar, 1939, 34, 35.

18. Antonio Spinoza, *Starace* (Milan, 1983), 50.

19. Peter Reichel, *Der schöne Schein des Dritten Reiches* (Munich, 1991), 257.

20. Bianda, Leone, Rossi, and Urso, *Atleti in Camicia Neri*, 34; Winfried Joch, *Politische Leibeserziehung und ihre Theorie im Nationalsozialistischen Deutschland* (Bern and Frankfurt a. Main, 1976), 91.

21. Feretti, *Essempi e Idee per L'Italiano Nuovo*, 179.

22. Michael Arthur Ledeen, *Universal Fascism* (New York, 1972), 62.

23. Cited from Kurt Liebermann, "Nietzsche und Mussolini," *Italien in Vergangenheit und Gegenwart*, Heft 8 (Leipzig, n.d.), in Hans Ulrich Gumbrecht, "I Redentori Della Victoria, Über Fiumes Ort in der Genealogie des Faschismus" (forthcoming as "On Fiume's Place in the Genealogy of Fascism," *Journal of Contemporary History* [April 1996]).

24. Renzo de Felice holds that the Ethiopian war was started for reasons of foreign policy rather than internal concerns. See his *Mussolini il duce: Gli anni del consenso, 1929–1936* (Turin, 1974), 615.

25. Renzo de Felice, *Mussolini il duce: Le Stato totalitario, 1936–1940* (Turin, 1981), 538.

26. Emilio Gentile, *Il Mito Dello Stato Nuovo Dall'Antigiolittismo al Fascismo* (Rome and Bari, 1982), 243.

27. De Felice, *Mussolini il duce*, 578.

28. Gioacchino Volpe, *Scritti sul fascismo, 1919–1938* (Rome, 1976), 1:60.

29. Pasquale Falco, *Letteratura populare fascista* (Cosenza, 1984), 50.

30. Bianda, Leone, Rossi, and Urso, *Atleti in Camicia Nera*, 35; De Grazia, *How Fascism Ruled Women*, 227.

31. George L. Mosse, *Nazi Culture* (New York, 1966), 31; Peter Paret, "'Kolberg' (1945) as Historical Film and Historical Document," *Journal of Film, Radio and Television* 14, no. 4 (1994): 437.

32. Feretti, *Essempi e Idee per L'Italiano Nuovo*, 189.

33. Sigrid Weigel, "Die geopferte Heldin und das Opfer als Heldin," in *Die Verborgene Frau*, ed. Inge Stephan and Siegrid Weigel, Sonderband, *Das Argument* (1983), 139–43.

34. Barbara Spackman, "The Fascist Rhetoric of Virility," *Stanford Italian Review* 8, nos. 1–2 (1990): passim.

35. Ibid., 85.

36. Ibid.

37. "Weg zum althellenischen Idealtypus des Menschen," *Neues Wiener Tageblatt*, no. 86 (27.3.1941) (Wiener Library Clipping Collection).

38. Hans F.-K. Günther, *Rassenkunde des deutschen Volkes* (Munich, 1935, first published, 1922), 56, 62, 63.

39. Friedrich Joachim Kluhn, "Von Sinn des SA-Wehrabzeichens," *Nationalsozialistische Monatshefte* 10, Heft 108 (March 1939): 189, 199.

40. George L. Mosse, *Toward the Final Solution: A History of European Racism* (New York, 1978), chap. 3.

41. See Justus H. Ulbricht, "Der Mythos vom Heldentod," *Jahrbuch des Archivs der Deutschen Jugendbewegung*, vol. 16, *1986–1987*, 141.

42. Renato Monteleone and Pino Sarasini, "I monumenti italiani ai caduti della Grande Guerra," in *La Grande Guerra*, ed. Diego Leoni and Camilo Zadra (Milan, 1986), 640.

43. For this and the following pages, see George L. Mosse, "National Socialism, Nudity and the Male Body," *Culturefront* 3, no. 1 (winter–spring 1994): 89–92; see also George L. Mosse, "Beauty without Sensuality/The Exhibition Entartete Kunst," in *Degenerate Art: The Fate of the Avant Garde in Nazi Germany*, ed. Stephanie Baron (Los Angeles, 1991), 25–31.

44. George L. Mosse, *Nationalism and Sexuality* (New York, 1985), 171, 172.

45. Cited in Klaus Wolbert, *Die Nackten und die Toten des Dritten Reiches* (Giessen, 1982), 20.

46. Arno Breker, *Im Strahlungsfeld der Ereignisse* (Preussisch-Oldendorf, 1972), 134; Johannes Sommer, *Arno Breker* (Bonn, 1942), 5; Arno Breker, *Schriften*, ed. Volker G. Probst (Bonn, Paris, and New York, 1983), 170.

47. Breker, *Schriften*, 98, 153.

48. For Gustav Stührk see the documentary film *Zeit der Götter, der Bildhauer Arno Breker*, von Lutz Dammbeck (Berlin: Filmcollage, 1993).

49. Werner Rittich, "Symbol Grosser Zeit, Zu dem Reliefswerk von Arno

Breker," *Die Kunst im Deutschen Reich* 6, Folge 1 (January 1942): 4; W. Lotz, "Ein Gang durch die Neue Reichskanzelei," ibid., 3, Folge 9, 305.

50. Michèle C. Cone, *Artists under Vichy* (Princeton, 1992), 162.

51. Ursula Böhmer, "Jean Cocteau und die "Breker Affaire," *Forum Homosexualität und Literatur* 16 (1992): 12.

52. Reichel, *Der schöne Schein des Dritten Reiches*, 369.

53. Cone, *Artists under Vichy*, 155.

54. *Rede des Reichsführer-SS anlässlich der Gruppenführer Besprechung in Töltz*, am 18.11.1937, Institut für Zeitgeschichte, Munich, Archive MA 311 BL 818,45.

55. Ibid., 53.

56. *Bildnisse Deutscher Männer* (Stuttgart, 1936), 19.

57. Günther, *Rassenkunde des deutschen Volkes*, 40.

58. Bianda, Leone, Rossi, and Urso, *Atleti in Camicia Nera*, 56; De Grazia, *How Fascism Ruled Women*, 181; Maria Fraddosio, "The Fallen Hero: The Myth of Mussolini and Fascist Women in the Italian Social Republic (1943–1954)," *Journal of Contemporary History* (January 1996), forthcoming.

59. Julian Petley, *Capital and Culture: German Cinema, 1933–45* (London: British Film Institute, 1979), 136.

60. Albert Cavaglion and Gian Paolo Romagnani, *Le interdizione del Duce. a cinguant'anni delle leggi razziali in Italia* (Turin, 1988), 37.

61. Jost Hermand, *Old Dreams of a New Reich: Volkish Utopias and National Socialism* (Bloomington, Ind., 1992), 253.

62. Sybil Milton, "Antechamber to Birkenau: The *Zigeunerlager* after 1933," in *Die Normalität des Verbrechens*, ed. Helge Grabitz, Klaus Bastlein, and Johannes Tuchel, with Peter Klein und Martina Voigt (Berlin, 1994), 243.

63. Karola Fings and Franz Sparing, "'tunlichst als erziehungsunfähig hinzustellen' Zigeunerkinder und Jugendliche: Aus der Fürsorge in die Vernichtung," *Dachauer Hefte* 9, Heft 9 (November 1993): 165.

64. See *Neues Volk* (February 1939), 8–9.

65. See Steven E. Aschheim, *The Nietzsche Legacy in Germany, 1890–1990* (Berkeley, 1992), 329 n. 42.

66. That there were a few cases of "Aryanization," where non-Aryans were transformed into members of the superior race by fiat, does not markedly affect this statement. This phenomenon has never been investigated, though I know of at least one case firsthand, that of Hans Lachmann-Mosse, a newspaper publisher to whom Herrmann Goering made such an offer in 1934. The offer was refused.

CHAPTER 9

1. See George L. Mosse, *Fallen Soldiers* (New York, 1990), 210–11.

2. *Der Spiegel*, May 29, 1989, 244.

3. Frederic Wertham, *Seduction of the Innocent* (New York, 1954), esp. chap. 4.

4. Igor Kon, *Sex and Russian Society* (Bloomington, Ind., 1993), esp. chapt. 7.

5. Ute Frevert, *Women in German History* (New York and Oxford, 1989), 287.

6. See Jack Zipes, "A Critical Commentary on Robert Bly's Iron John," *New German Critique*, no. 56 (winter 1992), 8ff.

7. Christopher Booker, *The Neophiliacs: The Revolution in English Life in the Fifties and Sixties* (London, 1969), 45.

8. Barry Gifford and Lawrence Lee, *Jack's Book: An Oral Biography of Jack Kerouac* (New York, 1978), 41.

9. Marjory Garber, *Vested Interests, Cross-Dressing and Cultural Anxiety* (New York, 1992), 384.

10. Todd Gitlin, *The Sixties: Years of Hope, Days of Rage* (Toronto and New York, 1989), 32.

11. Jack B. Moose, *Skinheads Shaved for Battle* (Bowling Green, Ohio, 1993), 34.

12. Ibid., 38.

13. Marlyn R. Farwell, "Virginia Woolf and Androgyny, *Contemporary Literature* 16, no. 4 (1975): 442.

14. Gertrude Himmelfarb, *The Demoralization of Society* (New York, 1995), 11ff.

15. Joachim S. Hohmann, *Männerfreundschaften: Die schönsten homosexuellen Liebesgeschichten der vergangenen siebzig Jahre* (Frankfurt a. Main, 1979), 106, 109.

16. Max Nordau, *Degeneration* (New York, 1968), 541; George L. Mosse, *Confronting the Nation: Jewish and Western Nationalism* (Hanover, N.H., 1993), chap. 11.

17. John C. Fout, "Sexual Politics in Wilhelmine Germany: The Male Gender Crisis, Moral Purity and Homophobia," *Journal of the History of Sexuality* 2, no. 3 (January 1992): 390, 391.

18. Carol Lee, *Talking Tough: The Fight for Masculinity* (London, 1993), 152.

19. See page 7.

INDEX

Page numbers in italics refer to illustrations.